Praise for *Managing the Supply Chain*

"In the last few years, supply chain management has become the subject of business columns as well as of interest to CEOs and CFOs, not only to logistics professionals and academics. For an in depth understanding of the concepts behind this important and complex topic, this well-written book provides an excellent introduction. The concise explanations and numerous examples allow readers to better appreciate the important trade-offs and opportunities in the supply chain."

—Hau L. Lee, Kleiner Perkins, Mayfield, Sequoia Capital Professor of the Department of Management Science and Engineering, and Professor of Operations, Information and Technology at the Graduate School of Business at Stanford University.

"A great reference for both the seasoned supply chain professional and those just entering the field. It's clear that supply chain excellence will continue to be the hallmark of corporate leaders of the 21st century. Using comprehensive functional writeups plus a wealth of real-world case examples, Dr. Simchi-Levi et al. show the reader all the foundational options for success."

—Gregory Cudahy, Global Leader, Supply Chain Management Cap Gemini Ernst & Young

MANAGING THE SUPPLY CHAIN

The Definitive Guide for the
Business Professional

David Simchi-Levi
Philip Kaminsky
and Edith Simchi-Levi

McGraw-Hill
New York   Chicago   San Francisco   Lisbon
London   Madrid   Mexico City   Milan   New Delhi
San Juan   Seoul   Singapore   Sydney   Toronto

The McGraw·Hill Companies

Library of Congress Cataloging-in-Publication Data

Simchi-Levi, David.
  Managing the supply chain : the definitive guide for the business
professional / by David Simchi-Levi, Philip Kaminsky, Edith Simchi-Levi.
      p. cm.
    ISBN 0-07-141031-7 (cloth : alk. paper)
      1. Business logistics. 2. Industrial procurement. I. Kaminsky,
Philip. II. Simchi-Levi, Edith. III. Title.

HD38.5.S56 2003
    658.7—dc21   2003012979

4 5 6 7 8 9 0   DOC/DOC   0 9 8 7 6 5

ISBN 0-07-141031-7

This publication is designed to provide accurate and authoritative information in regard
to the subject matter covered. It is sold with the understanding that neither the author
nor the publisher is engaged in rendering legal, accounting, or other professional
service. If legal advice or other expert assistance is required, the services of a competent
professional person should be sought.
> —*From a Declaration of Principles jointed adopted by a Committee*
> *of the American Bar Association and a Committee of Publisher*

McGraw-Hill books are available at special quantity discounts to use as premiums and
sales promotions, or for use in corporate training programs. For more information,
please write to the Director of Special Sales, Professional Publishing, McGraw-Hill,
Two Penn Plaza, New York, NY 10121-2298. Or contact your local bookstore.

 This book is printed on recycled, acid-free paper containing a minimum of 50%
recycled, de-inked fiber.

Dedication

*to our parents Shifra and Nathan Simchi-Levi,
Sylvia and Laurence Kaminsky, Ady Seidman,
and in memory of Lea Seidman*

D. S-L, P. K. and E. S-L

Contents

Preface

Interest in supply chain management has grown rapidly over the past several years, and continues to grow. A number of forces have contributed to this trend. First, in recent years it has become clear that many companies have reduced manufacturing costs as much as practically possible. Many of these companies are discovering the magnitude of savings that can be achieved by planning and managing their supply chain more effectively. Indeed, a striking example is Wal-Mart's success story, which is partly attributed to implementing new strategic partnerships with their suppliers, e.g. vendor managed inventory, as well as an innovative logistics strategy called crossdocking.

At the same time, information and communication systems have been widely implemented, and provide access to comprehensive data from all components of the supply chain. In particular, the influence of the Internet and e-commerce on the economy in general and business practice in particular, has been tremendous. For instance, the direct business model employed by industry giants such as Dell Computers and Amazon.com enables customers to order products over the Internet and thus allows companies to sell their products without relying on third-party distributors or conventional stores. New technologies such as RFID tags offer even more opportunities to further improve the management of the supply chain.

Also, in the 90s, outsourcing was the focus of many industrial manufacturers; firms considered outsourcing everything from the procurement function to production and manufacturing. Of course, outsourcing offers a variety of benefits but comes with new and considerable risks some of which have been realized in the last few years by companies such as Apple, Cisco or Nike.

Finally, the threat of terrorism exemplified by the horrendous attacks of September 11, 2001 on the World Trade Center and the Pentagon has profound implications for supply chain and manufacturing strategies. The near-term impacts—missed shipments, border-crossing delays, communications problems—are easily understood.

Less clear is the longer-term effect of increased uncertainty on lead times and demand, and the impact of that uncertainty on supply chain strategy.

It is therefore not surprising that many companies are involved in the analysis of their supply chains. In most cases, however, this analysis is performed based on experience and intuition; very few analytical models or planning tools have been used in this process. In contrast, in the last two decades the academic community has developed various models and tools for supply chain management. The first generation of this technology was not robust or flexible enough to allow industry to use it effectively. This, has changed over the last few years, during which improved analysis and insight, and effective models and decision-support systems, have been developed; however, these are not necessarily familiar to industry. Indeed, to our knowledge there is no published work (other than our textbook, *Designing and Managing the Supply Chain*, McGraw-Hill 2002, 2nd edition) that discusses these problems, models, concepts, and tools at an appropriate level.

In this book, we intend to fill this gap by providing state-of-the-art concepts that are important for the design, control, operation, and management of supply chain systems. In particular, we have attempted to convey the intuition behind many key supply chain concepts and to provide simple approaches that can be used to analyze various aspects of the supply chain. We have tried to emphasize an approach that is logical and succinct–we know our readers are busy people, and we have tried to convey the key concepts as efficiently as possible.

Of course, supply chain management is a very broad area, and it would be impossible for a single book to cover all of the relevant areas in depth. Indeed, there is considerable disagreement in academia and industry about exactly what these relevant areas are. Nevertheless, we have attempted to provide a broad introduction to many critical facets of supply chain management. Although many essential supply chain management issues are interrelated, we have strived wherever possible to make each chapter as self-contained as possible, so that the reader can refer directly to chapters covering topics of interest.

The discussion covers a wide range of topics starting with a chapter on the value of information that covers the bullwhip effect and the advantages of supply chain coordination. The chapter on supply chain integration develops concepts such as push, pull and push-pull systems and introduces a framework to identify the appropriate supply chain strategy for specific companies and individual products.

The chapter on network planning deals with three issues: the design of the logistics network, inventory positioning and management, and the effective allocation of resources and activities, such as manufacturing, distribution or warehousing, across the entire supply chain. The chapter on supply chain alliances delves into how to deal with partners such as suppliers and third part logistics companies.

The chapter on outsourcing, procurement and supply contracts characterizes the risk and benefit in outsourcing, introduces a framework for make-buy decisions as well as for selecting the appropriate procurement strategy. As we shall see, this framework implies that the procurement strategy is tightly linked to the firm's outsourcing strategy. The chapter also discusses effective supply contracts that ensure that both suppliers and buyers benefit from this relationship.

These chapters are followed by chapters on product design and its impact on supply chain performance; a chapter on customer value and its influence on the type of supply chain required; and a chapter on opportunities provided by international supply chains as well as problems and pitfalls. Finally, the chapter on information technology identifies information systems, technologies and decision support systems important in the management of the supply chain.

This book grew out of a textbook we wrote about five years ago. When we wrote that book, our objective was to present, in an easily accessible manner, supply chain concepts, strategies, and models. We are pleased to note that the text was very successful; we received a tremendous response from faculty, and industry professionals. The success of the first edition, as well as new concepts and recent technological changes, led to a second edition published last year, which built on the positive elements of the first edition, and included what we learned since we wrote the first edition. The goal of this book is to distill the various important concepts and ideas in the textbook, and to present them in a clear and succinct way for busy managers and consultants, who don't have time to take a full course on supply chain management, but who want to understand important supply chain management issues.

Many of the ideas developed in this book grew out of a number of supply chain management courses and Executive Education programs we taught at Northwestern University, Massachusetts Institute of Technology and the University of California, Berkeley over the past several years, as well as numerous consulting projects and supply chain decision support systems we developed at LogicTools (www.logic-tools.com). These courses have spawned many innovative and effective supply chain education concepts. The focus in these programs has always been on presenting, in an easily accessible manner, recently developed state-of-the-art models and solution methods important in the design, control, and operation of supply chains. Similarly, the consulting projects and decision-support systems developed by LogicTools have focused on applying these advanced techniques to solve specific problems faced by our clients. In the last several years, we have continued to add models and techniques to these courses, and we have started to put all of these techniques into perspective, and to develop frameworks to integrate all of these models and solution methods.

This book is extensively based on our textbook, *Designing and Managing the Supply Chain*. Parts of that book are based on other work we have done either together or with others, including *The Logic of Logistics*, written by Julien Bramel and David Simchi-Levi and published by Springer in 1997; an article by Chen, Drezner, Ryan, and Simchi-Levi in *Quantitative Models for Supply Chain Management*, edited by Sridhar Tayur, Ram Ganeshan, and Michael Magazine, and published by Kluwer Academic Publishers; and two papers, one written by the first and the third authors of this book and the second written by these two authors and M. Watson, that appeared in *The Practice of Supply Chain Management*, edited by C. Billington, T. Harrison, H. Lee, and J. Neale, published by Kluwer Academic Publishers.

ACKNOWLEDGMENTS

It is our pleasure to acknowledge all those who helped us with the various versions of this manuscript.

We are grateful to our colleagues at Massachusetts Institute of Technology; the University of California, Berkeley; and LogicTools who have provided us with opportunities to interact with some of the brightest minds in our field and to learn from their research and insights. Three people stand out in this regard: Professors Charles H. Fine and Stephen C. Graves (MIT), with whom Professor Simchi-Levi has closely collaborated in the last two years, and Dr. Michael S. Watson from LogicTools. We would also like to thank Dr. Larry Snyder from Lehigh University for his contribution.

Finally, we would like to thank Catherine Dassopoulos for picking up this project and supporting it through the long process and change of plans. We would also like to thank Daina Penikas and her staff for the excellent job on the manuscript preparation.

CHAPTER 1

Introduction

1.1 WHAT IS SUPPLY CHAIN MANAGEMENT?

Fierce competition in today's global markets, the introduction of products with shorter and shorter life cycles, and the heightened expectations of customers have forced business enterprises to invest in and focus attention on their supply chains. This, together with continuing advances in communications and transportation technologies (e.g., mobile communication, the Internet, and overnight delivery), has motivated the continuous evolution of the supply chain and of the techniques to manage it.

In a typical supply chain, raw materials are procured, and items are produced at one or more factories, shipped to warehouses for intermediate storage, and then shipped to retailers or customers. Consequently, to reduce cost and improve service levels, effective supply chain strategies must take into account the interactions at the various levels in the supply chain. The *supply chain*, which is also referred to as the *logistics network*, consists of suppliers, manufacturing centers, warehouses, distribution centers, and retail outlets, as well as raw materials, work-in-process inventory, and finished products that flow between the facilities (Fig. 1-1).

In this book we present and explain concepts, insights, practical tools, and decision support systems important for the effective

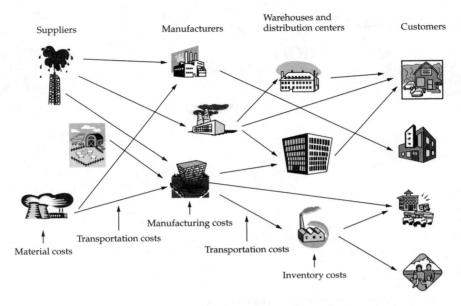

Suppliers   Manufacturers   Warehouses and   Customers
                                          distribution centers

Manufacturing costs

Transportation costs

Material costs

Transportation costs

Inventory costs

Figure 1-1   The logistics network.

management of the supply chain. But what exactly is *supply chain management?* We define it as follows:

> Supply chain management is a set of approaches used to efficiently integrate suppliers, manufacturers, warehouses, and stores so that merchandise is produced and distributed at the right quantities, to the right locations, and at the right time in order to minimize systemwide costs while satisfying service-level requirements.

This definition leads to several observations. First, supply chain management takes into consideration every facility that has an impact on cost and plays a role in making the product conform to customer requirements: from supplier and manufacturing facilities through warehouses and distribution centers to retailers and stores. Indeed, in some supply chain analysis, it is necessary to account for the suppliers' suppliers and the customers' customers because they have an impact on supply chain performance. Second, the objective of supply chain management is to be efficient and cost-effective across the entire system; total systemwide costs, from transportation and distribution to inventories of raw materials, work in process, and finished goods, are to be minimized. Thus the emphasis is not on simply minimizing transportation cost or reducing inventories but rather on taking a *systems approach* to supply chain management. Finally, because supply chain management revolves around efficient integration of suppliers, manufacturers, warehouses, and stores, it encompasses the firm's activities at many levels, from the strategic level through the tactical to the operational level.

What about logistics management? What is the difference between supply chain management and logistics management? While the answer to this question depends on who is addressing this issue, we will not distinguish between logistics and supply chain management in this text. Indeed, our definition of supply chain management is similar to the definition of *logistics management* given by the Council of Logistics Management:

> The process of planning, implementing, and controlling the efficient, cost-effective flow and storage of raw materials, in-process inventory, finished goods, and related information from point of origin to point of consumption for the purpose of conforming to customer requirements.

What makes supply chain management difficult? Although we will discuss a variety of reasons throughout this text, they can all be related to one or both of the following observations:

1. It is challenging to design and operate a supply chain so that total systemwide costs are minimized and systemwide service levels are maintained. Indeed, it is frequently difficult to operate *a single facility* so that costs are minimized and service level is maintained. The difficulty increases exponentially when an entire system is being considered. The process of finding the best *systemwide* strategy is known as *global optimization*.

2. Uncertainty is inherent in every supply chain; customer demand can never be forecast exactly, travel times will never be certain, and machines and vehicles will break down. Supply chains need to be designed to eliminate as much uncertainty as possible and to deal effectively with the uncertainty that remains.

In the next two sections we discuss each of these issues in detail.

1.2 GLOBAL OPTIMIZATION

What makes finding the best systemwide, or globally optimal, integrated solution so difficult? A number of factors make this a challenging problem:

1. The supply chain is a complex network of facilities dispersed over a large geography and, in many cases, all over the globe. The following example illustrates a network that is fairly typical of today's global companies.

EXAMPLE 1-1

National Semiconductor, whose list of competitors includes Motorola, Inc., and the Intel Corporation, is one of the world's largest chipmakers whose products are used in fax machines, cellular phones, computers, and cars. Currently, the company has four wafer fabrication facilities, three in the United States and one in Great Britain, and has test and assembly sites in Malaysia and Singapore. After assembly, finished products are shipped to hundreds of manufacturing facilities all over the world, including those of Compaq, Ford, IBM, and Siemens. Since the semiconductor industry is highly competitive, specifying short lead times and being able to deliver within the committed due date are critical capabilities. In 1994, 95 percent of National Semiconductor's customers received their orders within 45 days from the time the order was placed, whereas the remaining 5 percent received their orders within 90 days. These tight lead times required the company to involve 12 different airline carriers using about 20,000 different routes. The difficulty, of course, was that no customer knew in advance if they were going to be part of the 5 percent of customers who received their order in 90 days or the 95 percent who received their order within 45 days.[1]

2. Different facilities in the supply chain frequently have *different, conflicting objectives*. For instance, suppliers typically want manufacturers to commit themselves to purchasing large quantities in stable volumes with flexible delivery dates. Unfortunately, although most manufacturers would like to implement long production runs, they need to be flexible to their customers' needs and changing demands. Thus the suppliers' goals are in direct conflict with the manufacturers' desire for flexibility. Indeed, since production decisions typically are made without precise information about customer demand, the ability of manufacturers to match supply and demand depends largely on their ability to change supply volume as information about demand arrives. Similarly, the manufacturers' objective of making large production batches typically conflicts with the objective of both warehouses and distribution centers to reduce inventory. To make matters worse, this latter objective of reducing inventory levels typically implies an increase in transportation costs.

3. The supply chain is a dynamic system that evolves over time. Indeed, not only do customer demand and supplier capabilities change over time, but supply chain relationships also evolve over time. For example, as customers' power increases, there is increased pressure placed on manufacturers and suppliers to produce an enormous variety of high-quality products and, ultimately, to produce customized products.

4. System variations over time are also an important consideration. Even when demand is known precisely (e.g., because of contractual agreements), the planning process needs to account for demand and cost parameters varying over time due to the impact of seasonal fluctuations, trends, advertising and promotions, competitors' pricing strategies, and so forth. These time-varying demand and cost parameters make it difficult to determine the most effective supply chain strategy, i.e., the one that minimizes systemwide costs and conforms to customer requirements.

1.3 MANAGING UNCERTAINTY

Global optimization is made even more difficult because supply chains need to be designed for and operated in uncertain environments. A number of factors contribute to this:

1. Matching supply and demand is a major challenge:
    a. Boeing Aircraft announced a write-down of $2.6 billion in October 1997 due to "raw material shortages, internal and supplier parts shortages and productivity inefficiencies. . . ."[2]
    b. "Second quarter sales at U.S. Surgical Corporation declined 25 percent, resulting in a loss of $22 million. The sales and earnings shortfall is attributed to larger than anticipated inventories on the shelves of hospitals."[3]
    c. "IBM sells out New Aptiva PC; shortage may cost millions in potential revenue."[4]

Obviously, this difficulty stems from the fact that months before demand is realized, manufacturers have to commit themselves to specific production levels. These advance commitments imply huge financial and supply risks.

2. Inventory and back-order levels fluctuate considerably across the supply chain, even when customer demand for specific products does not vary greatly. To illustrate this issue, consider Figure 1-2, which suggests that in a typical supply chain, distributor orders to the factory fluctuate far more than the underlying retailer demand.

3. Forecasting does not solve the problem. Indeed, we argue in the first principle of all forecasts (see Chap. 2) that "forecasts are always wrong." Thus it is impossible to predict the precise demand for a specific item, even with the most advanced forecast techniques.

4. Demand is not the only source of uncertainty. Delivery lead times, manufacturing yields, transportation times, and component availability also can have significant supply chain

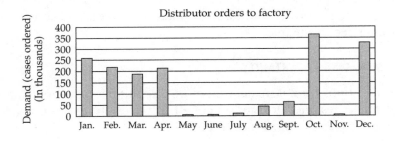

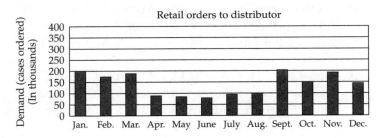

Figure 1-2   Order variations in the supply chain.

impact. As supply chains become larger and more geographically diverse, natural and human-made disasters can have tremendous impact.

EXAMPLE 1-2

In September 1999, a massive earthquake devastated Taiwan. Initially, 80 percent of the island's power was lost. Companies such as Hewlett-Packard and Dell, who source a variety of components from Taiwanese manufacturers, were affected by supply interruptions.[5] Similarly, fabric shipments from India were delayed in the wake of the January 26, 2001 earthquake in the Indian state of Gujarat, affecting many U.S. apparel manufacturers.[6]

Although uncertainty cannot be eliminated, we will explore various approaches that *minimize the effect* of uncertainty in the supply chain. When this is not possible, we will identify strategies that supply chain partners can apply so as to maintain or increase service level.

1.4 WHY SUPPLY CHAIN MANAGEMENT?

In the 1980s, companies discovered new manufacturing technologies and strategies that allowed them to reduce costs and better compete in different markets. Strategies such as just-in-time manufacturing, *kanban*, lean manufacturing, total quality management, and others became very popular, and vast quantities of resources were invested in implementing these strategies. In the last few years, however, it has become clear that many companies have reduced manufacturing costs as much as is practically possible. Many of these companies are discovering that effective supply chain management is the next step they need to take to increase profit and market share.

Indeed, in 1998 American companies spent $898 billion, or about 10 percent of the U.S. gross national product (GNP), on supply-related activities. During 2000, this cost increased to over $1 trillion, decreasing to $957 billion in 2001 and $910 billion in 2002.[7] This figure includes the cost of movement, storage, and control of products across the supply chain both within manufacturing plants and warehouses and between different components of the supply chain. Unfortunately, this huge investment typically includes many unnecessary cost components due to redundant stock, inefficient transportation strategies, and other wasteful practices in the supply chain. For instance, experts believe that the grocery industry can save about $30 billion, or 10 percent of its annual operating cost, by using more effective supply chain strategies.[1]

To illustrate this issue, consider the following two examples:

1. It takes a typical box of cereal more than 3 months to get from the factory to a supermarket.
2. It takes a typical new car, on average, 15 days to travel from the factory to the dealership. This lead time should be compared with the actual travel time, which is no more than 4 to 5 days.

Thus many opportunities exist to cut costs in the supply chain. Not surprisingly, a number of companies have been able to substantially increase revenue or decrease costs through effective supply chain management.

EXAMPLE 1-3

Procter & Gamble estimates that it saved retail customers $65 million in a recent 18-month supply chain initiative. "According to Procter & Gamble, the essence of its approach lies in manufacturers and suppliers working closely together . . . jointly creating business plans to eliminate the source of wasteful practices across the entire supply chain."[8]

This example suggests that *strategic partnerships* between suppliers and manufacturers may have a significant impact on supply chain performance. What are the types of *business plans* and *partnerships* that can best reduce costs and improve service levels? Which one is appropriate for the particular situation at hand? What incentives and performance measures should be used to make the partnership successful? Finally, how should the benefits resulting from the strategic partnerships be shared? Should the cost savings be transferred to the customers, split between the different partners, or kept by the most powerful player?

EXAMPLE 1-4

In 2 years, National Semiconductor reduced distribution costs by 2.5 percent, decreased delivery time by 47 percent, and increased sales by 34 percent by closing six warehouses around the globe and air-freighting microchips to customers from a new centralized distribution center in Singapore.[1]

Of course, by switching to air carriers, National Semiconductor increased transportation costs significantly. This increase was offset by a reduction in inventory costs resulting from the shift from a decentralized distribution system with a number of warehouses to a centralized system with a single warehouse. This example motivates the following question: What are the correct tradeoffs between inventory and transportation costs?

EXAMPLE 1-5

Nabisco, Inc., delivers 500 types of cookies and more than 10,000 candies to over 80,000 buyers and spends more than $200 million a year in transportation expenses. Unfortunately, too many trucks arrive at or depart from their destinations half empty. This is why Nabisco is pioneering a collaborative logistics effort so that it can share trucks and warehouse space with other companies in order to lower logistics costs. In a recent pilot program, Nabisco shared warehouses and trucks with 25 other manufacturers, including Dole and Lea & Perrins. In one test involving 8000 orders, grocer Lucky Stores reduced inventory costs by $4.8 million. Nabisco itself saved $78,000 in shipping costs, and combined, all the manufacturers involved in the test saved nearly $900,000.[9]

Of course, this type of cooperation with other companies requires advanced information systems and entails a number of risks. What systems are necessary for this approach to be a success? When should a company undertake this type of complicated partnership?

EXAMPLE 1-6

Dayton Hudson Corporation's Target stores rely on sophisticated relationships with suppliers. Target, for example, may agree that an

(continued)

earthenware manufacturer will supply a certain number of Italian bowls without specifying details of style and color. As the delivery date draws nearer, Target forecasts styles that are likely to sell. Based on these forecasts, the manufacturer can produce trial lots, which can be sold in select Target stores to determine if the particular styles manufactured will indeed sell.[10]

Clearly, this level of flexibility increases the complexity of the supplier's supply chain. Why would the supplier agree to this type of arrangement? How much does Target gain with this type of flexible ordering? Should Target be willing to pay more per bowl for this flexibility? If so, how much more? And finally, what type of information system needs to be employed by Target and its suppliers to support this level of flexibility?

EXAMPLE 1-7

In 1979, Kmart was one of the leading companies in the retail industry, with 1891 stores and average revenues per store of $7.25 million. At that time, Wal-Mart was a small niche retailer in the South with only 229 stores and average revenues about half those of Kmart stores. In 10 years, Wal-Mart had transformed itself; in 1992 it had the highest sales per square foot and the highest inventory turnover and operating profit of any discount retailer.[11] Today Wal-Mart is the largest and highest-profit retailer in the world. In fact, sales for year ending Jan. 2003 were $244.5 billion, and it is also the largest employer in the US. How did Wal-Mart do it? The starting point was a relentless focus on satisfying customer needs; Wal-Mart's goal was simply to provide customers with access to goods when and where they want them and to develop cost structures that enable competitive pricing. The key to achieving this goal was to make the way the company replenishes inventory the centerpiece of its strategy. This was done by using a logistics technique known as *cross-docking*. In this strategy, goods are continuously delivered to Wal-Mart's warehouses, from where they are dispatched to stores without ever sitting in inventory. This strategy reduced Wal-Mart's cost of sales significantly and made it possible to offer everyday low prices to their customers.[12]

If the cross-docking strategy works so well for Wal-Mart, shouldn't all companies use the same strategy? Indeed, *many success-*

ful retailers employ other distribution strategies; some keep inventory at their warehouses, whereas others ship directly to stores.

E X A M P L E 1-8

> The Home Depot, Inc., moves over 85 percent of its merchandise directly from suppliers to stores, avoiding warehouses altogether. In addition, since such a high volume of goods moves through its stores ($44 million in annual sales on average), the products frequently are shipped in full truck loads, for additional savings.[10]

These examples describe a number of supply chain management success stories. They suggest that in some industries, supply chain management is perhaps the single most important factor determining the success of the firm. Indeed, in the computer and printer industries, where most manufacturers use the same suppliers and identical technologies, companies compete on cost and service levels, the two key elements in our definition of supply chain management.

The examples also raise an important question. If these firms have improved supply chain performance by focusing on strategic partnering, using centralized warehousing, or employing the cross-docking strategy, what inhibits other firms from adopting the same techniques to improve their supply chain performance?

The earlier discussion suggests that the answer involves two major issues:

- The ability to replace traditional supply chain strategies, in which each facility or party in the chain makes decisions with little regard to their impact on other supply chain partners, by those which yield a *globally optimized* supply chain.
- The ability to effectively manage uncertainty. Unfortunately, the level of demand uncertainty has increased in the last few years. Indeed, in high-tech industries, product life cycles are becoming shorter and shorter. In particular, many computer and printer models have life cycles of only a few months, so the manufacturer may have only one order or production opportunity. Unfortunately, since these are new products, no historical data are available that allow the manufacturer to accurately predict customer demand. At the same time, the proliferation of products in these industries makes it

increasingly difficult to predict demand for a specific model. Finally, significant price declines in these industries are common, reducing the product value during its life cycle.[13]

EXAMPLE 1-9

A Korean manufacturer of electrical products such as industrial relays is facing a service level of about 70 percent; i.e., only about 70 percent of all orders are delivered on time. On the other hand, inventory keeps piling up, mostly of products that are not in demand. The manufacturer's *inventory turnover ratio*, defined as the ratio of the annual flow to average inventory at the manufacturer's main warehouse, is about four. However, in the electronics industry, leading companies turn inventory over about nine times a year. If the Korean manufacturer can increase its inventory turns to this level, it will be able to significantly reduce inventory levels. The manufacturer is thus searching for new strategies that will increase service levels over the next 3 years to about 99 percent and, at the same time, significantly decrease inventory levels and cost.

Just a few years ago, most analysts would have said that the two objectives described in Example 1-9, improved service and inventory levels, could not be achieved at the same time. Indeed, traditional inventory theory tells us that to increase service level, the firm must increase inventory and therefore cost. Surprisingly, recent developments in information and communications technologies, together with a better understanding of supply chain strategies, have led to innovative approaches that allow the firm to improve both objectives simultaneously.

Throughout the rest of this book we endeavor to present these approaches and strategies in detail. We will focus on demonstrating why certain strategies are adopted, what the tradeoffs are between different strategies, and how specific strategies are implemented in practice.

1.5 KEY ISSUES IN SUPPLY CHAIN MANAGEMENT

In this section we introduce some of the supply chain management issues that we discuss in much more detail throughout the remaining chapters. These issues span a large spectrum of a firm's activities, from the strategic through the tactical to the operational level:

- The *strategic level* deals with decisions that have a long-lasting effect on the firm. These include decisions regarding the number, location, and capacity of warehouses and manufacturing plants and the flow of material through the logistics network.
- The *tactical level* includes decisions that are typically updated anywhere between once every quarter and once every year. These include purchasing and production decisions, inventory policies, and transportation strategies, including the frequency with which customers are visited.
- The *operational level* refers to day-to-day decisions such as scheduling, lead time quotations, routing, and truck loading.

Below we introduce and discuss some of the key issues, questions, and tradeoffs associated with different decisions.

Network Planning Consider several plants producing products to serve a set of geographically dispersed retailers. The current set of warehouses is deemed inappropriate, and management wants to reorganize or redesign the distribution network. This may be due, for example, to changing demand patterns or the termination of a leasing contract for a number of existing warehouses. In addition, changing demand patterns may require a change in plant production levels, a selection of new suppliers, and a new flow pattern of goods throughout the distribution network. How should management select a set of warehouse locations and capacities, determine production levels for each product at each plant, and set transportation flows between facilities, either from plant to warehouse or warehouse to retailer, in such a way as to minimize total production, inventory, and transportation costs and satisfy service level requirements? This is a complex optimization problem, and advanced technology and approaches are required to find a solution.

Inventory Control Consider a retailer that maintains an inventory of a particular product. Since customer demand changes over time, the retailer can use only historical data to predict demand. How should the

retailer manage inventory? More fundamentally, why should the retailer hold inventory in the first place? Is it due to uncertainty in customer demand, uncertainty in the supply process, or some other reasons? If it is due to uncertainty in customer demand, is there anything
that can be done to reduce it?

Supply Contracts   In traditional supply chain strategies, each party in
the chain focuses on its own profit and hence makes decisions with little regard to their impact on other supply chain partners. Relationships between suppliers and buyers are established by means of supply
contracts that specify pricing and volume discounts, delivery lead
times, quality, returns, and so forth. The question, of course, is
whether supply contracts also can be used to replace the traditional
supply chain strategy with one that optimizes the entire supply chain
performance? In particular, what is the impact of volume discount and
revenue-sharing contracts on supply chain performance? Are there
pricing strategies that can be applied by suppliers to provide incentives
to buyers to order more products while at the same time increasing the
supplier profit?

Distribution Strategies   Wal-Mart's success story highlights the importance of a particular distribution strategy referred to as *cross-docking*. As observed earlier, this is a distribution strategy in which the
stores are supplied by central warehouses that act as coordinators of
the supply process and as transshipment points for incoming orders
from outside vendors but that do not keep stock themselves. We refer
to such warehouses as *cross-dock points*. Consider the following questions: How many cross-dock points are necessary? What are the savings achieved using a cross-docking strategy? How should a cross-
docking strategy; be implemented in practice? Is the cross-docking
strategy better than the classic strategy in which warehouses hold inventory? Which strategy should a particular firm employ: the cross-
docking strategy; the classic distribution strategy in which inventory is
kept at the warehouses; or direct shipping, a strategy in which items
are shipped from suppliers directly to stores?

Supply Chain Integration and Strategic Partnering   As observed earlier,
designing and implementing a globally optimal supply chain are quite
difficult because of the dynamics of the supply chain and the conflict-

ing objectives employed by different facilities and partners. Nevertheless, the National Semiconductor, Wal-Mart, and Procter & Gamble success stories demonstrate not only that an integrated, globally optimal supply chain is possible but also that it can have a huge impact on the company's performance and market share. Of course, one can argue that these three examples are associated with companies that are among the biggest companies in their respective industries; these companies can implement technologies and strategies that very few others can afford. However, in today's competitive markets, most companies have no choice; they are forced to integrate their supply chain and engage in strategic partnering. This pressure stems from both their customers and their supply chain partners. How can integration be achieved successfully? Clearly, information sharing and operational planning are the keys to a successfully integrated supply chain. But what information should be shared? How should it be used? How does information affect the design and operation of the supply chain? What level of integration is needed within the organization and with external partners? Finally, what types of partnerships can be implemented, and which type should be implemented for a given situation?

Outsourcing and Procurement Strategies Rethinking your supply chain strategy involves not only coordinating the different activities in the supply chain but also deciding what to make internally and what to buy from outside sources. How can a firm identify what manufacturing activities lie in its set of core competencies and thus should be completed internally and what products and components should be purchased from outside suppliers because these manufacturing activities are not core competencies? Is there any relationship between the answer to this question and product architecture? What are the risks associated with outsourcing, and how can these risks be minimized? When you do outsource, how can you ensure a timely supply of products? Finally, what is the impact of the Internet on procurement strategies? Should the firm use a private or public exchange when dealing with trading partners?

Product Design Effective design plays several critical roles in the supply chain. Most obviously, certain product designs may increase inventory holding or transportation costs relative to other designs, whereas other designs may facilitate a shorter manufacturing lead time. Unfortunately, product redesign is often expensive. When is it worthwhile to redesign products so as to reduce logistics costs or supply chain lead times? Is it possible to leverage product design to compensate for uncertainty in customer demand? Can one quantify the amount of savings resulting from such a strategy? What changes should be made in the supply chain to take advantage of the new product design? Finally, new concepts such as mass customization are increasingly popular. What role does supply chain management play in the successful implementation of these concepts?

Customer Value   Customer value is the measure of a company's contribution to its customer, based on the entire range of products, services, and intangibles that constitute the company's offerings. In recent years, this measure has superseded measures such as quality and customer satisfaction. Obviously, effective supply chain management is critical if a firm wishes to fulfill customer needs and provide value. But what determines customer value in different industries? How is customer value measured? How is information technology used to enhance customer value in the supply chain? How does supply chain management contribute to customer value? How do emerging trends in customer value, such as development of relationships and experiences, affect supply chain management? What is the relationship between product price and brand name in the conventional world and in the online world? Can "smart" pricing strategies be used to improve supply chain performance?

Information Technology and Decision-Support Systems   Information technology is a critical enabler of effective supply chain management. Indeed, much of the current interest in supply chain management is motivated by the opportunities that appeared due to the abundance of data and the savings that can be achieved by sophisticated analysis of these data. The primary issue in supply chain management is not whether data can be received, but what data should be transferred; i.e., which data are significant for supply chain management and which data can be ignored safely? How should the data be analyzed and used? What is the impact of the Internet? What infrastructure is required both internally and between supply chain partners? Finally, since information technology and decision-support systems are both available,

Table 1-1 Key Supply-Chain Management Issues

	Global Optimization	Managing Uncertainty
Network planning	x	
Inventory control		x
Supply contracts	x	
Distribution strategies	x	x
Strategic partnerships	x	
Outsourcing and procurement		x
Product design		x
Customer value	x	x
Information technology	x	x

can these technologies be viewed as the main tools used to achieve competitive advantage in the market? If they can, then what is preventing others from using the same technology?

Each of these issues and strategies is discussed in great detail in the remaining chapters. As you will see, the focus in each case is on either achieving a *globally optimized* supply chain or managing uncertainty in the supply chain or both. A summary is provided in Table 1-1.

1.6 BOOK OBJECTIVES AND OVERVIEW

For many reasons, interest in logistics and supply chain management has grown explosively in the last few years. This interest has led many companies to analyze their supply chains. In most cases, however, this has been done based on experience and intuition; very few analytical models or design tools have been used in this process. Meanwhile, in the last two decades, the academic community has developed various models and tools to assist with management of the supply chain. Unfortunately, the first generation of this technology was not robust or flexible enough to be used effectively by industry. This, however, has changed in the last few years. Analysis and insight have improved, and effective models and decision-support systems have been developed—but these may not be familiar to industry.

This book aims to fill the gap by presenting state-of-the-art models and solution methods, insights, and concepts important in the design, control, operation, and management of supply chain systems. Each chapter is mostly self-contained and includes numerous examples. We intend this book to be a reference for consultants and managers involved in any one of the processes that make up the supply chain. For example, transportation managers deciding which modes of transportation to use, inventory control managers wanting to ensure smooth production with as little inventory as possible, purchasing/supply managers designing contracts with their companies' suppliers and clients, and logistics managers in charge of their companies' supply chains can all benefit from the contents of this book.

CHAPTER 2

The Value of Information

2.1 INTRODUCTION

We live in the information age where data warehouses, Web services, XML, portals, and RFID tags are just a few of the technologies dominating the business pages of the daily newspaper. In Chapter 10 we examine these technologies in detail and look at the issues surrounding their implementation. In this chapter we consider the value of using any type of information technology; we deal specifically with the potential availability of more and more information throughout the supply chain and the implications that this availability has on effective design and management of the integrated supply chain.

The implications of this abundance of available information are enormous. The supply chain pundits and consultants like to use the phrase, *In modern supply chains, information replaces inventory.* We do not dispute this idea, but its meaning is vague. After all, at some point the customer needs products, not just information! Nevertheless, information changes the way supply chains can and should be managed effectively, and these changes may lead to, among other things, lower inventories. Indeed, our objective in this chapter is to characterize how information affects the design and operation of the supply chain. We show that by harnessing the information now available, one can design and operate the supply chain much more efficiently than ever before.

It should be apparent that having accurate information about inventory levels, orders, production, and delivery status throughout the supply chain should not make the managers of a supply chain less effective than if this information were not available. After all, they could choose to ignore it. As we will see, however, this information provides a tremendous opportunity to improve the way the supply chain is designed and managed. Unfortunately, using this information effectively does make the design and management of the supply chain more complex because many more issues must be considered.

We argue here that this abundant information

- Helps reduce variability in the supply chain.
- Helps suppliers make better forecasts, accounting for promotions and market changes.
- Enables the coordination of manufacturing and distribution systems and strategies.
- Enables retailers to better serve their customers by offering tools for locating desired items.
- Enables retailers to react and adapt to supply problems more rapidly.
- Enables lead time reductions.

The chapter is based on the seminal work in [1] and [2] as well as the recent work in [3] and [4]. In the next section, we follow the review article [5].

2.2 THE BULLWHIP EFFECT

In recent years, many suppliers and retailers have observed that while customer demand for specific products does not vary much, inventory and back-order levels fluctuate considerably across their supply chain. For instance, in examining the demand for Pampers disposable diapers, executives at Procter & Gamble noticed an interesting phenomenon. As expected, retail sales of the product were fairly uniform; there is no particular day or month in which the demand is significantly higher or lower than any other. However, the executives noticed that distributors' orders placed to the factory fluctuated much more than retail sales. In addition, Procter & Gamble's orders to its suppliers fluctuated even more. This increase in variability as we travel up in the supply chain is referred to as the *bullwhip effect*.

Figure 2-1 illustrates a simple four-stage supply chain: a single retailer, a single wholesaler, a single distributor, and a single factory. The retailer observes customer demand and places orders to the wholesaler. The wholesaler receives products from the distributor, who places orders to the factory. Figure 2-2 provides a graphic representation of orders, as a function of time, placed by different facilities. The figure clearly shows the increase in variability across the supply chain.

To understand the impact of the increase in variability on the supply chain, consider the second stage in our example, the wholesaler. The wholesaler receives orders from the retailer and places orders to its supplier, the distributor. To determine these order quantities, the wholesaler must forecast the retailer's demand. If the wholesaler does not have access to the customer's demand data, it must use orders placed by the retailer to perform the forecasting.

Since variability in orders placed by the retailer is significantly higher than variability in customer demand, as Figure 2-2 shows, the

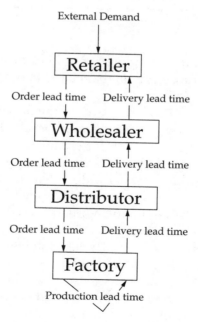

Figure 2-1   The supply chain.

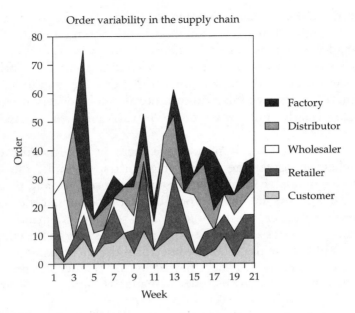

Figure 2-2 The increase in variability in the supply chain.

wholesaler is forced to carry more safety stock than the retailer or else to maintain higher capacity than the retailer in order to meet the same service level as the retailer.

This analysis can be carried over to the distributor as well as the factory, resulting in even higher inventory levels and therefore higher costs at these facilities. Consider, for example, a simple widget supply chain. A single factory, WidgetMakers, Inc., supplies a single retailer, theWidgetStore. Average annual widget demand at the WidgetStore is 5200 units, and shipments are made from WidgetMakers to the store each week. If the variability in orders placed by the WidgetStore is low, such that the shipment every week is about 100 units, Widget-Makers' production capacity and weekly shipping capacity need be only about 100 units. If weekly variability is very high, such that during certain weeks WidgetMakers must make and ship 400 units and some weeks no units at all, it is easy to see that production and shipping capacity must be much higher and that some weeks this capacity will be idle. Alternatively, WidgetMakers could build up inventory

THE VALUE OF INFORMATION

during weeks with low demand and supply these items during weeks with high demand, thus increasing inventory holding costs.

Thus it is important to identify techniques and tools that will allow us to control the bullwhip effect, i.e., to control the increase in variability in the supply chain. For this purpose, we need to first understand the main factors contributing to the increase in variability in the supply chain.

1. *Demand forecasting.* Traditional inventory management techniques practiced at each level in the supply chain lead to the bullwhip effect. To explain the connection between forecasting and the bullwhip effect, consider an approach that is used frequently to manage inventory, the *min-max inventory management policy* (see Chap. 4). Here, whenever the inventory at a facility is less than a given number, referred to as the *reorder point*, the facility orders a quantity that will increase its inventory to a given target level. This target level is set based on average demand and the variability of that demand. Typically, managers use *standard forecast smoothing techniques* to estimate average demand and demand variability. An important characteristic of all forecasting techniques is that as more data are observed, the more we modify the estimates of the average demand and demand variability. Since the order target level strongly depends on these estimates, the user is forced to change order quantities, thus increasing variability.

2. *Lead time.* It is easy to see that the increase in variability is magnified with increasing lead time. Indeed, as explained in Chapter 4, the reorder level consists of two quantities; the first is the average demand during lead time, and the second is the safety stock, which depends on lead time, demand variability, and service level. Thus, with longer lead times, a small change in the estimate of demand variability implies a significant change in reorder level, leading to a significant change in order quantities. This, of course, leads to an increase in variability.

3. *Batch ordering.* The impact of batch ordering is quite simple to understand. If the retailer orders in batches, then the wholesaler will observe a large order, followed by several periods of no orders, followed by another large order, and so on. Thus the wholesaler sees a distorted and highly variable pattern of orders.

Recall that firms use batch ordering for a number of reasons. As pointed out in Chapter 4, a firm that is faced with fixed ordering costs needs to minimize these costs, which leads to batch ordering. Second, as transportation costs become more significant, retailers may order quantities that allow them to take advantage of transportation discounts (e.g., full-truckload quantities). This may lead to some weeks with large orders and some with no orders at all. Finally, the quarterly or yearly sales quotas or incentives observed in many businesses also can result in unusually large orders observed on a periodic basis.

   4. *Price fluctuation.* Price fluctuation also can lead to the bullwhip effect. If prices fluctuate, retailers often attempt to stock up when prices are lower. This is accentuated by the prevailing practice in many industries of offering promotions and discounts at certain times or for certain quantities.

   5. *Inflated orders.* Inflated orders placed by retailers during shortage periods tend to magnify the bullwhip effect. Such orders are common when retailers and distributors suspect that a product will be in short supply and therefore anticipate receiving supply proportional to the amount ordered. When the period of shortage is over, the retailer goes back to its standard orders, leading to all kinds of distortions and variations in demand estimates.

   6. *Lack of centralized information.* One of the most frequent suggestions for reducing the bullwhip effect is to centralize demand information within a supply chain, i.e., to provide each stage of the supply chain with complete information on the actual customer demand. To understand why centralized demand information can reduce the bullwhip effect, note that if demand information is centralized, each stage of the supply chain can use the actual customer demand data to create more accurate forecasts rather than relying on the orders received from the previous stage, which can vary significantly more than the actual customer demand.

   Now consider two types of supply chains: one with centralized demand information and a second with decentralized demand information. In the first type of supply chain, the *centralized supply chain*, the retailer, or the first stage in the supply chain, observes customer demand, forecasts the average demand, determines its target inventory level, and places an order to the wholesaler. The wholesaler, or the second stage of the supply chain, receives the order along with the retailer's forecast average demand, uses this forecast to determine its target inventory level, and places an order to the distributor.

   Since the wholesaler has full information on the retailer inventory levels and customer demand, the wholesaler can predict an incoming order from the retailer and hence be ready for this order, thus reducing lead time. This lead time reduction leads to reduction in the increase in variability. Similarly, the distributors, or the third stage of the supply chain, has information about the wholesaler and the retailer inventory levels as well as customer demand and hence can significantly reduce lead time and as a result reduce the bullwhip effect.

The second type of supply chain that we consider is the *decentralized supply chain*. In this case the retailer does not make its forecast average demand available to the remainder of the supply chain. Instead, each stage of the supply chain must estimate mean demand based on the orders received from its customer, without knowledge of the retailer's forecast.

What can we conclude about the bullwhip effect in these two types of supply chains? For either type of supply chain, centralized or decentralized, the variability of the order quantities becomes larger as we move up the supply chain so that the orders placed by the wholesaler are more variable than the orders placed by the retailer, and so on. The difference in the two types of supply chains is in terms of the ability to respond to orders from down stream facilities. Centralized information allows to reduce lead time and hence variability in the supply chain.

Indeed, the variability of orders increases dramatically more in the decentralized system. In other words, a decentralized supply chain, in which only the retailer knows the customer demand, can lead to significantly higher variability than a centralized supply chain, in which customer demand information is available at each stage of the supply chain, particularly when lead times are large. We therefore conclude that *centralizing demand information can reduce the bullwhip effect significantly*.

2.2.1 Methods for Coping with the Bullwhip Effect

Our ability to identify the causes of the bullwhip effect leads to a number of suggestions for reducing the bullwhip effect or for eliminating its impact. These include reducing uncertainty, reducing the variability of the customer demand process, reducing lead times, and engaging in strategic partnerships.

1. *Reducing uncertainty.* One of the most frequent suggestions for decreasing or eliminating the bullwhip effect is to reduce uncertainty throughout the supply chain by centralizing demand information, i.e., by providing each stage of the supply chain with complete information on actual customer demand.

Note, however, that even if each stage uses the same demand data, each may still employ different forecasting methods and different buying practices, both of which may contribute to the bullwhip effect. In addition, even when each stage uses the same demand data, the same forecasting method, and the same ordering policy, the bullwhip effect will continue to exist, albeit at a significantly reduced level. Thus centralized demand information reduces the bullwhip effect but does not eliminate it.

2. *Reducing variability.* The bullwhip effect can be diminished by reducing the variability inherent in the customer demand process. For example, if we can reduce the variability of customer demand seen by the retailer, then even if the bullwhip effect occurs, the variability of demand seen by the wholesaler also will be reduced.

We can reduce the variability of customer demand through, for example, the use of an *everyday low pricing* (EDLP) strategy. When a retailer uses EDLP, it offers a product at a single consistent price rather than offering a regular price with periodic price promotions. By eliminating price promotions, a retailer can eliminate many of the dramatic shifts in demand that occur along with these promotions. Therefore, everyday low pricing strategies can lead to much more stable—i.e., less variable—customer demand patterns.

Of course, variability of customer demand depends not only on the retailer pricing strategy but also on its competitors' strategies. Thus, while EDLP is an important tool used to reduce demand variability, its impact can be limited.

3. *Lead-time reduction.* As we observed earlier, the longer the lead time, the larger is the increase in variability. Therefore, lead-time reduction can reduce the bullwhip effect significantly throughout a supply chain.

Observe that lead times typically include two components: order lead times (i.e., the time it takes to produce and ship the item) and information lead times (i.e., the time it takes to process an order). This distinction is important because order lead times can be reduced through the use of cross-docking, whereas information lead times can be reduced through the use of electronic data interchange (EDI).

4. *Strategic partnerships.* The bullwhip effect can be eliminated by engaging in any of a number of strategic partnerships. These strategic partnerships change the way information is shared and inventory is managed within a supply chain, possibly eliminating the impact of the bullwhip effect. For example, in vendor-managed inventory (VMI; see Chap. 5), the manufacturer manages the inventory of its product at the retailer outlet and therefore determines for itself how much inventory to keep on hand and how much to ship to the retailer in every period. Therefore, in VMI, the manufacturer does not rely on the orders placed by a retailer, thus avoiding the bullwhip effect entirely.

Other types of partnerships are also applied to reduce the bullwhip effect. As we discussed earlier, for example, centralizing demand information can dramatically reduce the variability seen by the upstream stages in a supply chain. Therefore, it is clear that these upstream stages would benefit from a strategic partnership that provides an incentive for the retailer to make customer demand data available to the rest of the supply chain.

2.3 EFFECTIVE FORECASTS

Information leads to more effective forecasts. The more factors that predictions of future demand can take into account, the more accurate these predictions can be. Of course, forecasts are never completely accurate. Indeed, the following rules of forecasting typically hold:[6]

1. *The forecast is always wrong.* In other words, it is very unlikely that actual demand will exactly equal forecast demand.

2. *The longer the forecast horizon, the worse is the forecast.* In other words, a forecast of demand far in the future is likely to be less accurate than a forecast of near-future demand.

3. *Aggregate forecasts are more accurate.* In other words, a forecast of aggregate demand (e.g., all Honda passenger cars) will be more accurate than a forecast for an individual end item (red two-door Honda Civic LX models).

Despite these rules, forecasting is a critical management tool. Over the next several chapters we will see that by correctly managing inventory, planners can make the best possible use of forecasts despite the inherent difficulties of forecasting. In addition, forecasts are not just for inventory decision making; decisions about whether to enter a particular market at all, about whether to expand production capacity, or about whether to implement a given promotional plan all can benefit from effective forecasting.

In this section we explore a number of the techniques that can be used, separately or in combination, to create forecasts. Of course, it would be possible to write an entire book on forecasting (and many such books exist); our goal here is to introduce the different approaches to forecasting and suggest when each of these approaches is appropriate.

Although there are many different forecasting tools and methods, they can be split into four general categories:[7]

- *Judgment methods* involve the collection of expert opinions.
- *Market research methods* involve qualitative studies of consumer behavior.
- *Time-series methods* are mathematical methods in which future performance is extrapolated from past performance.
- *Causal methods* are mathematical methods in which forecasts are generated based on a variety of system variables.

Below we discuss these methods in more detail.

2.3.1 Judgment Methods

Judgment methods strive to assemble the opinions of a number of experts in a systematic way. For example, salespeople (or dealers) frequently have a good understanding of expected sales because they are close to the market. A *salesforce composite* can be assembled that combines each salesperson's sales estimate in a logical way.

Panels of experts can be assembled in order to reach a consensus. This approach assumes that by communicating and openly sharing information, a superior forecast can be agreed on. These experts can be external experts or internal experts from a variety of functional areas within a company.

The *Delphi method* is a structured technique for reaching a consensus with a panel of experts without gathering them in a single location. Indeed, the technique is designed to eliminate the danger of one or a few strong-willed individuals dominating the decision-making process. In the Delphi method, each member of the group of experts is surveyed for his or her opinion, typically in writing. The opinions are compiled and summarized, and each individual is given the opportunity to change his or her opinion after seeing the summary. This process is repeated until consensus is achieved.

2.3.2 Market Research Methods

Market testing and *market surveys* can be valuable tools for developing forecasts, particularly of newly introduced products. In market testing, focus groups of potential customers are assembled and tested for their response to products, and this response is extrapolated to the entire market to estimate the demand for products. Market surveys involve gathering these data from a variety of potential customers, typically through interviews, telephone-based surveys, and written surveys.

2.3.3 Time-Series Methods

Time-series methods use a variety of past data (i.e., past values of the value being predicted) to estimate future data. There are a number of techniques that are used commonly, and each has different advantages and disadvantages. Below we discuss some common time-series methods.

Moving average. Each forecast is the average of some number of previous demand points. The key here is to select the number of points in the moving average so that the effect of irregularities in the data is minimized.

Exponential smoothing. Each forecast is a weighted average of the previous forecast and the last demand point. Thus this method is similar to the moving average, except that it is a weighted average of all past data points, with more recent points receiving more weight.

Methods for data with trends. The preceding approaches assume that there is no trend in the data. If there is a trend, methods such as *regression analysis* and *Holt's method* are more useful because they specifically account for trends in the data. Regression analysis fits a straight line to data points, whereas Holt's method combines the concept of exponential smoothing with the ability to follow a linear trend in the data.

Methods for seasonal data. A number of techniques account for seasonal changes in demand. For example, *seasonal decomposition* methods remove the seasonal patterns from the data and then apply the approaches listed earlier on these edited data. Similarly, *Winter's method* is a version of exponential smoothing that accounts for trends and seasonality.

More complex methods. A number of more complex methods have been proposed. However, these more complex methods are typically not used in practice, and indeed, there is some evidence that complex methods do not outperform simpler methods.[6]

2.3.4 Causal Methods

Recall that in the time-series methods just described, forecasts are based entirely on previous values of the data being predicted. In contrast, causal methods generate forecasts based on data *other than the data being predicted.* More specifically, the forecast is a function of some other pieces of data. For example, the causal sales forecast for the next quarter may be a function of inflation, gross national product (GNP), the unemployment rate, the weather, or anything besides the sales in this quarter.

2.3.5 Selecting the Appropriate Forecasting Technique

With so many forecasting techniques available, which one is appropriate for a given situation? Chambers, Mullick, and Smith (CMS),[8] in their seminal article pose three questions that help with this decision:

- *What is the purpose of the forecast? How is it to be used?* If gross sales estimates are sufficient, a less complex technique may be appropriate, whereas if detailed estimates are required, more advanced techniques may be necessary.
- *What are the dynamics of the system for which the forecast will be made?* Is the system sensitive to the type of economic data that would indicate that a causal model makes sense? Is the demand seasonal or trending upward or downward? All these affect the choice of forecasting tool.
- *How important is the past in estimating the future?* If the past is very important, time-series methods make sense. If significant systemwide changes render the past less important, judgment or market research methods may be indicated.

CMS also point out that at different stages of the product life cycle different forecast techniques are appropriate. In the product development phase, market research methods may indicate potential sales of different products and designs. In the testing and introduction phases, additional market research may be valuable, and judgment methods can be useful for predicting future demand of products. In the rapid growth phase of the product life cycle, time-series data may be the most valuable. Finally, once a product becomes mature, time-series analysis will be valuable, as will causal methods, which predict long-term sales performance based on estimates of economic data. Finally, the quality of forecasts frequently can be improved by combining a number of the techniques described in this section. Georgoff and Murdick[7] observe that "the results of combined forecasts greatly surpass most individual projections, techniques, and analysis by experts." This is particularly true because it is generally difficult to tell a priori which of several available forecasting techniques will work best for a given situation.

2.3.6   Forecasting in the Supply Chain

Of course, in a supply chain, each stage can affect the accuracy of the forecasts of the other stages. For example, consider retailer forecasts. These are typically based on an analysis of previous sales at the retailer. However, future customer demand is clearly influenced by such issues as pricing, promotions, and the release of new products. Some of these issues are controlled by the retailer, but some are controlled by the distributor, wholesaler, manufacturer, or competitors. If this

EXAMPLE 2-1

In fall 1996, Warner-Lambert, the consumer goods manufacturer, and Wal-Mart, the department store, began a pilot study of the collaborative planning, forecasting, and replenishment (CPFR) system. This software system facilitates collaboration in forecasting efforts between retailers and manufacturers. CPFR makes it easy to exchange drafts of forecasts as well as details of future sales promotions and past sales trends. The software "makes it easy for each side to review related messages and append new ones." Other companies, including Procter & Gamble, intend to adopt the CPFR system, and software companies intend to launch competing versions of this software. These systems go under the general name of *collaborative systems.*[9]

information is available to the retailer's forecasters, the forecasts obviously will be more accurate. Similarly, distributor and manufacturer forecasts are influenced by factors under retailer control. For example, the retailer may design promotions or set pricing. Also, the retailer may introduce new products into the stores, altering demand patterns. In addition, because a manufacturer or distributor has fewer products to consider than the retailer, the manufacturer may have more information about these products. For example, sales may be closely tied to some event. If a retailer is aware of this, it can increase inventories or raise prices to take advantage of this fact.

For all of these reasons, many supply chains are moving toward cooperative forecasting systems (see Ex. 2-1). In these supply chains, sophisticated information systems enable an iterative forecasting process in which all the participants in the supply chain collaborate to arrive at an agreed-on forecast. This implies that all components of the supply chain share and use the same forecasting tool, leading to a decrease in the bullwhip effect. We will discuss this in more detail in Chapter 10.

2.4   INFORMATION FOR THE COORDINATION OF SYSTEMS

Any supply chain includes many systems, such as manufacturing, storage, transportation, and retail systems. Clearly, managing any one of these systems involves a series of complex tradeoffs. For example, to run a manufacturing operation efficiently, setup and operating costs must be balanced with the costs of inventory and raw materials. Similarly, the appropriate inventory level requires a delicate balance between the cost of holding inventory, the costs associated with frequent orders, and the required service level. For instance, inventory management requires identifying the right balance between inventory holding costs and transportation costs because transportation typically involves quantity discounts of one type or another.

However, all these systems are connected. Specifically, the output from one system within the supply chain is the input to the next system. For example, the output from the manufacturing operation may be the input to a transportation or storage system or both. Thus, trying to find the best set of tradeoffs for any one stage is not sufficient. We need to consider the entire system and coordinate decisions.

This will be true whether or not there is a common owner for several of the systems in the supply chain. If there is, it is clearly in this owner's best interest to ensure that the overall cost is reduced, although this could lead to an increase in costs in one system if larger decreases occur elsewhere. Even if there is no common owner, however, the various systems still need some kind of coordination to operate effectively. The issue, of course, is whose best interest is it to reduce *overall* system cost, and how will these savings be shared among the system owners?

To explain this, observe that when the system is not coordinated—i.e., each facility in the supply chain does what is best for that facility—the result, as we discussed in Chapter 1, is *local optimization*. Each component of the supply chain optimizes its own operation without due respect for the impact of its policy on other components in the supply chain.

The alternative to this approach is *global optimization*, which implies that one identifies what is best for the entire system. In this case, two issues need to be addressed:

1. Who will optimize?
2. How will the savings obtained through the coordinated strategy be split among the different supply chain facilities?

These issues can be addressed in various ways. For example, supply contracts can be used (we discuss these in Chap. 6), or strategic partnerships can be employed (see Chap. 5).

To coordinate these facets of the supply chain, information must be available. Specifically, the knowledge of production status and costs, transportation availability and quantity discounts, inventory costs, inventory levels, and various capacities and customer demand is necessary to coordinate systems, especially in cost-effective ways.

2.5 LOCATING DESIRED PRODUCTS

There is more than one way to meet customer demand. Typically, for a make-to-stock system, we think of meeting customer demand from retail inventory if at all possible, but there are other options.

For example, suppose that you go to a retailer to buy a large appliance, and it is not available. Perhaps you will go to the retailer's competitor down the street. However, what if the retailer searches a database and promises to have the item delivered to your house within 24 hours. You probably will feel like you have received great customer service, even though the retailer is out of stock. Thus, being able to locate and deliver goods is sometimes as effective as having them in stock.

However, if the goods are located at the retailer's competitor, it is not clear whether this competitor would be willing to transfer the item.

2.6   LEAD-TIME REDUCTION

The importance of lead-time reduction cannot be overstated. It typically leads to

1. The ability to quickly fill customer orders that cannot be filled from stock
2. Reduction in the bullwhip effect
3. More accurate forecasts due to a decreased forecast horizon
4. Reduction in finished goods inventory levels (This is true because one can stock raw materials and packaging material or subassembly inventories to reduce finished-goods cycle time.)

For all these reasons, many firms are actively searching for suppliers with shorter lead times, and many potential customers consider lead time a very important criterion for vendor selection.

Much of the manufacturing revolution of the past 20 years has led to reduced lead times.[10] In Chapter 4 we discuss distribution network designs that reduce lead times; these designs can exist only because of the availability of information about the status of the entire supply chain. However, as discussed earlier, effective information systems cut lead times by reducing that portion of the lead time linked to order processing, paperwork, stock picking, transportation delays, and so on. Often these can be a substantial portion of the lead time, especially if there are many different stages in the supply chain and this information is transmitted one stage at a time. Clearly, if a retailer order *rapidly* propagates up the supply chain through the tiers of suppliers as far back as is necessary to meet the order, lead time can be reduced greatly.

Similarly, transferring point-of-sale (POS) data from the retailer to its supplier can help reduce lead times significantly because the supplier can anticipate an incoming order by studying POS data. These issues are covered in depth in Chapter 5, where we discuss strategic partnering between retailers and suppliers.

2.7   INFORMATION AND SUPPLY CHAIN TRADEOFFS

As observed in Chapter 1, a major challenge in supply chain management is replacing sequential planning processes with global optimization. In sequential planning, each stage of the supply chain optimizes its profit with no regard to the impact of its decisions on other supply chain stages. In contrast, in global optimization, the objective is to *coordinate* supply chain activities so as to maximize *supply chain performance.*

Unfortunately, as we discuss in detail below, the managers of different stages in the supply chain have conflicting goals, and it is exactly these conflicts that necessitate the integration and coordination of the different stages in the supply chain. Even within one stage, tradeoffs have to be made between reducing inventory and transportation costs or between increasing product variety and reducing inventory levels.

By carefully using the available information, the supply chain can move toward global optimization and, as a result, reduce systemwide cost while accounting for these conflicting goals and various tradeoffs. This is easier to do in a centralized system, but even in a decentralized system it may be necessary to find incentives to bring about the integration of supply chain facilities.

2.7.1 Conflicting Objectives in the Supply Chain[11]

We begin with the raw material suppliers. To operate and plan efficiently, these suppliers would like to see stable volume requirements, with little variation in the mix of required materials. In addition, they prefer flexible delivery times so that they can deliver efficiently to more than one customer. Finally, most suppliers would like to see large volume demands so that they can take advantage of economies of scope and scale.

Manufacturing management also has its own wish list. High production costs frequently limit the number of expensive changeovers as well as quality problems that may occur at the start of production runs. Typically, manufacturing management wants to achieve high productivity through production efficiencies, leading in turn to low production costs. These goals are facilitated if the demand pattern is known far into the future and has little variability.

The materials, warehousing, and outbound logistics managers also have lists of criteria. These include minimizing transportation costs by taking advantage of quantity discounts, minimizing inventory levels, and quickly replenishing stock. Finally, to satisfy their customers, retailers need short order lead times and efficient and accurate order delivery. The customers, in turn, demand in-stock items, enormous variety, and low prices.

2.7.2 Designing the Supply Chain for Conflicting Goals

In the past, for some of these goals to be met, others had to be sacrificed because the supply chain was viewed as a set of tradeoffs. Typically, high inventory levels and shipping costs and less product variety enabled manufacturers and retailers to come closer to meeting their goals. At the same time, customers' expectations were not as high as they are today. As we know, these expectations have increased dramatically in recent times as customers demand high variety and low cost, even as increased pressure to control inventory and transportation costs also has become prevalent. Fortunately, the large amount of information now available allows supply chains to be designed so that they come closer to meeting all these apparently conflicting goals. In effect, some of the tradeoffs that were considered several years ago to be inherent in any supply chain may not be tradeoffs at all.

In the following subsections we discuss many of these perceived tradeoffs and how, through the use of advanced information technology and creative network design, they do not have to be tradeoffs at all in a modern supply chain—or, at the very least, their impact can be reduced.

The Lot Size–Inventory Tradeoff As we have seen, manufacturers would like to have large lot sizes. Per-unit setup costs are reduced, manufacturing expertise for a particular product increases, and processes are easier to control. Unfortunately, typical demand does not come in large lot sizes, so large lot sizes lead to high inventory. Indeed, much of the focus of the manufacturing revolution of the 1980s involved switching to manufacturing systems with smaller lot sizes.

Setup time reduction, *kanban* and constant work-in-progress (CONWIP) systems, and other modern manufacturing practices typically were geared toward reducing inventories and improving system responsiveness. Although traditionally viewed in a manufacturing context, this approach to manufacturing has implications across the entire supply chain. Retailers and distributors would like short delivery lead times and wide product variety to respond to the needs of their customers. These advanced manufacturing systems make it possible for manufacturers to meet these needs by enabling them to respond more rapidly to customer needs.

This is especially true if information is available to ensure that the manufacturer has as much time as possible to react to the needs of downstream supply chain members. Similarly, if distributors or retailers have the ability to observe factory status and manufacturer inventory, they can quote lead times to customers more accurately. In addition, these systems enable retailers and distributors to develop an understanding of and confidence in the manufacturers' ability. This confidence allows the distributors and retailers to reduce the inventory they hold in anticipation of manufacturing problems.

The Inventory–Transportation Cost Tradeoff   There is a similar tradeoff between inventory and transportation costs. To see this, we need to review the nature of transportation costs. First, consider a company that operates its own fleet of trucks. Each truck has some fixed cost of operation (e.g., depreciation, driver time) and some variable cost (e.g., gas). If a truck is always full when it makes a delivery, the cost of operating the truck is spread out over the largest possible number of items. Since, in the end, the same total number of goods is always delivered (more or less equal to customer demand), carrying full truckloads minimizes transportation costs.

Similarly, if an outside firm is used for shipping, the firm typically provides quantity discounts. Also, it is usually cheaper to ship in quantities of full truckloads (TL shipping) than partial (less than full) truckloads (LTL shipping). Thus, in this case too, operating full trucks minimizes transportation costs.

In many cases, however, demand is in units of far less than a single truckload. Thus, when items are delivered in full truckloads, they typically have to wait for longer periods of time before they are consumed, leading to higher inventory costs.

Unfortunately, this tradeoff cannot be eliminated completely. However, we can use advanced information technology to reduce this effect. For example, advanced production control systems can be used to manufacture items as late as possible to ensure full truckloads. Similarly, distribution control systems may allow a materials manager to combine shipments of different products from warehouses to stores in order to fill trucks. This requires knowledge of orders and demand forecasts, as well as supplier delivery schedules.

Indeed, recent advances in decision-support systems allow the supply chain to find the appropriate balance between transportation and inventory costs by taking into account all aspects of the supply chain. Regardless of the transportation strategy selected, competition in the transportation industry will force costs down. This effect is enhanced by advanced transportation modes and carrier selection programs that ensure that the most cost-effective approach is used for each particular delivery, lowering overall transportation costs.

The Lead-Time–Transportation Cost Tradeoff   Total lead time is made up of time devoted to processing orders, to procuring and manufacturing items, and to transporting items between the various stages of the supply chain. As we mentioned earlier, transportation costs are lowest when large quantities of items are transported between stages of the supply chain. However, lead times often can be reduced if items are transported immediately after they are manufactured or arrive from suppliers. Thus there is a tradeoff between holding items until enough accumulate to reduce transportation costs and shipping them immediately to reduce lead time.

Again, this tradeoff cannot be eliminated completely, but information can be used to reduce its effect. Transportation costs can be controlled as described in the preceding section, reducing the need to hold items until a sufficient number accumulates. In addition, improved forecasting techniques and information systems reduce the other components of lead time so that it may not be essential to reduce the transportation component.

The Product Variety–Inventory Tradeoff   Evidently, product variety greatly increases the complexity of supply chain management. Manufacturers who make a multitude of different products with smaller lot sizes find that their manufacturing costs increase and their manufacturing efficiency decreases. To maintain the same lead times as a company may have had with fewer products, smaller amounts probably will be shipped, so warehouses will need to hold a larger variety of products. Thus increasing product variety increases both transportation and warehousing costs. Finally, since it is usually difficult to accurately forecast the demand for each product because all are competing for the same customers, higher inventory levels must be maintained to ensure the same service level.

The main issue that a firm supplying a variety of products needs to address is how to match supply and demand effectively. For instance, consider a manufacturer of winter ski jackets. Typically, 12 months before the selling season the firm introduces a number of designs that it will sell in the winter. Unfortunately, it is not clear how many ski jackets to produce from each design; therefore, it is not clear how to plan production.

One way to support the required product variety efficiently is to apply the concept called *delayed differentiation*, which we will discuss in Chapter 7. In a supply chain in which delayed differentiation is used, *generic products* are shipped as far as possible down the supply chain before variety is added. This could mean that a single product is received in the distribution center, and there it is modified or customized according to customer demand as seen by the warehouse.

The Cost–Customer Service Tradeoff All these tradeoffs are examples of the cost–customer service tradeoff. Reducing inventories, manufacturing costs, and transportation costs typically comes at the expense of customer service. In the preceding subsections we have seen that the level of customer service can be maintained while decreasing these costs by using information and appropriate supply chain designs. Implicitly, we have defined customer service as the ability of a retailer to meet a customer's demand from stock.

Of course, customer service could mean the ability of a retailer to meet a customer's demand quickly. We have discussed how transshipping may make this possible without increasing inventory. In addition, direct shipping from warehouses to the homes of retail customers is another way to achieve this. For example, Sears delivers a large proportion of the large appliances that it sells directly from warehouses to the end customer. This controls inventory cost at retail stores and allows warehouses to take direct advantage of risk-pooling effects. For this kind of system to work, information about warehouse inventories must be available at the stores, and order information should be transmitted rapidly to the warehouse. This is just one example of a system in which available information and appropriate supply chain design lead to decreased costs and increased service. In this case costs are lower when the inventory is stored in a centralized warehouse than when there is a larger inventory in the store. At the same time, customer service is improved because customers have a larger inventory to choose from, and appliances are delivered immediately to their homes.

Finally, it is important to point out that so far we have emphasized how supply chain technology and management can be applied to increase customer service levels *defined in some traditional sense* and to reduce costs. However, advanced supply chain management techniques and information systems could be used to provide customers with the kind of service that they have never been able to realize before and for which suppliers could charge a premium. One such example is the concept of *mass customization*, which involves delivering highly personalized goods and services to customers at reasonable prices and at high volume. Although this may not have been economically feasible in the past, improving logistics and information systems now makes this possible. The concept of mass customization is explained in more detail in Chapter 7.

2.8 SUMMARY

The bullwhip effect suggests that variability in demand increases as one moves up the supply chain. This increase in variability causes significant operational inefficiencies (e.g., it forces every facility in the supply chain to increase inventory significantly). Indeed, some authors[1] estimate that in certain industries, such as the pharmaceutical industry, this distorted information can cause the total inventory in the supply chain to exceed 100 days of supply. Thus it is important to identify strategies to efficiently cope with the bullwhip effect. In this chapter we have identified specific techniques to counteract the bullwhip effect, one of which is information sharing, i.e., centralized demand information.

Finally, we looked at the interaction of various supply chain stages. Typically, operating a supply chain is viewed as a series of tradeoffs both within and between the different stages. We concluded that information is the key enabler of integrating the different supply chain stages and discussed how information can be used to reduce the necessity of many of these tradeoffs.

CHAPTER 3

Supply Chain Integration

3.1 INTRODUCTION

In Chapter 1 we observed that supply chain management revolves around *efficient integration of suppliers, manufacturers, warehouses, and stores.* The challenge in supply chain integration, of course, is to coordinate activities across the supply chain so that the enterprise can improve performance: reduce cost, increase service level, reduce the bullwhip effect, better use resources, and respond effectively to changes in the marketplace. As many companies have recently realized, these challenges are met not only by coordinating production, transportation, and inventory decisions but more generally by integrating the *front end* of the supply chain, customer demand, to the *back end* of the supply chain, the production and manufacturing portion of the supply chain. The objective of this chapter is to illustrate the opportunities and the challenges associated with supply chain integration. We consider

- Various supply chain strategies, including push, pull, and a relatively new paradigm, the push-pull strategy
- A framework for matching products and industries with supply chain strategies
- Demand-driven supply chain strategies
- The impact of the Internet on supply chain integration
- Effective distribution strategies

Obviously, the availability of information plays an important role in supply chain integration. In some cases the supply chain must be designed to make this information available. In other cases the supply chain strategy must be designed to *take advantage* of information that is already available. And in many cases an expensive network must be designed to compensate for the lack of information.

3.2 PUSH, PULL, AND PUSH-PULL SYSTEMS

Traditional supply chain strategies often are categorized as push or pull strategies. Probably this stems from the manufacturing revolution of the 1980s, in which manufacturing systems were divided into these categories. Interestingly, in the last few years a number of companies have employed a hybrid approach, the push-pull supply chain paradigm. In this section we explain each one of the strategies.

3.2.1 Push-Based Supply Chain

In a *push-based supply chain*, production and distribution decisions are based on long-term forecasts. Typically, the manufacturer bases demand forecasts on orders received from the retailer's warehouses. It therefore takes much longer for a push-based supply chain to react to the changing marketplace, which can lead to

- The inability to meet changing demand patterns
- The obsolescence of supply chain inventory as demand for certain products disappears

In addition, we saw in Chapter 2 that the variability of orders received from the retailers and the warehouses is much larger than the variability in customer demand—the bullwhip effect. This increase in variability leads to

- Excessive inventories due to the need for large safety stocks (see Chap. 4)
- Larger and more variably sized production batches
- Unacceptable service levels
- Inventory obsolescence

Specifically, the bullwhip effect leads to inefficient resource utilization because planning and managing are much more difficult. For instance, it is not clear how a manufacturer should determine production capacity. Should it be based on peak demand, which implies that most of the time the manufacturer has expensive resources sitting idle, or should it be based on average demand, which requires extra—and typically expensive—capacity during periods of peak demand? Similarly, it is not clear how to plan transportation capacity. Should it be based on peak demand or on average demand? Thus, in a push-based supply chain, we often find increased transportation costs, high inventory levels, and/or high manufacturing costs due to the need for emergency production changeovers.

3.2.2 Pull-Based Supply Chain

In a *pull-based supply chain,* production and distribution are demand-driven so that they are coordinated with true customer demand rather than with forecast demand.[1] In a pure pull system, the firm does not hold any inventory and only responds to *specific orders.* This is enabled by fast information flow mechanisms that transfer information about customer demand (e.g., point of sale data) to the various supply chain participants. Pull systems are intuitively attractive because they lead to

- A decrease in lead times achieved through the ability to better anticipate incoming orders from retailers
- A decrease in inventory at retailers because inventory levels at these facilities increase with lead times (see Chap. 4)
- A decrease in variability in the system and, in particular, variability faced by manufacturers (see the discussion in Chap. 2) due to lead-time reduction
- Decreased inventory at the manufacturer due to the reduction in variability

EXAMPLE 3-1

A major apparel manufacturer recently changed its supply chain strategy to a pull-based system. Retailers order from this manufacturer about once a month but transfer point-of-sale (POS) data much more frequently, e.g., daily or weekly. These data allow the manufacturer to continuously adjust production quantities according to true customer demand.

Thus, in a pull-based supply chain, we typically see a significant reduction in system inventory level, enhanced ability to manage resources, and a reduction in system costs when compared with the equivalent push-based system. On the other hand, pull-based systems are often difficult to implement when lead times are so long that it is impractical to react to demand information. Also, in pull-based systems, it is frequently more difficult to take advantage of economies of scale in manufacturing and transportation because systems are not planned far ahead in time.

These advantages and disadvantages of push and pull supply chains have led companies to look for a new supply chain strategy that takes advantage of the best of both. Frequently, this is a push-pull supply chain strategy.

3.2.3 Push-Pull Supply Chain

In a *push-pull supply chain*, some stages of the supply chain, typically the initial stages, are operated in a push-based manner, whereas the remaining stages employ a pull-based strategy. The interface between the push-based stages and the pull-based stages is known as the *push-pull boundary*.

To better understand this strategy, consider the *supply chain time line*: the time that elapses between procurement of raw material, i.e., the beginning of the time line, and the delivery of an order to the customer, i.e., the end of the time line. The push-pull boundary is located somewhere along the time line and indicates the point in time when the firm switches from managing the supply chain using a push strategy to managing it using a pull strategy. This is illustrated in Figure 3-1.

Consider a personal computer (PC) manufacturer who builds to stock and thus makes all production and distribution decisions based on forecast. This is a typical push system. By contrast, an example of a push-pull strategy is one in which the manufacturer builds to order. This implies that component inventory is managed based on forecast but that final assembly is in response to a specific customer request. Thus the push portion of the manufacturer's supply chain is that portion prior to assembly, whereas the pull part of the supply chain starts with assembly and is performed based on actual customer demand. The push-pull boundary is at the beginning of assembly. Observe that in this case the manufacturer takes advantage of the fact that *aggregate*

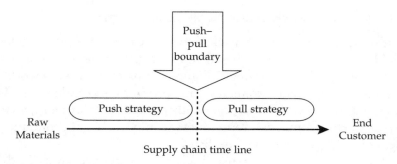

Figure 3-1   Push-pull supply chains.

forecasts are more accurate (see Chap. 2). Indeed, demand for a component is an aggregation of demand for all finished products that use this component.

Since aggregate forecasts are more accurate, uncertainty in component demand is much smaller than uncertainty in finished goods demand, and this leads to safety stock reduction. Dell Computers has used this strategy very effectively and is an excellent example of the impact of the push-pull strategy on supply chain performance.

Postponement, or delayed differentiation in product design (see Chap. 7), is also an excellent example of a push-pull strategy. In postponement, the firm designs the product and the manufacturing process so that decisions about which specific products are being manufactured can be delayed as long as possible. The manufacturing process starts by producing a generic or family product, which is differentiated to a specific end product when demand is revealed. The portion of the supply chain prior to product differentiation typically is operated using a push-based strategy. In other words, the generic product is built and transported based on a long-term forecast. Since demand for the generic product is an aggregation of demand for all its corresponding end products, forecasts are more accurate, and thus inventory levels are reduced. In contrast, customer demand for a specific end product typically has a high level of uncertainty, and thus product differentiation occurs only in response to individual demand. Thus the portion of the supply chain starting from the time of differentiation is pull-based.

3.2.4   Identifying the Appropriate Supply Chain Strategy

What is the appropriate supply chain strategy for a particular product? Should the firm use a push-based supply chain strategy, a pull-based strategy, or a push-pull strategy? Figure 3-2 provides a framework for matching supply chain strategies with products and industries. The vertical axis provides information on uncertainty in customer demand, whereas the horizontal axis represents the importance of economies of scale, either in production or in distribution.

Everything else being equal, higher demand uncertainty leads to a preference for managing the supply chain based on realized demand: a pull strategy. Alternatively, smaller demand uncertainty leads to an interest in managing the supply chain based on a long-term forecast: a push strategy.

Similarly, everything else being equal, the higher the importance of economies of scale in reducing cost, the greater is the value of aggregating demand, and thus the greater is the importance of managing the supply chain based on long-term forecast, a push-based strategy. If economies of scale are not important, aggregation does not reduce cost, so a pull-based strategy makes more sense.

In Figure 3-2 we partition the region spanned by these two dimensions into four boxes. Box I represents industries (or, more precisely, products) that are characterized by high uncertainty and by situations in which economies of scale in production, assembly, or distribution are not important, such as the computer industry. Our framework suggests that a high degree of pull-based supply chain strategy is appropriate for these industries and products. This is exactly the strategy employed by Dell Computers.

Box III represents products that are characterized by low demand uncertainty and important economies of scale. Products in the grocery industry such as beer, pasta, and soup belong to this category. Demand for these products is quite stable, whereas reducing transportation cost by shipping full truckloads is critical for controlling supply chain cost. In this case a pull strategy is not appropriate. Indeed, a traditional push-based retail strategy is appropriate because managing inventory based on long-term forecasts does not increase inventory holding costs, whereas delivery costs are reduced by leveraging economies of scale.

Boxes I and III represent situations in which it is relatively easy to identify an efficient supply chain strategy. In the remaining two cases there is a mismatch between the strategies suggested by the two

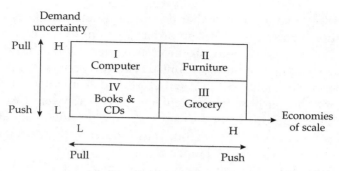

Figure 3-2 Matching supply chain strategies with products.

attributes, uncertainty and the importance of economies of scale. Indeed, in these boxes uncertainty "pulls" the supply chain toward one strategy, whereas economies of scale "push" the supply chain in a different direction.

For instance, box IV represents products characterized by low demand uncertainty, indicating a push-based supply chain, and low economies of scale, suggesting a pull-based supply chain strategy. Many high-volume/fast-moving books and CDs fall in this category. In this case a more careful analysis is required because both traditional retail push strategies and more innovative push-pull strategies may be appropriate, depending on the specific costs and uncertainties. We discuss this choice in more detail in Section 3.4.

Finally, box II represents products and industries for which uncertainty in demand is high, whereas economies of scale are important in reducing production and/or delivery costs. The furniture industry is an excellent example of this situation. Indeed, a typical furniture retailer offers a large number of similar products distinguished by shape, color, fabric, and so forth, and as a result, end-item demand uncertainty is very high. Unfortunately, these are bulky products, and hence delivery costs are also high.

Thus, in this case, there is a need to distinguish between the production and the distribution strategies. The production strategy has to follow a pull-based strategy because it is impossible to make production decisions based on long-term forecasts. On the other hand, the distribution strategy needs to take advantage of economies of scale in order to reduce transportation cost. This is exactly the strategy employed by many retailers that do not keep any inventory of furniture. When a customer places an order, it is sent to the manufacturer, who orders the fabric and produces to order. Once the product is ready, it is shipped, typically using truckload carriers, together with many other products, to the retail store and from there to the customer. For this purpose, the manufacturer typically has a fixed delivery schedule, and this is used to aggregate all products that are delivered to stores in the same region, thus reducing transportation costs due to economies of scale. Hence the supply chain strategy followed by furniture manufacturers is, in some sense, a pull-push strategy, where production is completed based on realized demand, a pull strategy, and delivery is according to a fixed schedule, a push strategy.

The automobile industry is another example of the conditions of box II. A typical car manufacturer offers a large number of similar products distinguished by functionality, motor power, shape, color, number of doors, sports wheels, and so forth, and as a result, demand uncertainty for a particular configuration is very high. Delivery costs are quite high as well. Traditionally, this industry has employed a push-based supply chain strategy, building inventory for the dealer distribution systems. Thus the automobile industry does not currently follow the model developed in Figure 3-2.

In 2000, however, General Motors (GM) announced a dramatic vision for restructuring the way it is designing, building, and selling its products.[2] The goal is to allow customers to customize and order cars online and have the cars delivered *to the customer's door* in less than 10 days. GM is moving exactly in the direction predicted by our model—toward a build-to-order strategy.

Unfortunately, lead times in the automobile industry are currently long: 50 to 60 days on average. To achieve its vision, GM has to redesign the entire supply chain, including the way it partners with suppliers, the way it manufactures products, and the way it distributes products. Reducing lead times to 10 days or below also may require a significant reduction in the number of options and configurations offered to buyers.

3.2.5 Implementing a Push-Pull Strategy

The framework developed in the preceding section attempts to characterize the appropriate level of pull and push for different products.

For instance, a high degree of pull is appropriate for products that belong to box I. Of course, achieving the design of the pull system depends on many factors, including product complexity, manufacturing lead times, and supplier-manufacturer relationships. Similarly, there are many ways to implement a push-pull strategy, depending on the location of the push-pull boundary. For instance, Dell locates the push-pull boundary at the assembly point, whereas furniture manufacturers locate the boundary at the production point.

EXAMPLE 3-2

Consider the automobile industry, known for its long transportation lead times. Prior to its latest effort to implement a make-to-order strategy, there were previous attempts to implement a push-pull strategy. In 1994, GM announced the establishment of a regional distribution center in Orlando, Florida, where an inventory of about 1500 Cadillacs was maintained. Dealers could order cars they did not have in their lots from the distribution center, and the cars would be delivered within 24 hours. GM was attempting to employ a push-pull strategy in which inventory at its regional distribution center was managed based on long-term forecasts, whereas delivery to dealers was based on realized demand. Thus the push-pull boundary was located at the manufacturer's distribution center. As discussed in Chapter 8, two major issues contributed to the failure of this strategy. First, the regional warehouse shifted inventory costs from the dealers to GM because it allowed dealers to reduce inventory levels. Second, the regional distribution center equalized small and large dealers. If all dealers have access to the regional warehouse, then there is no difference between small and large dealers. Thus it is difficult to see why large dealers would be interested in participating in such an arrangement.

The discussion so far suggests that the push strategy is applied to that portion of the supply chain where demand uncertainty is relatively small, and thus managing this portion based on long-term forecast is appropriate. On the other hand, the pull strategy is applied to the portion of the supply chain time line where uncertainty is high, and hence it is important to manage this portion based on realized demand. This distinction between the two portions of the supply chain has an important impact on the objectives of the supply chain strategy, as well as on organizational skills required to manage the system effectively.

Since uncertainty in the push portion of the supply chain is relatively small, service level is not an issue, so the focus can be on *cost minimization*. In addition, this portion of the supply chain is characterized not only by low demand uncertainty and economies of scale in production and/or transportation but also by long lead times and complex supply chain structures, including product assembly at various levels. Thus cost minimization is achieved by better using resources such as production and distribution capacities while minimizing inventory, transportation, and production costs.

On the other hand, the pull portion of the supply chain is characterized by high uncertainty, a simple supply chain structure, and a short cycle time. Hence the focus here is on service level. Specifically, high service level is achieved by deploying a *flexible* and *responsive* supply chain—a supply chain that can adapt quickly to changes in customer demand.[3]

This implies that different processes need to be used in different portions of the supply chain. Since the focus in the pull part of the supply chain is on service level, *order-fulfillment processes* typically are employed. Similarly, since the focus of the push part of the supply chain is on cost and resource utilization, supply chain *planning processes* are used here to develop an effective strategy for the next few weeks or months. In Chapter 4 we provide a detailed discussion of supply chain master planning that is applied to the push portion of the supply chain time line. Table 3-1 summarizes the characteristics of the push and pull portions of the supply chain.

Notice that the push portion and the pull portion of the supply chain interact only at the push-pull boundary. This is the point along

Table 3-1 Characteristics of the Push and Pull Portions of the Supply Chain

	Push	Pull
Objective	Minimize cost	Maximize service level
Complexity	High	Low
Focus	Resource allocation	Responsiveness
Lead time	Long	Short
Processes	Supply chain planning	Order fulfillment

EXAMPLE 3-3

Consider a supplier of fashion skiwear such as Sport Obermeyer.[3] Every year the company introduces many new designs, or products, for which forecast demand is highly uncertain. One strategy used successfully by Sport Obermeyer involves distinguishing between high-risk and low-risk designs. Low-risk products, i.e., those for which uncertainty and price are low, are produced in advance using long-term forecasts and focusing on cost minimization, a push-based strategy. However, decisions on production quantities for high-risk products are delayed until there is a clear market signal on customer demand for each style, a pull strategy. Since fabric lead times are long, the manufacturer typically orders fabric for high-risk products well in advance of receiving information about market demand, based only on long-term forecasts. In this case the manufacturer takes advantage of the same principle applied by Dell Computers: that aggregate forecasts are more accurate. Since demand for fabrics is an aggregation of demand for all products that use that fabric, demand uncertainty is low, and thus fabric inventory is managed based on push strategy. Thus Sport Obermeyer uses a push-pull strategy for the high-risk products and a push strategy for the low-risk products.

the supply chain time line where there is a need to coordinate the two supply chain strategies, typically through *buffer inventory*. However, this inventory plays a different role in each portion. In the push portion buffer inventory at the boundary is part of the output generated by the tactical planning process, whereas in the pull part it represents the input to the fulfillment process. Thus the interface between the push portion of the supply chain and the pull portion of the supply chain is forecast demand. This forecast, which is based on historical data obtained from the pull portion, is used to drive the supply chain planning process and to determine the buffer inventory.

3.3 DEMAND-DRIVEN STRATEGIES

The framework we have developed in this chapter requires integrating demand information into the supply chain planning process. This information is generated by employing two different processes:

- *Demand forecast.* A process in which historical demand data are used to develop long-term estimates of expected demand, i.e., forecasts (see Chap. 2 for more information about forecasting).

- *Demand shaping.* A process in which the firm determines the impact of various marketing plans such as promotion, pricing discounts, rebates, new product introduction, and product withdrawal on demand forecasts.

Of course, in either case the forecast is not completely accurate, and hence an important output from the demand-forecast and demand-shaping processes is an estimate of the *accuracy* of the forecast, the so-called forecast error, measured according to its *standard deviation.* This information provides insight into the likelihood that demand will be higher (or lower) than the forecast.

High demand forecast error has a detrimental impact on supply chain performance, resulting in lost sales, obsolete inventory, and inefficient use of resources. Can the firm employ supply chain strategies to increase forecast accuracy and thus decrease forecast error? We identify the following approaches:

- Select the push-pull boundary so that demand is aggregated over one or more of the following dimensions:
  - Demand is aggregated across products.
  - Demand is aggregated across geography.
  - Demand is aggregated across time.
  The objective is clear. Since aggregate forecasts are more accurate, the result is improved forecast accuracy.
- Use market analysis and demographic and economic trends to improve forecast accuracy (see Chap. 2 for details).
- Determine the optimal assortment of products by store so as to reduce the number of stock keeping units (SKUs) competing in the same market. Indeed, we are familiar with a large retailer who used to keep in each store more than 30 different types of garbage cans. It was relatively easy to predict aggregate demand across all SKUs in the garbage can category but very difficult to predict demand for an individual SKU.
- Incorporate collaborative planning and forecasting processes with customers so as to achieve a better understanding of market demand and the impact of promotions, pricing events, and advertising.

At the end of the demand planning process, the firm has a demand forecast by SKU by location. The next step is to analyze the supply chain and see if it can support these forecasts. This process, called *supply and demand management*, involves matching supply and demand by identifying a strategy that minimizes total production, transportation, and inventory costs or a strategy that maximizes profits. Along the way, the firm also determines the best way to handle volatility and risks in the supply chain. We describe this tactical planning process in Chapter 4.

Of course, demand planning and tactical planning have an impact on each other. Thus an iterative process must be used to identify

- The best way to allocate marketing budgets and associated supply and distribution resources
- The impact of deviations from forecast demand
- The impact of changes in supply chain lead times
- The impact of competitors' promotional activities on demand and supply chain strategies

The importance of the iterative process is demonstrated by the following example.

EXAMPLE 3-4

A classic example of the perils of not including supply chain analysis in market plans is the story of Campbell's Soup's winter promotion. In one unfortunate season the marketing department decided to promote chicken noodle soup in the winter. Of course, there is a seasonal spike in the demand for soup in winter anyway. By itself, this seasonal spike requires preparing and storing chicken and ingredients in huge quantities in the spring and fall in order to meet the demand. In addition, due to the promotion, production had to start early and use overtime capacity in order to meet the demand. Unfortunately, the cost of the excess production and inventory requirements far exceeded the revenue from the promotions.[4]

3.4 THE IMPACT OF THE INTERNET ON SUPPLY CHAIN STRATEGIES

The influence of the Internet and e-commerce on the economy in general and business practice in particular has been tremendous. Changes are happening rapidly. For instance, the direct-business model employed by industry giants such as Dell Computers and Amazon.com enables customers to order products over the Internet and thus allows companies to sell their products without relying on third-party distributors. Similarly, business-to-business e-commerce promises convenience and cost reduction.

In parallel, the Internet and the emerging e-business models have produced expectations that many supply chain problems will be resolved merely by using these new technology and business models. e-Business strategies were supposed to reduce cost, increase service level, and increase flexibility and, of course, profits, albeit sometime in the future. In reality, these expectations frequently have gone unmet because many of the new e-businesses have not been successful. In many cases the downfall of some of the highest-profile Internet businesses has been attributed to their logistics strategies.

Several examples follow.

EXAMPLE 3-5

The furniture industry seemed ripe for modernization and e-business when executives from Living.com purchased Shaw Furniture Gallery, the tenth largest furniture store in North Carolina, in March 1999. The purchase was intended to provide Living.com with access to top-line furniture manufacturers. After an investment of $70 million in capital and a spot as the exclusive Amazon.com furniture link, Living.com declared bankruptcy on August 29, 2000. Reasons for the failure included the investment in a new information system that did not function correctly and the switch to a carrier that had no experience with furniture delivery, leading to a stunning 30 percent return rate.

EXAMPLE 3-6

Furniture.com, launched in January 1999, offered thousands of products from many furniture makers. The company had $22 million in sales in the first 9 months of 2000 and 1 million visitors a month to its Web site. Its downfall (November 6, 2000) was due to logistics details and, in particular, inefficient delivery processes. Initially, Furniture.com used carriers to ship its products from a central warehouse to customers. Since transportation costs were too high, the firm formed an alliance with six regional distributors. Unfortunately, these relationships were hard to maintain and left many problems unsolved, including handling of repairs and returns.

EXAMPLE 3-7

Founded in 1989, Peapod is based in Skokie, Illinois, and is considered one of America's leading online grocers. As a highly experienced online grocer, the company serves more than 130,000 customers. In 1999, Peapod had sales of $73 million and generated a loss of $29 million. Peapod's mounting losses and inability to secure additional funding resulted in a buyout of a majority of its stock in April 2000 by Royal Ahold, the international food company. Peapod thus escaped the fate of Shoplink.com, Streamline.com, and Priceline's WebHouse Club, all of which have recently left the online grocery business. These failures generally are attributed to high delivery costs.

EXAMPLE 3-8

What started in 1995 as earth's biggest bookstore is rapidly becoming earth's biggest store. Amazon.com's main site offers millions of books, CDs, DVDs, videos, toys, tools, and electronics. In addition, Amazon.com conducts auctions for items ranging from art to real estate and provides schedulers, address books, and online greeting cards. Amazon also owns stakes in online sellers of pet supplies, prescription drugs, cars, groceries, and more. Although Amazon.com has become a model for Internet companies by placing market share ahead of profits and making acquisitions funded by its meteoric market capitalization, it has yet to make a profit. In 1996 the company had $16 million in sales and a $6 million loss; in 1999 it had $1.6 billion in sales and a $720 million loss; in 2000 it had $2.7 billion in sales and a $1.4 billion loss, hardly a financial success story. Losses have been lower in the last 2 years—$3.12 billion in sales and a $567,000 loss in 2001 and $3.93 billion in sales and $149,000 loss in 2002.

Some companies, of course, are extremely successful in developing new business models that allow them to increase profits significantly and capture a sizable market share. These companies use the Internet as the driver of business change.

EXAMPLE 3-9

According to the Stern Stewart EVA 1000 database, Dell Computers has outperformed its competition by over 3000 percent in terms of shareholder growth over the 8-year period 1988 to 1996. This example

(continued)

is important in our discussion because competition in the PC industry is not based on new technology. Indeed, most PC manufacturers use the same technology, the so-called Wintel standard. Competition in the PC industry is based primarily on price and service level. Dell's success is attributed to its virtual integration, a strategy that blurs the traditional boundaries between suppliers, manufacturers, and end users. Dell's decision to sell computers built from components produced by other manufacturers has relieved the firm of the burdens of owning assets, doing research and development, and managing a large workforce. At the same time, Dell only produces to order and thus keeps no finished goods inventory. These business decisions have allowed Dell to grow much faster than its competition and maintain only 8 days of inventory.

Despite its downturn in 2001 and the writeoff of $2.25 billion in excess inventory, Cisco is a good model of a company that makes innovative use of the Internet.

EXAMPLE 3-10

According to Peter Solvik, who is CIO of Cisco, "Cisco's Internet-based business model has been instrumental in its ability to quadruple in size from 1994 to 1998 ($1.3 billion to over $8 billion), hire approximately 1000 new employees per quarter while increasing their productivity, and save $560 million annually in business expenses." Over 80 percent of Cisco's customer business is performed over the Internet, and this is only a small part of the entire picture. Indeed, to differentiate itself from the competition in what is essentially a commodity business, Cisco acquires companies that have leading technology and integrates these companies rapidly with its systems. It also sells network solutions, not just components, to its customers. This requires coordination of hardware, software, and service components in many sales. The ability to provide these services and integrate comes from Cisco's single-enterprise system. This system provides the backbone for all activities in the company and not only connects customers and employees but also chip manufacturers, component distributors, contract manufacturers, logistics companies, and systems integrators. These participants can perform like one company because they all rely on the same Web-based data sources. All Cisco's suppliers see the same demand and do not rely on their own forecasts based on information flowing from multiple points in the supply chain. Cisco also built a dynamic

> replenishment system to help reduce supplier inventory. Cisco's average
> turns in 1999 were 10, compared with an average of 4 for competitors.
> Inventory turns for commodity items are even more impressive; they
> reach 25 to 35 turns a year.[5]

The preceding examples raise an important question: Why is it
that in some cases these new business models fail, whereas in other
cases they are incredibly successful? If Dell and Cisco can use the Internet to develop such effective business models, what inhibits other
firms from adopting similar techniques?

To answer this question, we require a better understanding of
Internet-based supply chain strategies.

3.4.1   What Is e-Business?

To better understand the impact of the Internet on supply chains, we
start by introducing our definitions of e-business and e-commerce:

- *E-business* is a collection of business models and processes
  motivated by Internet technology and focusing on
  improvement of extended enterprise performance.
- *E-commerce* is the ability to perform major commerce
  transactions electronically.

These definitions lead to several observations. First, e-commerce
is only part of e-business. Second, Internet technology is the force behind the business change. Finally, the focus in e-business is on the extended enterprise, i.e., intraorganizational, business-to-consumer
(B2C), and business-to-business (B2B) transactions. B2C refers to
businesses that are "direct to customer," especially retail activities over
the Internet, and includes products, insurance, banking, and so forth.
B2B refers to business conducted over the Internet predominantly
between businesses. This includes both the currently ubiquitous
exchanges and collaboration with suppliers and vendors to achieve
common goals.

Many companies have recognized that the Internet can have a
huge impact on supply chain performance. Indeed, these companies
have observed that the Internet can help them move away from the
traditional push strategies employed by most supply chains. Initially,

the move was toward a pull strategy, but eventually, many companies ended up with a push-pull supply chain.

3.4.2 The Grocery Industry

Consider the grocery industry. A typical supermarket employs a push-based strategy where inventory at the warehouses and stores is based on a forecast. When Peapod was founded in 1989, the idea was to establish a pure pull strategy with no inventory and no facilities. When a customer ordered groceries, Peapod would pick the products at a nearby supermarket. This strategy had significant service problems because stockout rates were very high (about 8 to 10 percent). In the last few years, Peapod has changed its business model to a push-pull strategy by setting up a number of warehouses; stockout rates are now less than 2 percent. Observe that in this case the push part is the portion of the Peapod supply chain prior to satisfying customer demand, and the pull part starts from a customer order. Also note that since a Peapod warehouse covers a large geographic area, clearly larger than the one covered by an individual supermarket, demand is aggregated over many customers and locations, resulting in better forecasts and inventory reduction.

Of course, in the online grocery industry there are other challenges, including reducing transportation costs and responding in a very short period of time, typically within 12 hours, in a tight delivery window. Unfortunately, no current online grocers have the density of customers that will allow them to control transportation costs and therefore compete successfully with traditional supermarkets. This is the reason why most online grocers have failed. Indeed, the framework developed in the preceding section suggests that this industry is characterized by low level of demand uncertainty for many products and high economies of scale in transportation cost, implying that a push-based strategy is more appropriate.

3.4.3 The Book Industry

The book industry is another excellent example of the evolution of supply chain strategies from push to pull and then to push-pull. Traditionally, book retailers such as Barnes and Noble had a push supply chain. When Amazon.com was established in 1995, its supply chain was a pure pull system with no warehouses and no stock. Indeed, at that time Ingram Book Group supplied most of Amazon's customer demand.

Ingram Book can aggregate across many customers and suppliers and take advantage of economies of scale. Thus the pull model employed by Amazon.com was an appropriate strategy when Amazon.com was building its brand name. As volume and demand increased, two issues became clear. First, Amazon.com's service level was affected by Ingram Book's distribution capacity, which was shared by many booksellers. Indeed, during periods of peak holiday demand, Amazon.com could not meet its service-level goals. Second, using Ingram Book in the first few years allowed Amazon.com to avoid inventory costs but significantly reduced profit margins. As demand increased, it became evident that Ingram Book did not provide any advantage for many of the book categories because Amazon.com's ability to aggregate across large geographic areas allowed the company to reduce uncertainties and hence inventory costs by itself without using a distributor.

As Amazon.com discovered these issues, the company changed its philosophy, and now Amazon.com has several warehouses around the country where most of the titles are stocked. Thus inventory at the warehouses is managed based on a push strategy, whereas demand is satisfied based on individual requests, a pull strategy.

3.4.4 The Retail Industry

The retail industry was in general late to respond to competition from virtual stores and to recognize the opportunities provided by the Internet. Recently, however, the landscape has changed as many so-called brick-and-mortar companies are adding an Internet shopping component to their offering. Enter click-and-mortar giants Wal-Mart, Kmart, Target, and Barnes and Noble, among others. These retailers recognize the advantage they have over pure Internet companies. Indeed, they already have the distribution and warehousing infrastructure in place. Thus they have established virtual retail stores serviced by their existing warehousing and distribution structures.

As a result of going online, click-and-mortar firms have changed their approach to stocking inventory. High-volume, fast-moving products, whose demand can be matched accurately with supply based on long-term forecasts, are stocked in stores, whereas low-volume, slow-moving products are stocked centrally for online purchasing. The low-volume products have highly uncertain demand levels and thus require high levels of safety stock. Centralized stocking reduces uncertainties by aggregating demand across geographic locations and thus reduces inventory levels. The analysis implies that these retailers use a push strategy for high-volume, fast-moving products and a push-pull strategy for low-volume, slow-moving products.

Of course, the move from brick-and-mortar to click-and-mortar stores is not an easy one and may require skills that the brick-and-mortar companies do not have.

EXAMPLE 3-11

Wal-Mart has always prided itself on its distribution operations. Thus it was a huge surprise when the company announced that it planned to hire an outside firm to handle order fulfillment and warehousing for its online store, Wal-Mart.com, which the retailer launched in the fall of 1999. Fingerhut Business Services filled orders behind the scenes at Wal-Mart's cyberstore. Indeed, with a background in handling individual orders, Fingerhut has emerged as a major provider of third-party distribution services to other retailers and e-tailers interested in home delivery. Fingerhut provided Internet order fulfillment, warehousing, shipment, payment processing, customer service, and merchandise returns for Wal-Mart.com when the service was launched.

3.4.5 Impact on Transportation and Fulfillment

This review of the evolution of supply chain strategies in various industries suggests the following insight: The Internet and the associated new supply chain paradigms introduce a shift in fulfillment strategies: from cases and bulk shipments to single items and smaller-size shipments and from shipping to a small number of stores to serving highly geographically dispersed customers. This shift also has increased the importance and complexity of reverse logistics.

Table 3-2   Traditional Fulfillment versus e-Fulfillment

	Traditional Fulfillment	e-Fulfillment
Supply chain strategy	Push	Push-pull
Shipment	Bulk	Parcel
Reverse logistics	Small part of the business	Important and highly complex
Delivery destination	Small number of stores	Large number of geographically dispersed customers
Lead times	Relatively long	Relatively short

Table 3-2 summarizes the impact of the Internet on fulfillment strategies. Specifically, the new developments in supply chain strategies are very good news for the parcel and LTL industries. Both pull and push-pull systems rely heavily on individual (e.g., parcel) shipments rather than bulk shipments. This is especially true in the B2C area, where a new term has been coined: *e-fulfillment.*

Another impact of e-fulfillment on the transportation industry is the significant increase in reverse logistics. Indeed, in the B2C arena, e-fulfillment typically means that the supplier needs to handle many returns, each of which consists of a small shipment. This is true because online retailers need to build customer trust through generous return terms. Parcel shipping is already set up to handle these returns, a major issue in B2C and in many cases in B2B commerce. This is a challenge for the LTL industry, which traditionally has not been very involved in door-to-door services.

e-Fulfillment logistics requires short lead times, the ability to serve globally dispersed customers, and the ability to reverse the flow easily from B2C to C2B. Only parcel shipping can do all this. Indeed, one important advantage of the parcel industry is the existence of an excellent information infrastructure that enables real-time tracking. Thus the future looks promising for the parcel shipping industry and, in particular, for those carriers and consolidators who work to modify their own systems to integrate them with their customers' supply chains.

3.5   DISTRIBUTION STRATEGIES

We now consider the portion of the supply chain beginning with the manufacturer and supplier and continuing, in the case of retail goods, to the retailer. Typically, three distinct outbound distribution strategies are used:

1. *Direct shipment.* In this strategy, items are shipped directly from the supplier to the retail stores without going through distribution centers.

2. *Warehousing.* This is the classic strategy in which warehouses keep stock and provide customers with items as required.

3. *Cross-docking.* In this strategy, items are distributed continuously from suppliers through warehouses to customers. However, the warehouses rarely keep the items for more than 10 to 15 hours.

We discuss traditional warehousing strategies in some depth in Chapter 4. Here we describe direct shipment and cross-docking.

3.5.1   Direct Shipment

Direct shipment strategies exist to bypass warehouses and distribution centers. Employing direct shipment, the manufacturer or supplier delivers goods directly to retail stores. The advantages of this strategy are

- The retailer avoids the expenses of operating a distribution center.
- Lead times are reduced.

This type of distribution strategy also has a number of important disadvantages:

- Risk-pooling effects, which we describe in Chapter 4, are negated because there is no central warehouse.
- The manufacturer and distributor transportation costs increase because it must send smaller trucks to more locations.

For these reasons, direct shipment is common when the retail store requires fully loaded trucks, which implies that the warehouse does not help in reducing transportation costs. It is most often mandated by powerful retailers or used in situations where lead time is critical. Sometimes the manufacturer is reluctant to be involved with direct shipping but may have no choice in order to keep the business. Direct shipment is also prevalent in the grocery industry, where lead times are critical because of perishable goods.

EXAMPLE 3-12

JCPenney has successfully implemented a direct shipping strategy. JCPenney sells general merchandise through nearly a thousand stores and millions of catalogs. With 200,000 items from more than 20,000 suppliers, managing the flow of goods is a formidable task. Each individual store retains total accountability for sales, inventory, and profit and is responsible for sales forecasts and releasing orders. Orders are communicated to buyers who coordinate the shipment with distribution personnel to ensure quick response, and an internal control and tracking system is used to monitor the flow of materials. In most cases products are shipped directly to Penney's stores.

3.5.2 Cross-Docking

Cross-docking is a strategy that Wal-Mart made famous. In this system, warehouses function as inventory coordination points rather than as inventory storage points. In typical cross-docking systems, goods arrive at warehouses from the manufacturer, are transferred to vehicles serving the retailers, and are delivered to the retailers as rapidly as possible. Goods spend very little time in storage at the warehouse—often less than 12 hours. This system limits inventory costs and decreases lead times by decreasing storage time.

Of course, cross-docking systems require a significant start-up investment and are very difficult to manage:

1. Distribution centers, retailers, and suppliers must be linked with advanced information systems to ensure that all pickups and deliveries are made within the required time windows.
2. A fast and responsive transportation system is necessary for a cross-docking system to work.
3. Forecasts are critical, necessitating the sharing of information.
4. Cross-docking strategies are effective *only* for large distribution systems in which a large number of vehicles are

delivering and picking up goods at the cross-dock facilities at any one time. In such systems, there is enough volume every day to allow shipments of fully loaded trucks from the suppliers to the warehouses. Since these systems typically include many retailers, demand is sufficient such that items that arrive at the cross-docking facilities can be delivered immediately to the retail outlets in full truckload quantities.

EXAMPLE 3-13

The tremendous market growth of Wal-Mart over the past 15 to 20 years highlights the importance of an effective strategy that coordinates inventory replenishment and transportation policies.[6] Over this time period, Wal-Mart developed into the largest and highest-profit retailer in the world. A number of major components in Wal-Mart's competitive strategy were critical to its success, but perhaps the most important has been its enthusiastic use of cross-docking. Wal-Mart delivers about 85 percent of its goods using cross-docking techniques, as opposed to about 50 percent for Kmart. To facilitate cross-docking, Wal-Mart operates a private satellite communications system that sends point-of-sale (POS) data to all its vendors, allowing them to have a clear picture of sales at all its stores. In addition, Wal-Mart has a dedicated fleet of 2000 trucks, and on average, stores are replenished twice a week. Cross-docking enables Wal-Mart to achieve economies of scale by purchasing full truckloads. It reduces the need for safety stocks and has cut the cost of sales by 3 percent compared with the industry average, a major factor explaining Wal-Mart's large profit margins.

Very few major retailers use one of these strategies exclusively. Typically, different approaches are used for different products, making it necessary to analyze the supply chain and determine the appropriate approach to use for a particular product or product family.

To evaluate these concepts, we proceed with a simple question: What are the factors that influence distribution strategies? Obviously, customer demand and location, service level, and costs, including transportation and inventory costs, all play a role. It is important to note the interplay of inventory and transportation costs (see Chap. 4). Both transportation and inventory costs depend on shipment size, but in opposite ways. Increasing lot sizes reduces the delivery frequency and enables the shipper to take advantage of price breaks in shipping volume, therefore reducing transportation costs. However, large lot sizes increase inventory cost per item because items remain in inventory for a longer period of time until they are consumed.

Demand variability also has an impact on the distribution strategy. Indeed, as we observed in Chapter 4, demand variability has a huge impact on cost; the larger the variability, the more safety stock is needed. Thus stock held at the warehouses provides protection against demand variability and uncertainty, and due to *risk pooling*, the more warehouses a distributor has, the more safety stock is needed. On the other hand, if the warehouses are not used for inventory storage, as in the cross-docking strategy, or if there are no warehouses at all, as in direct shipping, more safety stock is required in the distribution system. This is true because in both cases *each store* needs to keep enough safety stock. This effect is mitigated, however, by distribution strategies that enable better demand forecasts, smaller safety stocks, and transshipment strategies (described below). Any assessment of different strategies also must consider lead time and volume requirements, as well as the capital investment involved in the various alternatives.

Table 3-3 summarizes and compares the three distribution strategies discussed in this subsection. The inventory-at-warehouses strategy refers to the classic distribution strategy in which inventory is kept at the warehouses. The allocation row in the table refers to the point at which the allocation of different products to different retail outlets needs to be made. Clearly, in direct shipment, allocation decisions have to be made earlier than they do when cross-docking or

Table 3-3   Distribution Strategies

Strategy → Attribute ↓	Direct Shipment	Cross- Docking	Inventory at Warehouses
Risk pooling			Take advantage
Transportation costs		Reduced inbound costs	Reduced inbound costs
Holding costs	No warehouse costs	No holding costs	
Allocation		Delayed	Delayed

warehousing strategies are employed, so forecast horizons need to be longer.

3.5.3 Transshipment

The growth of rapid transportation options and advanced information systems has made transshipment an important option to consider when selecting supply chain strategies. By *transshipment*, we mean the shipment of items between different facilities *at the same level in the supply chain* to meet some immediate need.

Most often transshipment is considered at the retail level. As we mentioned earlier, transshipment capability allows the retailer to meet customer demand from *the inventory of other retailers*. To do this, the retailer must know what other retailers have in inventory and must have a rapid way to ship the items either to the store where the customer originally tried to make the purchase or to the customer's home. These requirements can be met only with advanced information systems, which allow a retailer to see what other retailers have in stock and facilitate rapid shipping between retailers.

It is easy to see that if the appropriate information systems exist, shipment costs are reasonable, and all the retailers have the same owner, transshipment makes sense. In this case the system is effectively taking advantage of the risk-pooling concept, even if no central warehouse exists, because one can view inventory in different retail outlets as part of a large, single pool.

Retailers that are independently owned and operated may want to avoid transshipment because they will be helping their competitors. In Chapter 5 we consider the issues associated with *distributor integration*, in which independent distributors cooperate in various ways, including transshipment of needed goods.

3.6 CENTRALIZED VERSUS DECENTRALIZED CONTROL

In a centralized system, decisions are made at a central location for the entire supply network. Typically, the objective is to minimize the total cost of the system subject to satisfying some service-level requirements. This is clearly the case when the network is owned by a single entity, but it is also true in a centralized system that includes many different organizations. In this case the savings, or profits, need to be allocated across the network using some contractual mechanism. We have already seen that centralized control leads to global optimization. Similarly, in a decentralized system, each facility identifies its most effective strategy without considering the impact on the other facilities in the supply chain. Thus a decentralized system leads to local optimization.

It is easy to see that, theoretically, a centralized distribution network will be at least as effective as a decentralized one because the centralized decision makers can make all the decisions that decentralized decision makers would make but also have the option of considering the interplay of decisions made at different locations in the supply network.

In a logistics system in which each facility can access only its own information, a centralized strategy is not possible. With advances in information technologies, however, all facilities in a centralized system can have access to the same data. Indeed, in Chapter 10 we discuss the concept of *single point of contact*. In this case information can be accessed from anywhere in the supply chain and is the same no matter what mode of inquiry is used or who is seeking the information. Thus centralized systems allow the sharing of information and, more important, the use of this information in ways that reduce the bullwhip effect (see Chap. 2) and improve forecasts. Finally, they allow the use of coordinated strategies across the entire supply chain—strategies that reduce systemwide costs and improve service levels.

Sometimes, of course, a system cannot be centralized "naturally." The retailers, manufacturers, and distributors might all have different owners and different objectives. In these cases it is often helpful to form partnerships to approach the advantages of a centralized system. We discuss these kinds of partnerships in Chapter 5. Also, detailed supply contracts can be useful, and we discuss these in more detail in Chapter 6.

3.7 CENTRAL VERSUS LOCAL FACILITIES

Another critical decision in supply chain design involves whether to use centralized or local production and warehousing facilities. We discuss certain elements of this decision in Chapter 4. Here we summarize additional important considerations:

> *Safety stock.* Consolidating warehouses allow the vendor to take advantage of risk pooling. In general, this means that the more centralized an operation is, the lower are the safety stock levels.

Overhead. Economies of scale suggest that operating a few large central warehouses leads to lower total overhead cost relative to operating many smaller warehouses.

Economies of scale. In many manufacturing operations, economies of scale can be realized if manufacturing is consolidated. It is often much more expensive to operate many small manufacturing facilities than to operate a few large facilities with the same total capacity.

Lead time. Lead time to market often can be reduced if a large number of warehouses are located closer to the market areas.

Service. This depends on how *service* is defined. As we indicated earlier, centralized warehousing enables the use of risk pooling, which means that more orders can be met with a lower total inventory level. On the other hand, shipping time from the warehouse to the retailer will be longer.

Transportation costs. Transportation costs are directly related to the number of warehouses used. As the number of warehouses increases, transportation costs between the production facilities and the warehouses also increase because total distance traveled is greater, and more important, quantity discounts are less likely to apply. However, transportation costs from the warehouses to the retailers are likely to fall because the warehouses tend to be much closer to the market areas.

Of course, it is possible that in an effective distribution strategy some products will be stored in a central facility, whereas others will be kept in various local warehouses. For instance, very expensive products with low customer demand may be stocked at a central warehouse, whereas low-cost products facing high customer demand may be stocked at many local warehouses. In addition, the use of centralized or local production and warehousing facilities is not necessarily an either-or decision. There are degrees of local and centralized operation, with varying degrees of the advantages and disadvantages listed earlier. Finally, advanced information systems help each type of system maintain some of the advantages of the other type. For example, lead times from central warehouses and safety stock for local warehouses can be reduced.

3.8 SUMMARY

In recent years many companies have improved performance, reduced cost, increased service levels, reduced the bullwhip effect, and improved responsiveness to changes in the marketplace by integrating the supply chain. In many cases this was facilitated by the implementation of push-pull strategies and by a focus on demand-driven strategies. In particular, the Internet has created the opportunity to revolutionize supply chain strategies. Indeed, the success of giants such as Dell Computers and Cisco and the significant market capitalization of newly established companies such as Amazon.com can be attributed to sophisticated Internet-based supply chain strategies.

At the same time, the collapse of many Internet companies sends an alarming message that e-business presents not only opportunities but also great challenges. Key to these challenges is the ability to identify the appropriate supply chain strategy for a particular company and individual products. Indeed, the premise on which many of the Internet companies were built, that in the new economy there is no need for either physical infrastructure or inventory, has in many cases been disastrous. The new supply chain paradigm, push-pull strategy, advocates holding inventory, although it pushes the inventory upstream in the supply chain.

Of course, even traditional firms need to have an effective distribution strategy. Depending on the details of the situation, traditional warehouses, cross-docking, direct shipment, and transshipment all can be effective tools for managing inventory and distribution costs.

CHAPTER 4

Network Planning

4.1 INTRODUCTION

The supply chain consists of suppliers, plants, warehouses, distribution centers, and retail outlets, as well as raw materials, work-in-process inventory, and finished products that flow between the facilities. Unfortunately, as we discussed in Chapter 1, optimizing supply chain performance is difficult due to

- Different conflicting objectives and tradeoffs
- Inherent uncertainties in both supply and demand
- Supply chain dynamics, i.e., the bullwhip effect

In this chapter we focus on what we call *network planning*—the process by which a firm structures and manages the supply chain in order to

- Find the right balance among inventory, transportation, and manufacturing costs
- Match supply and demand under uncertainty by positioning and managing inventory effectively
- Use resources effectively in a dynamic environment

Of course, this is a complex process that requires a hierarchical approach in which decisions on network design, inventory positioning and management, and resource utilization are combined to reduce cost and increase service level. Thus we divide the network planning process into three steps:

1. *Network design.* This includes decisions on the number, locations, and size of manufacturing plants and warehouses; the assignment of retail outlets to warehouses; and so on. Major sourcing decisions are also made at this point, and the typical planning horizon is a few years.

2. *Inventory positioning and management.* This includes identifying stocking points as well as selecting facilities that will produce to stock and thus keep inventory and facilities that will produce to order and hence keep no inventory. It also includes inventory management strategies that take into account demand and supply uncertainties, lead times, cost, and so on.

3. *Resource allocation.* Given the structure of the logistics network and the location of stocking points, the objective in this step is to determine when and how much to produce or purchase and where and when to store inventory. These decisions require identifying the optimal tradeoff between setup costs and times and inventory and transportation costs, taking into account production, sourcing, and warehousing capacities, as well as other business rules and constraints.

In this chapter we analyze each of these steps and provide examples of the processes involved.

4.2   NETWORK DESIGN

Network design determines the physical configuration and infrastructure of the supply chain. As explained in Chapter 1, network design is a strategic decision that has a long-lasting effect on the firm. Network design involves decisions relating to plant and warehouse location as well as distribution and sourcing.

The supply chain infrastructure typically needs to be reevaluated due to changes in demand patterns, product mix, production processes, sourcing strategies, or the cost of running facilities. In addition, mergers and acquisitions may mandate the integration of different logistics networks.

In this section, we concentrate on the following key strategic decisions:

1. Determining the appropriate number of facilities such as plants and warehouses
2. Determining the location of each facility
3. Determining the size of each facility
4. Allocating space for products in each facility
5. Determining the production requirements in each plant
6. Determining sourcing requirements
7. Determining distribution strategies

The objective is to design or reconfigure the logistics network in order to minimize annual systemwide cost, including production and purchasing costs, inventory holding costs, facility costs (storage, handling, and fixed costs), and transportation costs subject to a variety of *service-level requirements*. In this setting, the tradeoffs are clear. Increasing the number of warehouses typically yields

- An improvement in service level due to the reduction in average travel time to the customers
- An increase in inventory costs due to increased safety stocks required to protect each warehouse against uncertainties in customer demands
- An increase in overhead and setup costs
- A reduction in outbound transportation costs—transportation costs from the warehouses to the customers
- An increase in inbound transportation costs—transportation costs from the suppliers and/or manufacturers to the warehouses

In essence, the firm must balance the costs of opening new warehouses with the advantages of being *close* to the customer. Thus warehouse location decisions are crucial determinants of whether the supply chain is an efficient channel for the distribution of products.

We describe below some of the issues related to data collection and the calculation of costs required for the optimization models. Some of the information provided is based on logistics textbooks.[1,2,3]

Figures 4-1 and 4-2 present two screens of a typical decision-support system (DSS); the user would see these screens at different

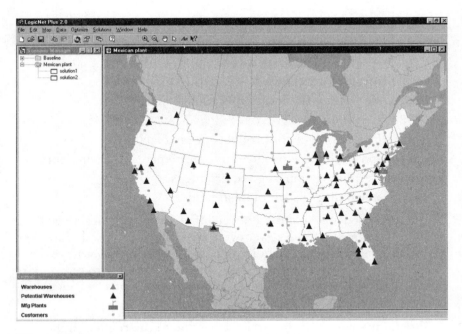

Figure 4-1 The DSS screen representing data prior to
optimization.

stages of optimization. One screen represents the network prior to optimization, and the other represents the optimized network.

4.2.1 Data Collection

A typical network configuration problem involves large amounts of
data, including information on

1. Locations of customers, retailers, existing warehouses and
   distribution centers, manufacturing facilities, and suppliers
2. All products, including volumes, and special transport modes
   (e.g., refrigerated)
3. Annual demand for each product by customer location
4. Transportation rates by mode

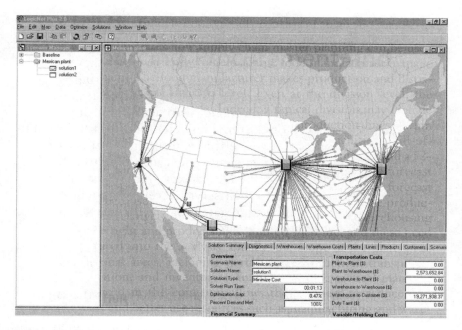

Figure 4-2 The DSS screen representing the optimized logistics network.

5. Warehousing costs, including labor, inventory carrying charges, and fixed operating costs
6. Shipment sizes and frequencies for customer delivery
7. Order-processing costs
8. Customer service requirements and goals
9. Production and sourcing costs and capacities

4.2.1.1 Data Aggregation A quick look at the preceding list suggests that the amount of data involved in any optimization model for this problem is overwhelming. For instance, a typical soft drink distribution system has between 10,000 and 120,000 accounts (customers). Similarly, in a retail logistics network, such as Wal-Mart or JC Penney, the number of different products that flow through the network is in the thousands or even hundreds of thousands.

For this reason, an essential first step is data aggregation. This is carried out using the following procedure:

1. Customers located in close proximity to each other are aggregated using a grid network or other clustering technique. All customers within a single cell or a single cluster are replaced by a single customer located at the center of the cell or cluster. This cell or cluster is referred to as a *customer zone*. A very effective technique that is used commonly is to aggregate customers according to the five- or three-digit ZIP code. Observe that if customers are classified according to their service levels or frequency of delivery, they will be aggregated together by classes. That is, all customers within the same class are aggregated independently of the other classes.

2. Items are aggregated into a reasonable number of product groups based on
   a. *Distribution pattern.* All products picked up at the same source and destined to the same customers are aggregated together. Sometimes there is a need to aggregate not only by distribution pattern but also by logistics characteristics, such as weight and volume. That is, consider all products having the same distribution pattern. Within these products, we aggregate those SKUs with similar volume and weight into one product group.
   b. *Product type.* In many cases different products simply might be variations in product models or style or might differ only in the type of packaging. These products are typically aggregated together.

An important consideration, of course, is the impact on the model's effectiveness of replacing the original detailed data with the aggregated data. We address this question in two ways:

1. Even if the technology exists to solve the logistics network design problem with the original data, it may still be useful to aggregate data because our ability to forecast customer demand at the account and product levels is usually poor. Because of the reduction in variability achieved through aggregation, forecast demand is significantly more accurate at the aggregated level.

2. Various researchers report that aggregating data into about 150 to 200 points usually results in no more than a 1 percent error in the estimation of total transportation costs.[1,4]

In practice, the following approach is typically used when aggregating the data:

- Aggregate demand points for 150 to 200 zones. If customers are classified into classes according to their service levels or frequency of delivery, each class will have 150 to 200 aggregated points.
- Make sure that each zone has approximately an equal amount of total demand. This implies that the zones may be of different geographic sizes.
- Place the aggregated points at the center of the zone.
- Aggregate the products into 20 to 50 product groups.

Figure 4-3 presents information about 3220 customers all located in North America, whereas Figure 4-4 shows the same data after

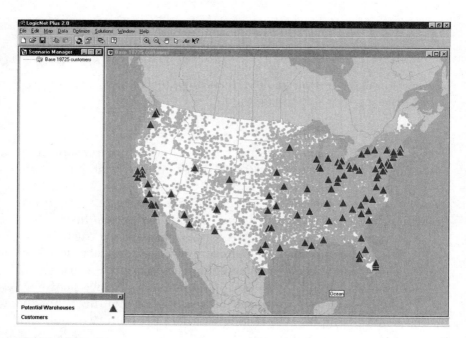

Figure 4-3   The DSS screen representing data prior to aggregation.

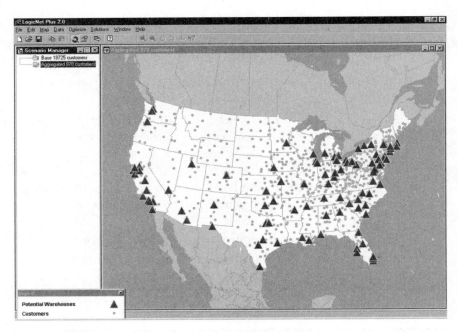

Figure 4-4 The DSS screen representing data after aggregation.

aggregation using a three-digit ZIP code, resulting in 217 aggregated points.

4.2.1.2 Transportation Rates The next step in constructing an effective distribution network design model is to estimate transportation costs. An important characteristic of most transportation rates, including truck, rail, and others, is that the rates are almost linear with distance but not with volume. We distinguish here between transportation costs associated with an *internal* and an *external* fleet.

Estimating transportation costs for company-owned trucks is typically quite simple. It involves annual costs per truck, annual mileage per truck, annual amount delivered, and the truck's effective capacity. All this information can be used to easily calculate cost per mile per SKU.

Incorporating transportation rates for an external fleet into the model is more complex. We distinguish here between two modes of transportation: truckload, referred to as *TL*, and less than truckload, referred to as *LTL*.

In the United States, TL carriers subdivide the country into zones. Almost every state is a single zone, except for certain big states, such as Florida and New York, which are partitioned into two zones. The carriers then provide their clients with zone-to-zone table costs. This database provides the cost per mile per truckload between any two zones. For example, to calculate TL cost from Chicago, Illinois, to Boston, Massachusetts, one needs to get the cost per mile for this pair and multiply it by the distance from Chicago to Boston. An important property of the TL cost structure is that it is not symmetric; i.e., it is typically more expensive to ship a fully loaded truck from Illinois to New York than from New York to Illinois.

In the LTL industry, the rates typically belong to one of three basic types of freight rates: *class*, *exception*, and *commodity*. The class rates are standard rates that can be found for almost all products or commodities shipped. They are found with the help of a *classification tariff* that gives each shipment a *rating* or a *class*. For instance, the railroad classification includes 31 classes ranging from 400 to 13 that are obtained from the widely used *Uniform Freight Classification*. The *National Motor Freight Classification*, on the other hand, includes only 23 classes ranging from 500 to 35. In all cases, the higher the rating or class, the greater is the relative charge for transporting the commodity. There are many factors involved in determining a product's specific class. These include product density, ease or difficulty of handling and transporting, and liability for damage.

Once the rating is established, it is necessary to identify the *rate basis number*. This number is the approximate distance between the load's origin and destination. With the commodity rating or class and the rate basis number, the specific rate per hundred pounds (hundred weight, or cwt) can be obtained from a carrier tariff table (i.e., a freight rate table).

The two other freight rates, namely, *exception* and *commodity*, are specialized rates used to provide either less expensive rates (exception) or commodity-specific rates (commodity).[2,5] Most carriers provide a database file with all their transportation rates; these databases typically are incorporated into decision-support systems.

The proliferation of LTL carrier rates and the highly fragmented nature of the trucking industry have created the need for sophisticated rating engines. An example of such a rating engine that is used widely is SMC3's RateWare (see *www.smc3.com*). This engine can work with various carrier tariff tables as well as SMC3's CzarLite, one of the most widely used and accepted forms of nationwide LTL ZIP code–based rates. Unlike an individual carrier's tariff, CzarLite offers a market-based price list derived from studies of LTL pricing on a regional, interregional, and national basis. This provides shippers with a fair pricing system and prevents any individual carrier's operational and marketing bias from overtly influencing the shipper choice. Consequently, CzarLite rates are often used as a base for negotiating LTL contracts between shippers, carriers, and third-party logistics providers.

In Figure 4-5 we provide LTL cost charged by one carrier for shipping 4000 pounds as a function of the distance from Chicago. The cost is given for two classes, class 100 and class 150. As you can see, in this case the transportation cost function is not linear with distance.

4.2.1.3 Warehouse Costs Warehousing and distribution center costs include three main components:

1. *Handling costs.* These include labor and utility costs that are proportional to annual flow through the warehouse.
2. *Fixed costs.* These capture all cost components that are not proportional to the amount of material that flows through the warehouse. The fixed cost is typically proportional to warehouse size (capacity) but in a nonlinear way (Fig. 4-6).

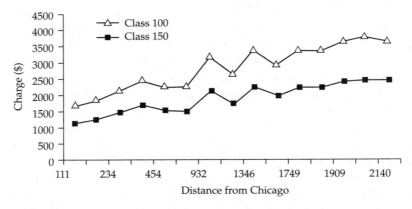

Figure 4-5 Transportation rates for shipping 4000 lb.

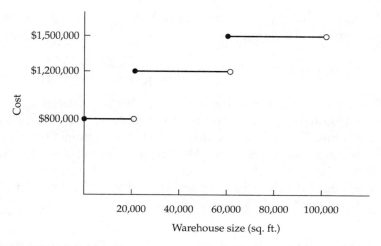

Figure 4-6 Warehouse fixed costs as a function of the warehouse capacity.

As the figure shows, this cost is fixed in certain ranges of warehouse size.

3. *Storage costs.* These represent inventory holding costs, which are proportional to *average* positive inventory levels.

Thus, estimating the warehouse handling costs is fairly easy, whereas estimating the other two cost values is quite difficult. To see this difference, suppose that during the entire year 1000 units of product are required by a particular customer. These 1000 units are not required to flow through the warehouse *at the same time*, so the average inventory level likely will be significantly lower than 1000 units. Thus, when constructing the data for the DSS, we need to convert these annual flows into actual inventory amounts over time. Similarly, annual flow and average inventory associated with this product tell us nothing about how much space is needed for the product in the warehouse. This is true because the amount of space that the warehouse needs is proportional to peak inventory, not annual flow or average inventory.

An effective way to overcome this difficulty is to use the *inventory turnover ratio*. This is defined as

$$\text{Inventory turnover ratio} = \frac{\text{annual sales}}{\text{average inventory level}}$$

Specifically, in our case the inventory turnover ratio is the ratio of the total annual outflow from the warehouse to the average inventory level. Thus the average inventory level is total annual flow divided by the inventory turnover ratio. Multiplying the average inventory level by the inventory holding cost gives the annual storage costs. Finally, to calculate the fixed cost, we need to estimate the warehouse capacity. This is done in the next subsection.

4.2.1.4 Warehouse Capacities Another important input to the distribution network design model is the actual warehouse capacity. It is not immediately obvious, however, how to estimate the actual space required, given the specific annual flow of material through the warehouse. Again, the inventory turnover ratio suggests an appropriate approach. As before, annual flow through a warehouse divided by the inventory turnover ratio allows us to calculate the average inventory level. Assuming a regular shipment and delivery schedule, such as that given in Figure 4-7, it follows that the required storage space is approximately *twice* that amount. In practice, of course, every pallet stored in a warehouse requires an empty space to allow for access

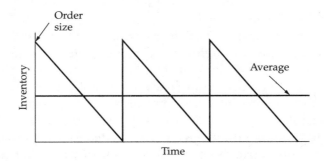

Figure 4-7 Inventory level as a function of time.

and handling; thus, considering this space as well as space for aisles, picking, sorting, and processing facilities, and automatic guided vehicles (AGVs), we typically multiply the required storage space by a factor. This factor depends on the specific application and allows us to assess the amount of space available in the warehouse more accurately. A typical factor used in practice is 3. This factor would be used in the following way. Consider a situation where the annual flow through the warehouse is 1000 units, and the inventory turnover ratio is 10.0. This implies that the average inventory level is about 100 units, and hence, if each unit takes 10 square feet of floor space, the required space for the products is 2000 square feet. Therefore, the total space required for the warehouse is about 6000 square feet.

4.2.1.5 Potential Facility Locations It is also important to effectively identify potential locations for new plants and warehouses. Typically, these locations must satisfy a number of conditions:

- Geographic and infrastructure conditions
- Natural resources and labor availability
- Local industry and tax regulations
- Public interest

As a result, only a limited number of locations would meet all the requirements. These are the potential location sites for the new facilities.

4.2.1.6 Service-Level Requirements There are various ways to define service levels in this context. For example, we might specify a maximum distance between each customer and the warehouse serving it. This ensures that a warehouse will be able to serve its customers within a reasonable time. Sometimes we must recognize that for some customers, such as those in rural or isolated areas, it is harder to provide the same level of service that most other customers receive. In this case it is often helpful to define the service level as the proportion of customers whose distance to their assigned warehouse is no more than a given distance. For instance, we might require that 95 percent of the customers be situated within 200 miles of the warehouses serving them.

4.2.1.7 Future Demand As observed in Chapter 1, decisions at the strategic level, which include distribution network design, have a long-lasting effect on the firm. In particular, decisions regarding the number, location, and size of facilities have an impact on the firm for at least the next 3 to 5 years. This implies that changes in customer demand over the next few years should be taken into account when designing the network. This is addressed most commonly using a scenario-based approach incorporating net-present-value calculations. For example, various possible scenarios representing a variety of possible future demand patterns over the planning horizon can be generated. These scenarios can then be incorporated directly into the model to determine the best distribution strategy.

Recently, advanced Decision Support Systems (DSS) have been developed and implemented that allow companies to consider multiple planning periods in a single model. In this case, users identify future demand by product by location for the new few years. The DSS generates a network strategy including not only the size and locations of facilities but also the best time to establish the new facilities.

4.2.2 Model and Data Validation

The preceding subsections document the difficulties in collecting, tabulating, and cleaning the data for a network configuration model. Once this is done, how do we ensure that the data and model accurately reflect the network design problem?

The process used to address this issue is known as *model and data validation*. This is typically done by reconstructing the existing network configuration using the model and collected data and comparing the output of the model to existing data.

The importance of validation cannot be overstated. Valuable output of the model configured to duplicate current operating conditions includes all costs—warehousing, inventory, production, and transportation—generated under the current network configuration. These data can be compared with the company's accounting information. This is often the best way to identify errors in the data, problematic assumptions, modeling flaws, and so forth.

In one project we are aware of, for example, the transportation costs calculated during the validation process were consistently underestimating the costs suggested by the accounting data. After a careful review of the distribution practices, the consultants concluded that the effective truck capacity was only about 30 percent of the truck's physical capacity; i.e., trucks were being sent out with very little load. Thus the validation process not only helped calibrate some of the parameters used in the model but also suggested potential improvements in the use of the existing network.

It is often also helpful to make local or small changes in the network configuration to see how the system estimates their impact on costs and service levels. Specifically, this step involves positing a variety of what-if questions. This includes estimating the impact of closing an existing warehouse on system performance. Or, to give another example, it allows the user to change the flow of material through the existing network and see the changes in the costs. Often managers have good intuition about what the effect of these small-scale changes on the system should be, so they can more easily identify errors in the model. Intuition about the effect of radical redesign of the entire system is often much less reliable.

To summarize, the model validation process typically involves answering the following questions:

- Does the model make sense?
- Are the data consistent?
- Can the model results be fully explained?
- Did you perform sensitivity analysis?

Validation is critical for determining the validity of the model and data, but the process has other benefits. In particular, it helps the user make the connection between the current operations, which were modeled during the validation process, and possible improvements after optimization.

4.2.3 Solution Techniques

Once the data are collected, tabulated, and verified, the next step is to optimize the configuration of the logistics network. In practice, two techniques are employed:

    1. Mathematical optimization techniques that include
        a. Exact algorithms that are guaranteed to find optimal solutions, i.e., least-cost solutions

   b. Heuristic algorithms that find *good* solutions, not
   necessarily optimal solutions
2. Simulation models that provide a mechanism to evaluate
   specified design alternatives created by the designer

Most DSSs for logistics network design employ mathematical optimization techniques that guarantee to find the least-cost network configuration. Unfortunately, mathematical optimization techniques described earlier have some important limitations. They deal with static models—typically by considering annual, or average, demand—and they do not take into account changes over time. Simulation-based tools take into account the dynamics of the system and are capable of characterizing system performance for a *given design*. Thus it is up to the user to provide the simulation model with a number of design alternatives.

This implies that simulation models allow the user to perform a micro-level analysis. Indeed, the simulation model may include[6]

1. Individual ordering pattern
2. Specific inventory policies
3. Inventory movements inside the warehouse

Unfortunately, simulation models only model a prespecified logistics network design. In other words, given a particular configuration of warehouses, retailers, and so forth, a simulation model can be used to help estimate the costs associated with operating that configuration. If a different configuration is considered (e.g., a few of the customers are to be served by a different warehouse), the model has to be rerun.

As we detail in Chapter 10, simulation is not an optimization tool. It is useful for characterizing the performance of a particular configuration but not for determining an effective configuration from a large set of potential configurations. In addition, a detailed simulation model that incorporates information about individual customer ordering patterns, specific inventory and production policies, daily distribution strategies, and so on may require enormous computational time to achieve a desired level of accuracy in system performance. This implies that typically one can consider *very few* alternatives using a simulation tool.

Thus, if system dynamics is not a key issue, a static model is appropriate, and mathematical optimization techniques can be applied.

In our experience, this type of model accounts for almost all the network configuration models used in practice. When detailed system dynamics is an important issue, it makes sense to use the following two-stage approach,[6] which takes advantage of the strengths of both simulation- and optimization-based approaches:

1. Use an optimization model to generate a number of least-cost solutions at the macro level, taking into account the most important cost components.
2. Use a simulation model to evaluate the solutions generated in the first phase.

4.2.4 Key Features of a Network Configuration DSS

One of the key requirements of any DSS for network design is flexibility. In this context, we define *flexibility* as the ability of the system to incorporate a large set of preexisting network characteristics. Indeed, depending on the particular application, a whole spectrum of design options may be appropriate. At one end of this spectrum is the complete reoptimization of the existing network. This means that each warehouse can be either opened or closed and all transportation flows can be redirected. At the other end of the spectrum, it may be necessary to incorporate the following features in the optimization model:

1. *Customer-specific service-level requirements.*
2. *Existing facilities.* In most cases, facilities such as plants and warehouses already exist, and their leases have not yet expired. Therefore, the model should not permit the closing of these facilities.
3. *Expansion of existing warehouses.* Existing warehouses may be expandable.
4. *Specific flow patterns.* In a number of situations, specific flow patterns (e.g., from a particular warehouse to a set of customers) should not be changed, or perhaps more likely, a certain manufacturing location does not or cannot produce certain SKUs.
5. *Warehouse-to-warehouse flow.* In some cases, material may flow from one warehouse to another warehouse.

6. *Production and bill of materials.* In some cases, assembly is required and needs to be captured by the model. For this purpose, the user needs to provide information on the components used to assemble finished goods. In addition, production information down to the line level can be included in the model.

It is not enough for the DSS to incorporate all the features just described. It also must have the capability to deal with all these issues with little or no reduction in its *effectiveness.* The latter requirement is related directly to the so-called robustness of the system. This stipulates that the relative quality of the solution generated by the system (i.e., cost and service level) should be independent of the specific environment, the variability of the data, and the particular setting. If a particular DSS is not robust, it is difficult to determine how effective it will be for a particular problem.

4.3 INVENTORY MANAGEMENT

The importance of inventory positioning and the need for the coordination of inventory decisions and transportation policies have long been evident. Unfortunately, managing inventory in complex supply chains is typically difficult and may have a significant impact on the customer service level and supply chain systemwide cost.

As we discussed in Chapter 1, a typical supply chain consists of suppliers and manufacturers, who convert raw materials into finished products, and distribution centers and warehouses, from which finished products are distributed to customers. This implies that inventory appears in the supply chain in several forms:

- Raw material inventory
- Work-in-process (WIP) inventory
- Finished product inventory

Each of these needs its own inventory control mechanism. Unfortunately, determining these mechanisms is difficult because efficient production, distribution, and inventory control strategies that reduce systemwide costs and improve service levels must take into account the interactions of the various levels in the supply chain. Nevertheless, the benefits of determining these inventory control mechanisms can be enormous.

EXAMPLE 4-1

> General Motors (GM) has one of the largest production and distribution networks in the world. In 1984, GM's distribution network consisted of 20,000 supplier plants, 133 parts plants, 31 assembly plants, and 11,000 dealers. Freight transportation costs were about $4.1 billion with 60 percent for material shipments. In addition, GM inventory was valued at $7.4 billion, of which 70 percent was work in progress (WIP), and the rest was finished vehicles. GM has implemented a decision tool capable of reducing the combined corporate cost of inventory and transportation. Indeed, by adjusting shipment sizes (i.e., inventory policy) and routes (i.e., transportation strategy), costs could be reduced by about 26 percent annually.[7]

Of course, the key question is: Why hold inventory at all? Some of the reasons include

1. Unexpected changes in customer demand. Customer demand has always been hard to predict, and uncertainty in customer demand has increased in the last few years due to
   a. The short life cycle of an increasing number of products. This implies that historical data about customer demand may not be available or may be quite limited (see Chap. 1).
   b. The presence of many competing products in the marketplace. This proliferation of products makes it increasingly difficult to predict demand for a specific model. Indeed, while it is relatively easy to forecast demand across product groups—i.e., to forecast demand for all products competing in the same market—it is much more difficult to estimate demand for individual products.
2. The presence in many situations of a significant uncertainty in the quantity and quality of the supply, supplier costs, and delivery times.
3. The presence of long delivery lead times, even if there is no uncertainty in demand or supply.
4. Economies of scale offered by transportation companies that encourage firms to transport large quantities of items and therefore hold large inventories. Indeed, many of the transportation providers try to encourage large-size shipments by offering all sorts of discounts to shippers.

5. Limited production capacities and volume discounts offered by suppliers.

Unfortunately, managing inventory effectively in this environment is often difficult, as the following examples illustrate:

- In 1993, Dell Computer's stock plunged after the company predicted a loss. Dell acknowledged that the company was sharply off in its forecast of demand, resulting in inventory write-downs.[8]
- In 1993, Liz Claiborne experienced an unexpected earnings decline as a consequence of higher-than-anticipated excess inventories.[9]
- In 1994, IBM struggled with shortages in the ThinkPad line due to ineffective inventory management.[10]
- In 2001, Cisco took a $2.25 billion excess inventory charge due to declining sales.

These examples lead to an important issue: What are the important considerations when selecting an approach to managing inventory? Since demand is uncertain in most situations, forecast demand is a critical element in determining order quantity. However, given a particular forecast, how should inventory be managed? The approach to managing inventory is typically called the *inventory policy*.

What are the key factors affecting inventory policy?

1. First and foremost is customer demand, which may be known in advance or may be random. In the latter case, forecasting tools may be used in situations in which historical data are available to estimate the average customer demand, as well as the amount of variability in customer demand (often measured as the standard deviation).
2. Replenishment lead time, which may be known at the time we place the order, or may be uncertain.
3. The number of different products.
4. The length of the planning horizon.
5. Costs, including order cost and inventory holding cost.
   a. Typically, order cost consists of two components: the cost of the product and the transportation cost.
   b. Inventory holding cost, or inventory carrying cost, consists of

i. State taxes, property taxes, and insurance on inventories.
ii. Maintenance costs.
iii. Obsolescence cost, which derives from the risk that an item will lose some of its value because of changes in the market.
iv. Opportunity costs, which represent the return on investment that one would receive had money been invested in something else (e.g., the stock market) instead of inventory.

6. Service-level requirements. In situations where customer demand is uncertain, it is often impossible to meet customer orders 100 percent of the time, so management needs to specify an acceptable level of service.

4.3.1 The Effect of Demand Uncertainty

Many companies treat the world as if it were predictable, making production and inventory decisions based on forecasts of the demand made far in advance of the selling season. Although these companies are aware of demand uncertainty when they create a forecast, they design their planning processes as if the initial forecast was an accurate representation of reality. In this case one needs to remember the following principles of all forecasts (see Chap. 2):

1. The forecast is always wrong.
2. The longer the forecast horizon, the worse is the forecast.
3. Aggregate forecasts are more accurate.

Thus the first principle implies that it is difficult to match supply and demand, and the second one implies that it is even more difficult if one needs to predict customer demand for a long period of time, e.g., the next 12 to 18 months. The third principle suggests, for instance, that while it is difficult to predict customer demand for individual SKUs, it is much easier to predict demand across all SKUs within one product family. This is an example of the *risk-pooling concept*.

Indeed, the risk-pooling concept affects inventory management in many ways. The essence of risk pooling is that if end demand is just as likely to be high as to be low, aggregate demand is easier to predict than individual end-item demand. For example, Ford can more easily predict sales of trucks than of a particular model of truck, say, the

F-150. Likewise, Ford can more easily predict the sales of F-150 trucks than of blue F-150 trucks with a particular option package. The same concept applies to aggregate demand across markets or stores. It is easier for Proctor and Gamble to estimate sales for Tide across an entire state than to predict sales for Tide in a particular store.

To illustrate the importance of incorporating demand uncertainty and forecast demand into the analysis, and to characterize the impact of demand uncertainty on the inventory policy, consider the following example.

E X A M P L E   4-2

A TV set distributor faces random demand for the product and receives supply from the manufacturer. Of course, the manufacturer cannot instantaneously satisfy orders placed by the distributor; there is a fixed lead time for delivery whenever the distributor places an order. Since demand is random and the manufacturer has a fixed delivery lead time, the distributor needs to hold inventory even if no fixed setup cost is charged for ordering the products.

There are several reasons why the distributor holds inventory:

1. To satisfy demand occurring during lead time. Since orders are not met immediately, inventory must be on hand to meet customer demand during the period between the time the distributor orders and when the order arrives.

2. To protect against uncertainty in demand and, in particular, to protect against situations in which demand during lead time is much larger than the forecast.

3. To balance annual inventory holding costs and annual fixed order costs. That is, more frequent orders lead to lower inventory levels and thus lower inventory holding costs, but they also lead to higher annual fixed order costs.

While these issues are clear intuitively, the specific inventory policy that the distributor should apply is not simple. To manage inventory effectively, the distributor needs to decide when and how many TV sets to order. We distinguish between two types of policies:

- *Continuous review policy*, in which inventory is reviewed every day, and a decision is made about whether and how much to order

- *Periodic review policy,* in which inventory is reviewed at regular intervals, and an appropriate quantity is ordered after each review

In both cases the inventory policy is based on the concept of *inventory position.* The inventory position at any point in time is the actual inventory at the warehouse plus items ordered by the warehouse but not yet arrived minus items that are back ordered. We are ready to describe effective continuous and periodic review policies.

Continuous Review Policy   An effective inventory policy is characterized by two parameters, the reorder point s and the order-up-to level S; whenever the inventory position is below the reorder point s, an order is placed to increase the inventory level to the order-up-to level S. Such a policy is called an (s, S) *policy* or a *min-max policy.* Figure 4-8 illustrates the inventory level over time when the min-max policy is implemented.

The reorder point consists of two components. The first is the average demand during lead time, and the second is the *safety stock.* The safety stock is the amount of inventory that the distributor needs to keep at the warehouse and in the pipeline to protect against deviations from average demand during lead time.

Periodic Review Policy   In many real-life situations, the inventory level is reviewed periodically, at regular intervals, and an appropriate quantity is ordered after each review. For instance, the inventory level

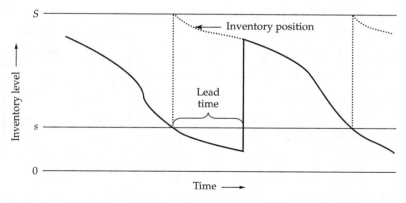

Figure 4-8   Min-max policy.

may be reviewed at the start of each month or the end of each week, and an order may be placed at that time. Since inventory levels are reviewed at a periodic interval, the fixed cost of placing an order is a sunk cost and hence can be ignored; presumably, the fixed cost was used to determine the review interval. The quantity ordered arrives after the appropriate lead time.

What inventory policy should the warehouse use in this case? Since fixed cost does not play a role in this environment, the inventory policy is characterized by one parameter, the *base-stock level*. That is, the warehouse determines a target inventory level, the base-stock level, and each review period the inventory position is reviewed, and the warehouse orders enough to raise the inventory position to the base-stock level. Figure 4-9 illustrates the inventory level over time when this type of policy is implemented.

The base-stock level includes two components: (1) average demand during an interval of time equal to the review period plus the lead time and (2) safety stock, which is the amount of inventory that the warehouse needs to protect against deviations from average demand during that period of time, i.e., during the review period plus the lead time.

Of course, the appropriate safety stock level is affected by a number of different system characteristics. The service level, or likelihood of meeting customer demand, is directly related to the level of safety stock. If a higher service level is desired, more safety stock will be required. Also, if demand is highly variable (frequently much higher or

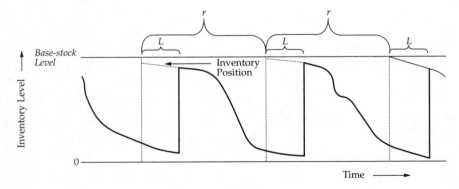

Figure 4-9   Inventory level in a periodic review policy.

lower than average), it is important to hold more safety stock. Similarly, if lead times are long, safety stock needs to be higher to guard against stockouts during lead times.

4.4 STRATEGIC SAFETY STOCK

The analysis in the preceding section has focused on a single facility (e.g., a warehouse or a retail outlet) managing its inventory in order to minimize the facility's own cost as much as possible. In this section we consider a multifacility supply chain that belongs to a single firm. The objective of the firm is to manage inventory so as to reduce systemwide cost; thus it is important to consider the interaction of the various facilities and the impact this interaction has on the inventory policy that should be employed by each facility.

Of course, important questions when managing inventory in a complex supply chain are *where to keep safety stock? which facilities should produce to stock?* and *which should produce to order?* The answer to these questions clearly depends on the desired service level, the supply network, lead times, and a number of operational issues and constraints. Thus our focus is on a strategic model that allows the firm to position safety stock effectively in its supply chain and identify facilities that should produce to stock and those that should produce to order.

To illustrate the tradeoffs and the impact of strategically positioning safety stock in the supply chain, consider the following example.

4.4.1 An Illustrative Example

ElecComp, Inc.,[11] is a large contract manufacturer of circuit boards and other high-tech parts. The company sells about 27,000 high-value products whose life cycle is relatively short. Competition in this industry forces ElecComp to commit to short lead times to its customers; this committed service time to the customers is typically much shorter than manufacturing lead time. Unfortunately, the manufacturing process is quite complex, including a complex sequence of assemblies at different stages.

Because of the long manufacturing lead time and the pressure to provide customers with a short response time, ElecComp kept inventory of finished products for many of its SKUs. Thus the company managed its supply chain based on long-term forecast, the so-called push-based supply chain strategy (see Chap. 3 for the difference between push and pull strategies). This make-to-stock environment required the company to build safety stock and resulted in huge financial and shortage risks.

Executives at ElecComp had long recognized that this push-based supply chain strategy was not the appropriate strategy for their supply chain. Unfortunately, because of the long lead time, a pull-based supply chain strategy, in which manufacturing and assembly are done based on realized demand, was not appropriate either.

Thus ElecComp focused on developing a new supply chain strategy whose objectives are

1. Reducing inventory and financial risks
2. Providing customers with competitive response times.

This could be achieved by

- Determining the optimal *location* of inventory across the various stages of the manufacturing and assembly process
- Calculating the optimal *quantity* of safety stock for each component at each stage.

Thus the focus of redesigning ElecComp's supply chain was on a hybrid strategy in which one portion of the supply chain is managed based on push, i.e., a make-to-stock environment, whereas the remaining portion of the supply chain is managed based on pull, i.e., a make-to-order strategy. Evidently, the supply chain stages that produce to stock will be the locations where the company keeps safety stock, whereas the make-to-order stages will keep no stock at all. Hence the challenge was to identify the location in the supply chain in which the strategy is switched from a push-based, i.e., a make-to-stock strategy, to a pull-based, i.e., a make-to-order, supply chain strategy. This location is referred to as the *push-pull boundary*.

ElecComp developed and implemented the new push-pull supply chain strategy, and the impact was dramatic! For the same customer lead times, safety stock was reduced by 40 to 60 percent, depending on product line. More important, with the new supply chain structure, ElecComp concluded that it could cut lead times to its customers by 50 percent and still enjoy a 30 percent reduction in safety stock.

Below we describe how this was achieved for a number of product lines.

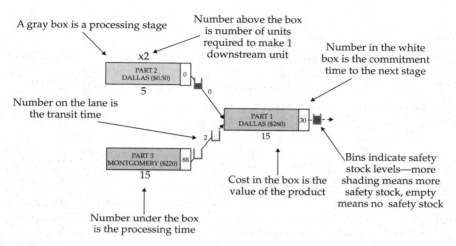

Figure 4-10 How to read the diagrams.

To understand the analysis and the benefit experienced by ElecComp, consider Figure 4-10, in which a finished product (part 1) is assembled in a Dallas facility from two components, one produced in the Montgomery facility and one in a different facility in Dallas. Each box provides information about the value of the product produced by that facility; numbers under each box are the processing time at that stage; bins represent safety stock. Transit times between facilities are provided as well. Finally, each facility provides committed response time to the downstream facilities. For instance, the assembly facility quotes 30 days response time to its customers. This implies that any order can be satisfied in no more than 30 days. The Montgomery facility quotes an 88-day response time to the assembly facility. As a result, the assembly facility needs to keep inventory of finished products in order to satisfy customer orders within its 30-day committed service time.

Observe that if somehow ElecComp can reduce the committed service time from the Montgomery facility to the assembly facility from 88 days to, say, 50 or perhaps 40 days, the assembly facility will be able to reduce its finished good inventory, whereas the Montgomery facility will need to start building inventory. Of course, ElecComp's objective is to minimize systemwide inventory and manufacturing costs; this is precisely what strategic inventory optimization tools do. By looking at the entire supply chain, the tools determine the appropriate inventory level at each stage.

For instance, if the Montgomery facility reduces its committed lead time to 13 days, then the assembly facility does not need any inventory of finished goods. Any customer order will trigger an order for parts 2 and 3. Part 2 will be available immediately because the facility producing part 2 holds inventory, whereas part 3 will be available at the assembly facility in 15 days (13 days committed response time by the manufacturing facility plus 2 days transportation lead time). It takes another 15 days to process the order at the assembly facility, and therefore, the order will be delivered to the customers within the committed service time. Thus, in this case, the assembly facility produces to order, i.e., a pull-based strategy, whereas the Montgomery facility needs to keep inventory and hence is managed based on push, i.e., a make-to-stock strategy.

Now that the tradeoffs are clear, consider the product structure depicted in Figure 4-11. Light boxes (parts 4, 5, and 7) represent outside suppliers, whereas dark boxes represent internal stages within ElecComp's supply chain. Observe that the assembly facility is committed to a 30-day response time to customers and keeps inventory of finished goods. More precisely, the assembly facility and the facility manufacturing part 2 both produce to stock. All other stages produce to order.

Figure 4-12 depicts the optimized supply chain that provides customers with the same 30-day response time. Observe that by adjusting the committed service time of various internal facilities, the assembly system starts producing to order and keeps no finished good inventory. On the other hand, the Raleigh and Montgomery facilities need to reduce their committed service time and hence keep inventory.

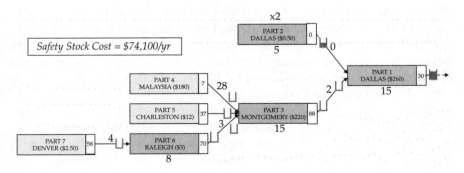

Figure 4-11   Current safety stock location.

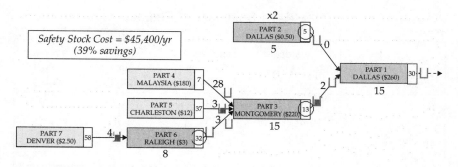

Figure 4-12 Optimized safety stock.

So where is the push and where is the pull in the optimized strategy? Evidently, the assembly facility and the Dallas facility that produces part 2 both operate now in a make-to-order fashion, i.e., a pull strategy, whereas the Montgomery facility operates in a make-to-stock fashion, a push strategy. The impact on the supply chain is a 39 percent reduction in safety stock!

At this point it was appropriate to analyze the impact of a more aggressive quoted lead time to the customers. That is, ElecComp executives considered reducing quoted lead times to the customers from 30 to 15 days. Figure 4-13 depicts the optimized supply chain strategy in this case. The impact was clear. Relative to the baseline (Fig. 4-11) inventory was down by 28 percent, whereas response time to the customers is halved. See Table 4-1 for a summary of the results of this study.

Finally, Figures 4-14 and 4-15 present a more complex product structure. Figure 4-14 provides information about the supply chain

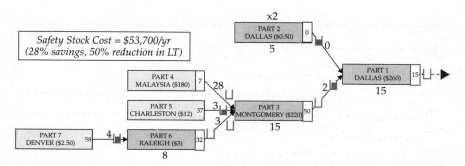

Figure 4-13 Optimized safety stock with reduced lead time.

Table 4-1 Summary of Results

Scenario	Safety Stock Holding Cost ($/yr)	Lead Time to Customer (days)	Cycle Time (days)	Inventory Turns (turns/yr)
Current	74,100	30	105	1.2
Optimized	45,400	30	105	1.4
Shorten lead time	53,700	15	105	1.3

strategy before optimization, and Figure 4-15 depicts the supply chain strategy after optimizing the push-pull boundary as well as inventory levels at different stages in the supply chain. Again, the benefit is clear. By correctly selecting which stage is going to produce to order and which is producing to stock, inventory cost was reduced by more than 60 percent while maintaining the same quoted lead time to customers.

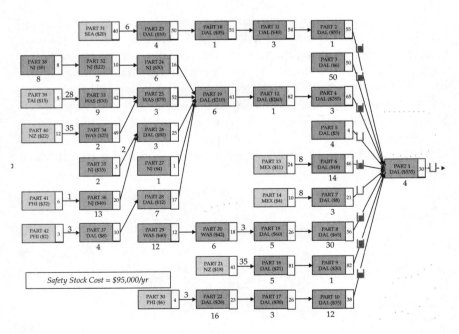

Figure 4-14 Current supply chain.

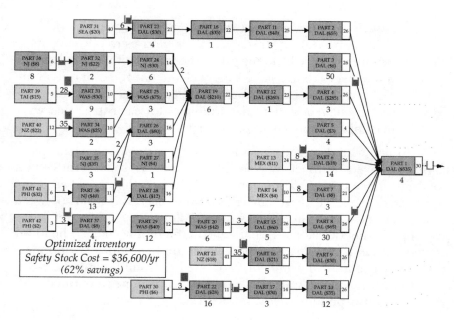

Figure 4-15 Optimized supply chain.

4.4.2 Summary

Using a multistage inventory optimization technology ElecComp was able to significantly reduce inventory cost while maintaining and sometimes significantly decreasing quoted service times to customers. This is achieved by

1. Identifying the push-pull boundary, i.e., identifying supply chain stages that should operate in a make-to-stock fashion and hence keep safety stock. The remaining supply chain stages operate in a make-to-order fashion and thus keep no inventory. This is done by pushing inventory to less costly locations in the supply chain.

2. Taking advantage of the risk-pooling concept. This concept suggests that demand for a component used by a number of finished products has smaller variability and uncertainty than that of the finished goods.

3. Replacing traditional supply chain strategies that are typically referred to as *sequential,* or *local, optimization* by a

globally optimized supply chain strategy. In a sequential, or
local, optimization strategy, each stage tries to optimize its
profit with very little regard to the impact of its decisions on
other stages in the same supply chain. On the other hand, in
a global supply chain strategy, one considers the entire
supply chain and identifies strategies for each stage that will
maximize supply chain performance.

To better understand the impact of the new supply chain paradigm employed by ElecComp, consider Figure 4-16, where we plot
total inventory cost against quoted lead time to the customers. The
upper tradeoff curve represents the traditional relationship between
cost and quoted lead time to customers. This curve is a result of locally optimizing decisions at each stage in the supply chain. The lower
tradeoff curve is the one obtained when the firm globally optimizes
the supply chain by locating correctly the push-pull boundary.

Observe that this shift of the tradeoff curve, due to optimally locating the push-pull boundary, implies that

1. For the same quoted lead time, the company can
   significantly reduce cost or
2. For the same cost, the firm can significantly reduce lead time.

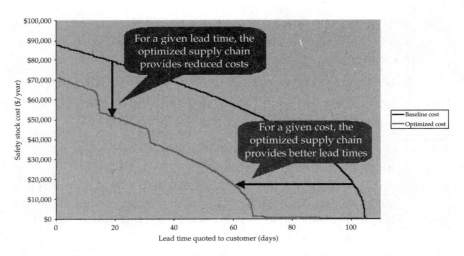

Figure 4-16 Tradeoff between quoted lead time and safety stock.

Finally, notice that the curve representing the traditional relationship between cost and customer quoted lead time is smooth, whereas the new tradeoff curve representing the impact of optimally locating the push-pull boundary is not, with jumps in various places. These jumps represent situations in which the location of the push-pull boundary changes, and significant cost savings are achieved.

Our experience is that those employing the new supply chain paradigm, such as ElecComp, typically choose a supply chain strategy that reduces both cost and customer quoted lead time. This strategy allows ElecComp to satisfy demand much faster than its competitors and develop a cost structure that enables competitive pricing.

4.5 RESOURCE ALLOCATION

As observed in Chapter 3, different processes need to be applied to different portions of the supply chain. Since the focus in the pull part of the supply chain is on service level, order fulfillment processes are typically applied. Similarly, since the focus of the push part of the supply chain is on cost and resource allocation, *supply chain master planning processes* are used here to develop an effective strategy for the next few months.

Supply chain master planning is defined as the process of coordinating and allocating production and distribution strategies and resources to maximize profit or minimize systemwide cost. In this process the firm considers forecast demand for the entire planning horizon, e.g., the next 52 weeks, as well as safety stock requirements. The latter are determined, for instance, based on models similar to the one analyzed in the preceding section.

The challenge of allocating production, transportation, and inventory resources in order to satisfy demand can be daunting. This is especially true when the firm is faced with seasonal demand, limited capacities, competitive promotions, or high volatility in forecasting. Indeed, decisions such as when and how much to produce, where to store inventory, and whether to lease additional warehouse space may have enormous impact on supply chain performance.

Traditionally, the supply chain planning process was performed manually with a spreadsheet and was done by each function in the company independently of other functions. That is, the production plan would be determined at the plant, independently from the inventory plan, and typically would require the two plans to be somehow coordinated at a later time. This implies that divisions typically end up "optimizing" just one parameter, usually production costs.

In modern supply chains, however, this sequential process is replaced by a process that takes into account the interaction between the various levels of the supply chain and identifies a strategy that maximizes supply chain performance. This is referred to as *global optimization*, and it necessitates the need for an optimization-based DSS. These systems, which model the supply chain as large-scale mixed-integer linear programs, are analytic tools capable of considering the complexity and dynamic nature of the supply chain.

Typically, the output from the tool is an effective supply chain strategy that coordinates production, warehousing, transportation, and inventory decisions. The resulting plan provides information on production quantities, shipment sizes, and storage requirements by product, location, and time period. This is referred to as the *supply chain master plan*.

In some applications, the supply chain master plan serves as an input for a detailed production scheduling system. In this case the production scheduling system employs information about production quantities and due dates received from the supply chain master plan. This information is used to propose a detailed manufacturing sequence and schedule. This allows the planner to integrate the back end of the supply chain, i.e., manufacturing and production, and the front end of the supply chain, i.e., demand planning and order replenishment (Fig. 4-17). The figure illustrates an important issue. The focus of order replenishment systems, which are part of the pull portion of the supply chain, is on service level. Similarly, the focus of the tactical planning, i.e., the process by which the firm generates a supply chain master plan, which is in the push portion of the supply chain, is on cost minimization or profit maximization. Finally, the focus in the detailed manufacturing scheduling portion of the supply chain is on *feasibility*. That is, the focus is on generating a detailed production schedule that satisfies all production constraints and meets all the due-date requirements generated by the supply chain master plan.

Of course, the output from the tactical planning process, i.e., the supply chain master plan, is shared with supply chain participants to improve coordination and collaboration. For example, the distribution center managers can now better use this information to plan their labor

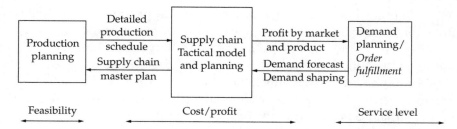

Figure 4-17 The extended supply chain: from manufacturing to order fullfillment.

and shipping needs. Distributors can share plans with their suppliers and customers in order to decrease costs for all partners in the supply chain and promote savings. Specifically, distributors can realign territories to better serve customers, store adequate amounts of inventory at the customer site, and coordinate overtime production with suppliers.

In addition, supply chain master planning tools can identify potential supply chain bottlenecks *early* in the planning process, allowing the planner to answer such questions as

- Will leased warehouse space alleviate capacity problems?
- When and where should the inventory for seasonal or promotional demand be built and stored?
- Can capacity problems be alleviated by rearranging warehouse territories?
- What impact do changes in the forecast have on the supply chain?
- What will be the impact of running overtime at the plants or outsourcing production?
- What plant should replenish each warehouse?
- Should the firm ship by sea or by air? Shipping by sea implies long lead times and therefore requires high inventory levels. On the other hand, using air carriers reduces lead times and hence inventory levels but significantly increases transportation cost.
- Should we rebalance inventory between warehouses or replenish from the plants to meet unexpected regional changes in demand?

Another important capability that tactical planning tools have is the ability to analyze demand plans and resource utilization to maximize profit. This enables balancing the effect of promotions, new product introductions, and other planned changes in demand patterns and supply chain costs. Planners now are able to analyze the impact of various pricing strategies as well as identify markets, stores, or customers that do not provide the desired profit margins.

A natural question is, when should one focus on cost minimization and when to focus on profit maximization? While the answer to this question may vary from instance to instance, it is clear that cost minimization is important when the structure of the supply chain is fixed or at times of a recession and therefore in a state of oversupply. In this case the focus is on satisfying all demand at the lowest cost by allocating resources effectively. On the other hand, profit maximization is important at time of growth, i.e., at time when demand exceeds supply. In this case capacity can be limited because of use of limited natural resources or because of expensive manufacturing processes that are hard to expand, as is the case in the chemical and electronic industries. In these cases, deciding who to serve and for how much is more critical than cost savings.

Finally, an effective supply chain master planning tool also must be able to help the planners improve the accuracy of the supply chain model. This, of course, is counterintuitive because the accuracy of the supply chain master planning model depends on the accuracy of the demand forecast that is an input to the model. However, notice that the accuracy of the demand forecast is typically time-dependent. That is, the accuracy of forecast demand for the first few time periods, e.g., the first 10 weeks, is much higher than the accuracy of demand forecast for later time periods. This suggests that the planner should model the early portion of the demand forecast at a great level of detail, i.e., apply weekly demand information. On the other hand, demand forecasts for later time periods are not as accurate, and hence the planner should model the later demand forecast month by month or by groups of 2 to 3 weeks each. This implies that later demand forecasts are aggregated into longer time buckets, and hence, due to the risk-pooling concept, the accuracy of the forecast improves.

In summary, supply chain master planning helps address fundamental tradeoffs in the supply chain such as setup cost versus holding costs or production lot sizes versus capacities. It takes into account

EXAMPLE 4-4

This example illustrates how supply chain master planning can be used dynamically and consistently to help a large food manufacturer manage the supply chain. The food manufacturer makes production and distribution decisions at the division level. Even at the division level, the problems tend to be large scale. Indeed, a typical division may include hundreds of products, multiple plants, many production lines within a plant, multiple warehouses (including overflow facilities), bill-of-material structures to account for different packaging options, and a 52-week demand forecast for each product for each region. The forecast accounts for seasonality and planned promotions. The annual forecast is important because a promotion late in the year may require production resources relatively early in the year. Production and warehousing capacities are tight and products have limited shelf life, and these need to be integrated into the analysis. Finally, the scope of the plan spans many functional areas, including purchasing, production, transportation, distribution, and inventory management. The tactical planning DSS introduced in the company allows the planners to reduce systemwide cost and better use resources such as manufacturing and warehousing. Indeed, a detailed comparison of the plan generated by the tactical tool with the spreadsheet strategy suggests that the optimization-based tool is capable of reducing total costs across the entire supply chain. See Figure 4-18 for illustrative results.

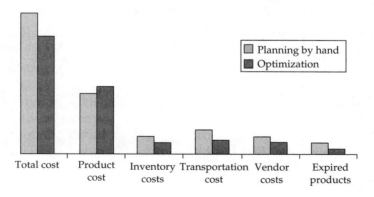

Figure 4-18 Comparison of manual versus optimized scenarios.

supply chain costs such as production, supply, warehousing, transportation, taxes, and inventory, as well as capacities and changes in the parameters over time.

4.6 SUMMARY

Optimizing supply chain performance is difficult because of conflicting objectives, because of demand and supply uncertainties, and because of supply chain dynamics. However, through network planning, which combines network design, inventory positioning and management, and resource allocation, the firm can globally optimize supply chain performance. This is achieved by considering the entire network, taking into account production, warehousing, transportation, and inventory costs as well as service-level requirements.

Table 4-2 summarizes the key dimensions of each of the planning activities—network design, inventory positioning/management, and resource allocation. The table shows that network design involves long-term plans (typically over years), is done at a high level, and can yield high returns. The planning horizon for resource allocation is months or weeks; the frequency of replanning is high, e.g., every

Table 4-2 Network Planning Characteristics

	Network Design	Inventory Positioning and Management	Resource Allocation
Decision focus	Infrastructure	Safety stock	Production Distribution
Planning horizon	Years	Months	Months
Aggregation level	Family	Item	Classes
Frequency	Yearly	Monthly/weekly	Monthly/weekly
Return on investment	High	Medium	Medium
Implementation	Very short	Short	Short
User	Very few	Few	Few

week; and it typically delivers quick results as well. Inventory planning is focused on short-term uncertainty in demand, lead time, processing time, or supply. The frequency of replanning is high, e.g., monthly planning to determine appropriate safety stock based on the latest forecast and forecast error. Inventory planning also can be used more strategically to identify locations in the supply chain where the firm keeps inventory, as well as to identify stages that produce to stock and those which produce to order.

CHAPTER 5

Supply Chain Alliances

5.1 INTRODUCTION

One of the paradoxes of business today is that at the same time that complex business practices (such as the ones we have discussed in the preceding chapters) are becoming essential for firms to survive and thrive, the necessary financial and managerial resources to implement these practices are becoming increasingly scarce. This is one reason why it may not always be effective to perform all these key business functions in-house. Frequently, a company may find it effective to use other firms with special resources and technical knowledge to perform these functions.

Even if a firm has the available resources to perform a particular task, another firm in the supply chain sometimes may be better suited to perform that task simply because its relative location in the supply chain better positions it to do so. Often a combination of position in the supply chain, resources, and expertise determines the most appropriate firm in the supply chain to perform a particular function. Of course, it is not enough to *know* who in the supply chain should perform a particular function—steps must be taken so that the function is actually performed by the appropriate firm.

As with any business function, there are four basic ways for a firm to ensure that a logistics-related business function is completed:[1]

1. *Internal activities.* A firm can perform the activity using internal resources and expertise, if they are available. As we

will discuss more completely in the next section, if this activity is one of the *core strengths* of the firm, this may be the best way to perform the activity.

2. *Acquisitions.* If a firm does not have the expertise or specialized resources internally, it can acquire another firm that does. This certainly gives the acquiring firm full control over the way the particular business function is performed, but it has several possible drawbacks. For one thing, acquiring a successful company can be difficult and expensive. The culture of the acquired company may clash with that of the acquiring company, and the effectiveness of the acquired company could be lost in the assimilation process. The acquired company may have dealt previously with the acquiring company's competitors, and it could lose this business. This may hurt its overall effectiveness. For these reasons, as well as many others, an acquisition may not be appropriate.

3. *Arm's-length transactions.* Most business transactions are of this type. A firm needs a specific item or service, such as the delivery of a load of items, the maintenance of a vehicle, or the design and installation of logistics management software, and purchases or leases the item or service. Many times an arm's-length transaction is the most effective and appropriate arrangement. Of course, the goals and strategies of the supplier might not match those of the buyer. In general, this kind of short-term arrangement fulfills a particular business need but does not lead to long-term strategic advantages.

4. *Strategic alliances.* These are typically multifaceted, goal-oriented, long-term partnerships between two companies in which both risks and rewards are shared. In many cases the problems of outright acquisition can be avoided, whereas at the same time mutual goals can lead to the commitment of many more resources than in the case of arm's-length transactions. Strategic alliances typically lead to long-term strategic benefits for both partners.

This chapter focuses on *strategic alliances* related to supply chain management. In the next section we introduce a framework for analyzing the advantages and disadvantages of strategic alliances. In the following three sections the three most important types of supply chain–related strategic alliances are discussed in greater detail: third-party logistics (3PL), retailer-supplier partnerships (RSPs), and distributor integration (DI).

5.2 A FRAMEWORK FOR STRATEGIC ALLIANCES

There are many difficult strategic issues that play a part in the selection of appropriate *strategic alliances*. In his classic book, *Partnerships for Profit*, Jordan Lewis[1] introduces an effective general framework for analyzing strategic alliances. This framework, which we briefly introduce in this section, is very helpful for considering the kinds of supply chain–related strategic alliances that we address in the rest of this chapter.

To determine whether a particular strategic alliance is appropriate for your firm, consider how the alliance will help address the following issues:

Adding value to products. A partnership with the appropriate firm can help add value to existing products. For example, partnerships that improve time to market, distribution times, or repair times help to increase the perceived value of a particular firm. Similarly, partnerships between companies with complementary product lines can add value to both companies' products.

Improving market access. Partnerships that lead to better advertising or increased access to new market channels can be beneficial. For example, complementary consumer product manufacturers can cooperate to address the needs of major retailers, increasing sales for everyone.

Strengthening operations. Alliances between appropriate firms can help to improve operations by lowering system costs and cycle times. Facilities and resources can be used more efficiently and effectively. For example, companies with complementary seasonal products can effectively use warehouses and trucks year round.

Adding technological strength. Partnerships in which technology is shared can help add to the skills base of both partners. Also, the

difficult transitions between old and new technologies can be
facilitated by the expertise of one of the partners. For example,
a supplier may need a particular enhanced information system
to work with a certain customer. Partnering with a firm that
already has expertise in this system makes it easier to address
difficult technological issues.

Enhancing strategic growth. Many new opportunities have high
entry barriers. Partnerships might enable firms to pool expertise
and resources to overcome these barriers and explore new
opportunities.

Enhancing organizational skills. Alliances provide a tremendous
opportunity for organizational learning. In addition to learning
from one another, partners are forced to learn more about
themselves and to become more flexible so that these alliances
work.

Building financial strength. In addition to addressing these
competitive issues, alliances can help to build financial strength.
Income can be increased, and administrative costs can be shared
between partners or even reduced owing to the expertise of one
or both of the partners. Of course, alliances also limit
investment exposure by sharing risk.

Strategic alliances have their downsides. The preceding list is
useful for determining these. Each company has its *core strengths* or
competencies—specific talents that differentiate the company from its
competitors and give it an advantage in the eyes of its customers.
These core strengths must not be weakened by the alliance, which can
happen if resources are diverted from these strengths or if technological or strategic strengths are compromised to make the partnership
successful. Similarly, key differences with competitors must not be diminished. This is possible if key technology is shared or if entry barriers are reduced for the competition.

Determining these core strengths is clearly very important; unfortunately, it is also very difficult. What they are depends on the nature of the business and of the firm. Core strengths do not necessarily
correspond to a large investment of resources, and they may be intan-
gible items such as management skills or brand image. To determine a
firm's core strengths, consider how the firm's internal capabilities

contribute to differentiating it from its competition in each of the seven key items listed above. Now, how will *strategic alliances* help or hurt in each of these areas?

The following example illustrates the advantages and disadvantages of strategic alliances. Consider how IBM, Intel, and Microsoft benefited and were hurt by the relationships described in this example.

EXAMPLE 5-1

Although not specifically related to logistics, the story of the IBM personal computer (PC) highlights the advantages and the disadvantages of outsourcing key business functions. When IBM decided to enter the PC market in late 1981, the company did not have the infrastructure in place to design and build a PC. Rather than take the time to develop these capabilities, IBM outsourced almost all the major components of the PC. For example, the microprocessor was designed and built by Intel, and the operating system was provided by a small company in Seattle called Microsoft. IBM was able to release this computer to market within 15 months of beginning its design by tapping the expertise and resources of other companies. Furthermore, within 3 years, IBM replaced Apple Computer as the number one supplier of personal computers. By 1985, IBM's market share was more than 40 percent. However, the downside to IBM's strategy soon became clear as competitors such as Compaq were able to enter the market by using the same suppliers as IBM. Furthermore, when IBM tried to regain control of the market by introducing its PS/2 line of computers, featuring a new, proprietary design and an operating system called OS/2, other companies did not follow IBM's lead, and the original architecture remained dominant in the market. By the end of 1995, IBM's market share had fallen to less than 8 percent, behind market leader Compaq's 10 percent.[2]

Although strategic alliances are becoming increasingly prevalent in all walks of business, three types are particularly significant in supply chain management. Third-party logistics (3PL), retailer-supplier partnerships (RSPs), and distributor integration (DI) are discussed in detail in the next three sections. As you read about these issues, try to place them in the framework described earlier.

5.3 THIRD-PARTY LOGISTICS

The use of third-party logistics (3PL) providers to take over some or all of a company's logistics responsibilities is becoming more prevalent. Indeed, the 3PL industry, which essentially began in the 1980s, was a $45.48 billion industry in 1999 and grew by 24 percent to $56.4 billion in 2000 and by 7.4 percent to $60.6 billion in 2001 and 6.9 percent in 2002.[3]

5.3.1 What Is 3PL?

3PL is simply the use of an outside company to perform all or part of a firm's materials management and product distribution functions. 3PL relationships are typically more complex than traditional logistics supplier relationships; they are true strategic alliances.

Although companies have used outside firms to provide particular services, such as trucking and warehousing, for many years, these relationships had two typical characteristics: They were *transaction-based*, and the companies hired often were *single-function* companies. Modern 3PL arrangements involve long-term commitments and often multiple functions or process management. For example, Ryder Dedicated Logistics has a 5-year agreement to design, manage, and operate all of Whirlpool Corporation's inbound logistics.[4]

3PL providers come in all sizes and shapes, from small companies with a few million dollars in revenues to huge companies with revenues in the billions. Most of these companies can manage many stages of the supply chain.

Surprisingly, the use of 3PL is most prevalent among large companies. Firms such as Minnesota Mining & Manufacturing Co. (3M), Eastman Kodak, Dow Chemical, Time Warner, and Sears Roebuck are turning over large portions of their logistics operations to outside suppliers. 3PL providers are finding it hard to persuade small companies to employ their services, although this may change as the use of 3PL becomes more prevalent and as 3PL providers make a larger effort to develop relationships with smaller companies.[5]

5.3.2 Advantages and Disadvantages of 3PL

Most of the general advantages and disadvantages of strategic alliances described in Section 5.2 apply here.

Focus on core strengths. The most frequently cited benefit of using 3PL providers is that they allow a company to focus on its core competencies. With corporate resources becoming increasingly limited, it is often difficult to be an expert in every facet of a business. Logistics outsourcers provide a company with the opportunity to focus on that company's particular area of expertise, leaving the logistics expertise to the logistics companies. (Of course, if logistics is one of the company's areas of expertise, then outsourcing may not make sense.)

EXAMPLE 5-2

The partnership between Ryder Dedicated Logistics and General Motors' Saturn division is a good example of these benefits. Saturn focuses on automobile manufacturing, and Ryder manages most of Saturn's other logistics considerations. Ryder deals with vendors; delivers parts to the Saturn factory in Spring Hill, Tennessee; and delivers finished vehicles to the dealers. Saturn orders parts using electronic data interchange (EDI) and sends the same information to Ryder. Ryder makes all the necessary pickups from 300 different suppliers in the United States, Canada, and Mexico, using special *decision-support software* to effectively plan routes to minimize transportation costs.[6]

EXAMPLE 5-3

British Petroleum (BP) and Chevron Corp. wished to stick to their core competencies. To do this, they formed Atlas Supply, a partnership of about 80 suppliers, to deliver items such as spark plugs, tires, window-washing fluid, belts, and antifreeze to their 6500 service stations. Rather than use the distribution networks of either BP or Chevron or create a new one, Atlas outsourced all logistics to GATX, which is responsible for running five distribution centers and maintaining inventory of 6500 SKUs at each service station. Each service station orders supplies through its oil company, which forwards the order to Atlas and then to GATX. Each station has a preassigned ordering day to avoid system bottlenecks. GATX systems determine appropriate routes and configurations and transmit orders to the distribution center. The next day, the distribution center selects and packs the orders, and trucks are loaded in the appropriate order based on the delivery schedule. As deliveries are made, returns and deliveries from Atlas suppliers are picked

(continued)

up. GATX electronically informs Atlas, Chevron, and BP of the status of all deliveries. The companies save enough on transportation costs alone to justify this partnership, and the two oil companies have managed to reduce the number of distribution centers from 13 to 5 and significantly improve service levels.[7]

Provides technological flexibility. The ever-increasing need for technological flexibility is another important advantage of the use of 3PL providers. As requirements change and technology advances, the better 3PL providers constantly update their information technology and equipment. Often individual companies do not have the time, resources, or expertise to constantly update their technology. Different retailers may have different, and changing, delivery and information technology requirements, and meeting these requirements may be essential to a company's survival. 3PL providers often can meet these requirements in a quicker, more cost-effective way.[8] Also, 3PL providers already may have the capability to meet the needs of a firm's potential customers, allowing the firm access to certain retailers that might not otherwise be possible or cost-effective.

Provides other flexibilities. 3PL providers also may provide greater flexibility to a company. One example is flexibility in geographic locations. Increasingly, suppliers are requiring rapid replenishment, which in turn may require regional warehousing. By using 3PL providers for this warehousing, a company can meet customer requirements without committing capital and limiting flexibility by constructing a new facility or committing to a long-term lease. Also, flexibility in service offerings may be achieved through the use of third parties, which may be equipped to offer retail customers a much larger variety of services than the hiring firm. In some cases, the volume of customers demanding these services may be low to the firm, but higher to the 3PL provider, who may be working for several different firms across different industries.[9] In addition, flexibility in resource and workforce size can be achieved through outsourcing. Managers can change what would be fixed costs into variable costs in order to react more quickly to changing business conditions.

EXAMPLE 5-4

Working with the Simmons Company, a mattress manufacturer, Ryder Dedicated Logistics provided new technology that allowed Simmons to completely change the way it does business. Before its involvement with Ryder, Simmons warehoused between 20,000 and 50,000 mattresses at each of its manufacturing facilities to meet customer demand in a timely fashion. Now Ryder maintains an on-site logistics manager at Simmons' manufacturing plant. When orders arrive, the logistics manager uses special software to design an optimal sequence and route to deliver the mattresses to customers. This logistics plan is then transmitted to the factory floor, where the mattresses are manufactured in the exact quantity, style, and sequence required—all in time for shipment. This logistics partnership has virtually eliminated the need for Simmons to hold inventory at all.[6]

EXAMPLE 5-5

SonicAir, a division of UPS, provides an even more sophisticated third-party service. This company serves specialized customers who supply equipment for which every hour of downtime is very expensive; SonicAir rapidly delivers service parts where they are needed. SonicAir maintains 67 warehouses and uses specialized software to determine the appropriate inventory level for each part at each warehouse. When an order is placed, the system determines the best way to deliver the part and sends it out, usually on the next flight, from which it is delivered by one of the company's ground couriers. This service enables customers to store fewer parts at each field service bureau than otherwise would be necessary—and still provide the same level of service. With some parts valued at hundreds of thousands of dollars, this is clearly a cost savings to the customer. At the same time, this business is very profitable for SonicAir because customers are willing to pay well for this level of service.[6]

Important disadvantages of 3PL. The most obvious disadvantage of the use of 3PL providers is the *loss of control* inherent in outsourcing a particular function. This is especially true for outbound logistics, where 3PL company employees themselves might interact with a firm's customers. Many 3PL firms work very hard to address these concerns. Efforts include painting company logos on the sides of trucks, dressing 3PL employees in the uniforms of the hiring company, and providing extensive reporting on each customer interaction.

Also, if logistics is one of the core competencies of a firm, it makes no sense to outsource these activities to a supplier who may not be as capable as the firm's in-house expertise. For example, Wal-Mart built and manages its own distribution centers, and Caterpillar runs its parts supply operations. These are competitive advantages and core competencies of these firms, so outsourcing is unnecessary. In particular, if certain logistics activities are within the core competencies of the firm and others are not, it might be wise to employ 3PL providers for only those areas which outside providers can handle better than the hiring firm. For example, if vendor-managed inventory (VMI) replenishment strategies and materials handling are core competencies of a company but transportation is not, a 3PL firm could be contacted to handle shipments from the dock to the customer exclusively. Similarly, pharmaceutical companies build and own distribution centers for controlled drugs but often use public warehouses located closer to the customer for items that are less expensive and easier to control.[10]

5.3.3   3PL Issues and Requirements

A 3PL contract is typically a major and complex business decision. Other than the pros and cons listed earlier, there are many considerations that are critical in deciding whether an agreement should be entered into with a particular 3PL provider.

1. *Know your own costs.* Among the most basic issues to consider in selecting a 3PL provider is to know your own costs so that they can be compared with the cost of using an outsourcing firm. Often it is necessary to use activity-based costing techniques, which involve tracing overhead and direct costs back to specific products and services.[8]

2. *Customer orientation of the 3PL.* Of course, it is not enough to select a provider based on cost alone. Many of the advantages listed earlier involve intangibles such as flexibility. Therefore, the strategic logistics plan of the

company and how a 3PL provider would fit into this plan must be considered carefully. A 1995 survey of 3PL providers[4] identified the following characteristics as most critical to the success of a 3PL agreement. The most important was the customer orientation of the provider; i.e., the value of a 3PL relationship is directly related to the ability of the provider to understand the needs of the hiring firm and to adapt its services to the special requirements of that firm. The second most important factor was reliability. The flexibility of the provider, or its ability to react to the changing needs of the hiring firm and the needs of that firm's customers, was third. Significantly farther down the list were cost savings.

3. *Specialization of the 3PL.* When choosing a potential 3PL provider, some experts suggest that companies should consider firms whose roots lie in the particular area of logistics that is most relevant to the logistics requirements in question. For example, Roadway Logistics, Menlo Logistics, and Yellow Logistics evolved from major LTL carriers; Exel Logistics, GATX, and USCO started as warehouse managers; and UPS and Federal Express have expertise in the timely handling of small packages. Some firms have even more specialized requirements, and these should be considered carefully when choosing a 3PL partner.[10] Sometimes a firm can use one of its trusted core carriers as its 3PL provider. For example, Schneider National, a firm that already worked closely with Baxter Healthcare Corp., recently agreed to take over Baxter's dedicated fleet routes.[11]

4. *Asset-owning versus non-asset-owning 3PL.* There are also advantages and disadvantages to using an asset-owning versus a non-asset-owning 3PL company. Asset-owning companies have significant size, access to human resources, a large customer base, economies of scope and scale, and systems in place, but they may tend to favor their own divisions in awarding work, to be bureaucratic, and to have a long decision-making cycle. Non-asset-owning companies may be more flexible and able to tailor services and have the freedom to mix and match providers. They also may have low overhead costs and specialized industry expertise at the same time but limited resources and lower bargaining power.[10]

5.3.4 3PL Implementation Issues

Once a potential partner has been selected, the process has only begun. Agreements need to be reached, and appropriate efforts must be made by both companies to initiate the relationship effectively. Experts point to one lesson in particular that has come from failed 3PL agreements: Devote enough time to startup considerations; i.e., starting the relationship effectively during the first 6 months to a year is both the most difficult and the most critical part of any 3PL alliance. The company purchasing the services must identify exactly what it needs for the relationship to be successful and be able to provide specific performance measures and requirements to the 3PL firm. The logistics provider, in turn, must consider and discuss these requirements honestly and completely, including their realism and relevance.[5] Both parties must be committed to devoting the time and effort needed to making a success of the relationship. It is critical that both parties remember that this is a mutually beneficial third-party alliance, with shared risk and reward. The parties are partners—neither party can take a "transaction pricing" mentality.[12]

In general, *effective communication* is essential for any outsourcing project to succeed. First, within the hiring company, managers must communicate to each other and to their employees exactly why they are outsourcing and what they expect from the outsourcing process so that all relevant departments are on the "same page" and can become appropriately involved. Obviously, communication between the firm and the 3PL provider is also critical. It is easy to speak in generalities, but specific communication is essential if both companies are to benefit from the outsourcing arrangement.[5] On a technological level, it is usually necessary to enable communications between the 3PL suppliers' systems and those of the hiring customer. Along the same line, a firm should avoid 3PL providers who use proprietary information systems because these are much more difficult to integrate with other systems.

Other important issues to discuss with potential 3PL providers include the following:

- The third party and its service providers must respect the confidentiality of the data that you provide them.
- Specific performance measures must be agreed on.
- Specific criteria regarding subcontractors should be discussed.

- Arbitration issues should be considered before entering into a contract.
- Escape clauses should be negotiated into the contract.
- Methods of ensuring that performance goals are being met should be discussed.[12]

5.4 RETAILER-SUPPLIER PARTNERSHIPS

The formation of strategic alliances between retailers and their suppliers is becoming ubiquitous in many industries. We saw in Chapter 2 that variation in orders placed by retailers to suppliers in traditional retailer-supplier relationships is typically far greater than the variation in demand seen by retailers. In addition, suppliers have far better knowledge of their lead times and production capacities than do retailers. Thus, as margins get tighter and customer satisfaction becomes even more important, it makes sense to create cooperative efforts between suppliers and retailers in order to leverage the knowledge of both parties.

5.4.1 Types of RSPs

The types of retailer-supplier partnerships (RSPs) can be viewed on a continuum. At one end is information sharing, which helps the vendor plan more efficiently, and at the other is a consignment scheme, where the vendor completely manages and owns the inventory until the retailer sells it.

In a basic *quick-response strategy*, suppliers receive point-of-sale (POS) data from retailers and use this information to synchronize their production and inventory activities with actual sales at the retailer. In this strategy, the retailer still prepares individual orders, but the POS data are used by the supplier to improve forecasting and scheduling and to reduce lead time.

EXAMPLE 5-6

Among the first companies to use this scheme was Milliken and Company, a textile and chemicals company. Milliken worked with several clothing suppliers and major department stores, all of which agreed to use POS data from the department stores to "synchronize" their

(continued)

ordering and manufacturing plans. The lead time from order receipt at Milliken's textile plants to final clothing receipt at the department stores was reduced from 18 to 3 weeks.[13]

In a *continuous-replenishment strategy*, sometimes called *rapid replenishment*, vendors receive POS data and use these data to prepare shipments at previously agreed-on intervals to maintain specific levels of inventory. In an advanced form of continuous replenishment, suppliers gradually may decrease inventory levels at the retail store or distribution center as long as service levels are met. Thus, in a structured way, inventory levels are improved continuously. In addition, the inventory levels need not be simple levels but could be based on sophisticated models that change the appropriate level based on seasonal demand, promotions, and changing consumer demand.[14]

In a *vendor-managed inventory* (VMI) *system*, sometimes called a *vendor-managed replenishment* (VMR) *system*, the supplier decides on the appropriate inventory levels of each of the products (within previously agreed-on bounds) and the appropriate inventory policies to maintain these levels. In the initial stages, vendor suggestions must be approved by the retailer, but eventually, the goal of many VMI programs is to eliminate retailer oversight on specific orders. This type of relationship is perhaps most famously exemplified by Wal-Mart and Procter & Gamble, whose partnership, begun in 1985, has improved P&G's on-time deliveries toWal-Mart dramatically while increasing inventory turns.[15] Other discount stores followed suit, including Kmart, which by 1992 had developed over 200 VMI partners.[13] These VMI projects in general have been successful: Projects at Dillard Department Stores, JCPenney, and Wal-Mart have shown sales increases of 20 to 25 percent and 30 percent inventory turnover improvements.[15]

EXAMPLE 5-7

First Brands, Inc., the maker of such products as Glad sandwich bags, has successfully partnered with Kmart. In 1991, the company entered Kmart's Partners in Merchandise Flow program, in which vendors are responsible for ensuring appropriate inventory levels to Kmart at all times, at Kmart's insistence. Initially, Kmart provided a 3-year sales history, followed later by daily POS data to First Brands, which uses special software to convert these data into a production and delivery plan to each of Kmart's 13 distribution centers.[16]

The main characteristics of RSPs are summarized in Table 5-1.

5.4.2 Requirements for RSPs

The most important requirement for an effective RSP, especially one toward the VMI end of the partnership spectrum, is *advanced information systems* on both the supplier and retailer sides of the supply chain. Electronic data interchange (EDI) or Internet-based private exchanges—to relay POS information to the supplier and delivery information to the retailer—are essential to cut down on data transfer time and entry mistakes. Bar coding and scanning are essential to maintain data accuracy. And inventory, production control, and planning systems must be online, accurate, and integrated to take advantage of the additional information available.

As in all initiatives that can radically change the way a company operates, top management commitment is required for the project to succeed. This is especially true because information that has been kept confidential up to this point will now have to be shared with suppliers and customers, and cost allocation issues will have to be considered at a very high level (this is covered in more detail below). It is also true because such a partnership may shift power within the organization from one group to another. For instance, when implementing a VMI partnership, the day-to-day contacts with retailers shift from sales and marketing personnel to logistics personnel. This implies that incentives for and compensation of the sales force have to be modified because

Table 5-1 Main Characteristics of RSP

Criteria → Type ↓	Decision Maker	Inventory Ownership	New Skills Employed by Vendors
Quick response	Retailer	Retailer	Forecasting skills
Continuous replenishment	Contractually agreed-to levels	Either party	Forecasting and inventory control
Advanced continuous replenishment	Contractually agreed-to and continuously improved levels	Either party	Forecasting and inventory control
VMI	Vendor	Either party	Retail management

retailers' inventory levels are driven by supply chain needs, not by pricing and discount strategies. This change in power may require significant involvement of top management.

Finally, RSP requires the partners to develop a certain level of trust without which the alliance is going to fail. In VMI, for example, suppliers need to demonstrate that they can manage the entire supply chain; i.e., they can manage not only their own inventory but also that of the retailer. Similarly, in quick response, confidential information is provided to the supplier, which typically serves many competing retailers. In addition, strategic partnering in many cases results in significant reduction in inventory at the retailer outlet. The supplier needs to make sure that the additional available space is not used to benefit the supplier's competitors. Furthermore, the top management at the supplier must understand that the immediate effect of decreased inventory at the retailer will be a *one-time loss in sales revenue*.

5.4.3   Inventory Ownership in RSPs

Several important issues must be considered when entering into an RSP. One major issue is the decision concerning who makes the replenishment decisions. This places the partnership on the continuum of strategic partnership possibilities described earlier. This can be done in stages, first with information and later with decision making that is shared between the partners.

Inventory ownership issues are critical to the success of this kind of strategic alliance effort, especially one involving VMI. Originally, ownership of goods transferred to the retailer when goods were received. Now some VMI partnerships are moving to a consignment relationship in which the supplier owns the goods until they are sold. The benefit of this kind of relationship to the retailer is obvious: lower inventory costs. Furthermore, since the supplier owns the inventory, it will be more concerned with managing it as effectively as possible. One possible criticism of the original VMI scheme is that the vendor has an incentive to move to the retailer as much inventory as the contract allows. If this is a fast-moving item and the partners had agreed on 2 weeks of inventory, this may be exactly what the retailer wants to see in stock. If, however, this is a more complex problem of inventory management, the vendor needs to have an incentive to keep inventories as low as possible, subject to some agreed-on service level. For example,

Wal-Mart no longer owns the stock for many of the items it carries, including most of its grocery purchases. It only owns them briefly as they are being passed through the checkout scanner.[17]

It is less clear, however, why this consignment arrangement is beneficial to the supplier because the supplier owns inventory for a longer period of time. Many times, as in the case of Wal-Mart, the supplier has no choice because the market dictates this kind of arrangement. Even if this is not the case, such an arrangement is beneficial to the supplier because it allows the supplier to coordinate distribution and production, thus reducing total cost. To better understand this issue, recall from Chapter 4 the discussion of the difference between *global optimization* and *local optimization*. In the traditional supply chain, each facility does what is best for that facility; i.e., the retailer manages its own inventory without regard to the impact on the supplier. The supplier, in turn, identifies a policy that will optimize its own cost subject to satisfaction of the retailer demand. In VMI, one tries to optimize the entire system by coordinating production and distribution. In addition, the supplier can further decrease total cost by coordinating production and distribution for several retailers. This is precisely why global optimization allows for significant reductions in total system costs.

Sometimes, depending on the relative power of the supplier and the retailer, the supply contract must be negotiated so that the supplier and the retailer share *overall system savings*. Retailers also must take this into account when comparing the cost of competing vendors: Different logistics schemes have different costs.

EXAMPLE 5-8

Ace Hardware, a retail hardware dealer coop, has successfully implemented a consignment VMI scheme for lumber and building materials. In this program, Ace maintains financial ownership of these goods at the retailer, but the retailer has custodial ownership that makes it responsible if the product is damaged or destroyed.[18] The program is considered extremely successful, with service levels increasing from 92 to 96 percent on VMI items. Ace eventually would like to expand it to other product lines.[19]

In addition to inventory and ownership issues, advanced strategic alliances can cover many different areas. Issues such as joint forecasting, meshed planning cycles, and even joint product development are sometimes considered.[20]

5.4.4   Issues in RSP Implementation

For any agreement to succeed, performance measurement criteria also must be agreed to. These criteria should include nonfinancial measures as well as the traditional financial measures. For example, nonfinancial measures could include POS accuracy, inventory accuracy, shipment and delivery accuracy, lead times, and customer fill rates.

When information is being shared between retailers and suppliers, *confidentiality* becomes an issue. Specifically, a retailer who deals with several suppliers within the same product category may find that category information is important to the supplier in making accurate forecasts and stocking decisions. Similarly, there may be a relationship between stocking decisions made by several suppliers. How can these potential conflicts be managed with the retailer maintaining the confidentiality of each partner?

When entering any kind of strategic alliance, it is important for both parties to realize that initially there will be problems that can only be worked out through *communication* and *cooperation*. For example, when First Brands started partnering with Kmart, Kmart often claimed that its supplier was not living up to its agreement to keep 2 weeks of inventory on hand at all times. It turned out that the problem arose from different forecasting methods employed by the two companies. This problem was solved eventually by direct communication between Kmart's forecasting experts and those from First Brands—this type of communication would have occurred through salespeople before the VMI partnership began.[16]

In many cases the supplier in a partnership commits to fast response to emergencies and situational changes at the retailer. If the manufacturing technology or capacity do not currently exist at the supplier, they may need to be added. For example, VF Mills, the maker of Wrangler jeans and a pioneer of quick-response methods in the clothing industry, had to completely reengineer its production processes, including retraining and additional capital investment.[15]

5.4.5 Steps in RSP Implementation

The important points listed earlier can be summarized in the following steps in VMI implementation:[21]

1. Initially, the contractual terms of the agreement must be negotiated. These include decisions concerning ownership and when it is to be transferred, credit terms, ordering responsibilities, and performance measures such as service or inventory levels, when appropriate.

2. Next, the following three tasks must be executed:

   a. If they do not exist, integrated information systems must be developed for both supplier and retailer. These information systems must provide easy access to both parties.

   b. Effective forecasting techniques to be used by the vendor and the retailer must be developed.

   c. A tactical decision-support tool to assist in *coordinating* inventory management and transportation policies must be developed. The systems developed, of course, will depend on the particular nature of the partnership.

5.4.6 Advantages and Disadvantages of RSPs

One advantage of VMI relationships is nicely illustrated by the following example.

EXAMPLE 5-9

Whitehall Robbins (WR), which makes over-the-counter drugs such as Advil, has an RSP relationship with Kmart. Like First Brands, WR initially disagreed with Kmart about forecasts. In this case it turned out that WR forecasts were more accurate because the company has a much more extensive knowledge of its products than Kmart does. For example, Kmart's Chap Stick forecasts did not take the seasonality of the product into account. In addition, WR planners can take production issues, such as planned downtime, into account when planning shipments.

Also, WR benefits in another way. In the past Kmart would order large quantities of seasonal items at the beginning of the season, often linked to a promotion. This practice often led to returns because it was

(continued)

difficult for Kmart to accurately forecast the amount it would sell. Now WR supplies weekly demand at an "everyday low cost," so large orders and preseason promotions have been eliminated, which in turn has greatly reduced returns. Inventory turns for seasonal items have gone from 3 to more than 10 and for nonseasonal items from 12 to 15 to 17 to 20.[16]

Thus, in general, a huge advantage of RSPs is the knowledge the supplier has about order quantities, implying an ability to control the bullwhip effect (see Chap. 2). This, of course, varies from one type of partnership to another. In quick response, for instance, this knowledge is achieved through transfer of customer demand information that allows the supplier to reduce lead time, whereas in VMI the retailer provides demand information and the supplier makes ordering decisions, thus completely controlling the variability in order quantities. Of course, this knowledge can be leveraged to reduce overall system costs and improve overall system service levels. The benefits to the supplier in terms of better service levels, decreased managerial expenses, and decreased inventory costs are obvious. The vendor should be able to reduce forecast uncertainties and thus better coordinate production and distribution. To be more specific, reduced forecast uncertainties lead to reduced safety stocks, reduced storage and delivery costs, and increased service levels,[21] as we noted in our discussion of the bullwhip effect in Chapter 2.

In addition to the important benefits listed earlier, implementing a strategic partnership provides a variety of side benefits. It provides a good opportunity for the reengineering of the retailer-supplier relationship. For example, redundant order entries can be eliminated, manual tasks can be automated, tasks such as ticketing merchandise and designing displays can be reassigned for systemwide efficiency, and unnecessary control steps can be eliminated from the process.[15] Many of these advantages stem from the same changes and technology needed to implement partnerships in the first place.

Many of the problems with RSPs were discussed earlier and are summarized here:

- It is necessary to employ advanced technology, which is often expensive.
- It is essential to develop trust in what once may have been an adversarial supplier-retailer relationship.

- In a strategic partnership, the supplier often has much more responsibility than formerly. This may force the supplier to add personnel to meet this responsibility.
- Finally, and perhaps most critically, expenses at the supplier often increase as managerial responsibilities increase. Also, inventory initially may be shifted back to the supplier; if a consignment arrangement is used, inventory costs in general may increase for the supplier. Thus it may be necessary to work out a contractual relationship in which the retailer shares decreased system inventory costs with the supplier.

Float is another issue with any EDI implementation, and it needs to be carefully considered when committing to a VMI partnership. Retailers who have become accustomed to waiting 30 to 90 days to pay for goods may now have to pay on delivery. Even if they pay only when their goods are sold, this could be much sooner than their usual period of float.[22]

5.4.7 Successes and Failures

We have cited several examples of RSPs in the preceding sections. We include several other examples of successes—and one example of a failure—next.

EXAMPLE 5-10

Western Publishing is using VMI for its Golden Books line of children's books at several retailers, including more than 2000 Wal-Mart locations. In this program, POS data automatically trigger reorders when inventory falls below a reorder point. This inventory is delivered either to a distribution center or, in many cases, directly to a store. In this case ownership of the books shifts to the retailer once deliveries have been made. In the case of Toys "R" Us, Western Publishing has even managed the entire book section for the retailer, including inventory from suppliers other than Western Publishing. The company has generated significant additional sales in both cases, although the program has increased costs significantly. These are costs related to the additional inventory management duties, as well as the extra freight costs incurred by shipping directly to stores. Nonetheless, management believes that VMI has provided a net benefit for the company.[18]

EXAMPLE 5-11

After Wal-Mart included supplier Mead-Johnson in its VMI program, the results were dramatic. Mead-Johnson has complete POS information to which it reacts instead of orders. Since this program was implemented, inventory turns at Wal-Mart have gone from under 10 to more than 100, and at Mead-Johnson, from 12 to 52. Similarly, Scott Paper Company has been managing inventory in 25 of its customer distribution centers. In this effort, inventory turns at the customers have increased from about 19 to somewhere between 35 and 55, inventory levels have been reduced, and service levels have improved. One caveat can be drawn from the experiences of Schering-Plough Healthcare Products (SPHP) with Kmart's Partners in the Merchandise Flow program. In the first year of implementation, SPHP did see decreased stockouts at Kmart but not substantially improved sales or profits. By patiently continuing with the program, however, SPHP eventually did realize substantial benefits in these areas.[23]

EXAMPLE 5-12

VF Corporation's Market Response System provides another success story of VMI. The company, which has many well-known brand names (e.g., Wrangler, Lee, and Girbaud), began its program in 1989. Currently, about 40 percent of its production is handled through some type of automatic replenishment scheme. This is particularly notable because the program encompasses 350 different retailers, 40,000 store locations, and more than 15 million levels of replenishment. Each division uses automatic software to manage the huge influx of data and special techniques developed at VF to cluster the data so that they are more manageable. VF's program is considered to be one of the most successful in the apparel industry.[24]

EXAMPLE 5-13

Spartan Stores, a grocery chain, shut down its VMI effort about 1 year after its inception. In examining the reasons for the failure of the program, some important ingredients for a successful VMI program became clear. One problem was that buyers were not spending any less time on reorders than they had before because they did not trust the suppliers enough to stop their careful monitoring of the inventories and deliveries of the VMI items. Buyers intervened at the slightest hint of trouble. Further, the suppliers did not do much to allay these fears. The problems were not with the suppliers' forecasts; instead, they were due to the suppliers' inability to deal with product promotions, which are a key part of the grocery business. Because suppliers were unable to account for promotions appropriately, delivery levels often were unacceptably low during these periods of peak demand. In addition, Spartan executives felt that the inventory levels achieved by the VMI program were no lower than the levels the company could have achieved with a well-managed traditional supplier program. It should be noted that Spartan considered the VMI program successful with some suppliers. These were the suppliers with better forecasting skills. In addition, Spartan intends to maintain the continuous replenishment programs, in which inventory levels automatically trigger fixed delivery quantities with some of its suppliers.[25]

5.5 DISTRIBUTOR INTEGRATION

For years, business experts have advised manufacturers, particularly industrial manufacturers, to treat their distributors like partners.[26] Typically, this meant appreciating the value of the distributors and their relationship with the end users and providing them with the necessary support to be successful. Distributors have a wealth of information about customer needs and wants, and successful manufacturers use this information when developing new products and product lines. Similarly, distributors typically rely on manufacturers to supply the necessary parts and expertise.

EXAMPLE 5-14

The chairman and CEO of Caterpillar Corporation, Donald Fites, credits Caterpillar dealers with much of his company's recent success.

(continued)

Fites points out that dealers are much closer to customers than to the corporation and can respond more rapidly to customer needs. They arrange financing when the product is purchased and carefully monitor, repair, and service the product. Fites says that "the dealer creates the image of a company that doesn't just stand behind its products but with its products anywhere in the world." Caterpillar believes that its dealer network gives the company a tremendous advantage over its competition, especially the big Japanese construction and mining equipment manufacturers such as Komatsu and Hitachi.[27]

This view of distributors is changing, however, as customer service needs present new challenges and information technology rises to meet these challenges. Even a strong and effective distributor network cannot always meet the needs of customers. A rush order might be impossible to meet from inventory, or the customer might require some specialized technical expertise that the distributor does not have. In the past these issues were addressed by adding inventory and personnel, either to each distributor or to the manufacturer. Modern information technology leads to a third solution, in which distributors are integrated so that the expertise and inventory located at one distributor are available to the others.

5.5.1 Types of Distributor Integration

Distributor integration (DI) can be used to address both inventory-related and service-related issues. In terms of inventory, DI can be used to create a large pool of inventory across the entire distributor network, lowering total inventory costs while raising service levels. Similarly, DI can be used to meet a customer's specialized technical service requests by steering these requests to the distributors best suited to address them.

As we pointed out in earlier chapters, increased inventory traditionally is used to meet unusual rush orders and to provide spare parts quickly to facilitate repairs. In more sophisticated companies, risk-pooling concepts might be used to keep inventory earlier in the supply chain, where it can be distributed as needed. In a DI arrangement, each distributor can check the inventories of other distributors to locate a needed product or part. Dealers are contractually bound to exchange the part under certain conditions and for agreed-on remuneration. This type of arrangement improves service levels at each of the distributors and lowers the total system inventory required. Of course, this type of arrangement is possible only because sophisticated information systems allow distributors to review each others' inventory and integrated logistics systems allow parts to be delivered cheaply and efficiently.

EXAMPLE 5-15

Machine tool builder Okuma America Corporation has implemented a DI system. Okuma carries many expensive machine tools and repair parts, but the high cost of carrying the full line makes it impossible for Okuma's 46 distributors in North and South America to do so. Instead, Okuma requires each of its dealers to carry a minimum number of machine tools and parts. The company manages the entire system so that each tool and part is in stock somewhere in the system, either in one of the company's two warehouses or at one of the distributors. A system called Okumalink allows each of the distributors to check the warehouse inventories and to communicate with other distributors in finding a required part. Once a part is found, the company ensures that it is delivered quickly to the requesting dealer. There are plans to upgrade the system so that each distributor has full knowledge of the inventory held by all distributors. Since the system's implementation, inventory costs throughout the system have been reduced, the chance that a distributor will lose a sale because of inventory shortages has decreased, and customer satisfaction has increased.[28]

Similarly, DI can be used to improve each distributor's perceived technical ability and ability to respond to unusual customer requests. In this kind of alliance, different distributors build expertise in different areas. A customer's specific request is routed to the distributor with the most expertise. For example, Otra, a large Dutch holding company with about 70 electrical wholesale subsidiaries, has designated some of them as *centers of excellence* in particular areas, such as warehouse layouts or POS materials. The other subsidiaries, as well as customers, are directed to these centers of excellence to meet particular requests.[28]

5.5.2 Issues in DI

There are two major issues involved in implementing a DI alliance. First, distributors may be skeptical of the rewards of participating in such a system. There is the chance that they will feel that they are providing some of their expertise in inventory control to less skilled partners, especially when some of the distributors are larger and have bigger inventories than others. In addition, participating distributors will be forced to rely on other distributors, some of whom they may not know, to help them provide good customer service.

This new kind of relationship also tends to take certain responsibilities and areas of expertise away from certain distributors and concentrate them on a few distributors. It is not surprising that distributors might be nervous about losing these skills and abilities. This explains why establishing a DI relationship requires a large commitment of resources and effort on the part of the manufacturing company. Distributors must feel sure that this is a long-term alliance. Organizers must work hard to build trust among the participants. Finally, the manufacturer may have to provide pledges and guarantees to ensure distributor commitment.

EXAMPLE 5-16

Dunlop-Enerka is a Dutch company that supplies conveyer belts to mining and manufacturing companies worldwide. Traditionally, the company met maintenance and repair requirements by storing vast quantities of inventory at distributors throughout Europe. To reduce inventories, the company installed a computer-based information system, Dunlocomm, to monitor inventory at the warehouses of each of its distributors. When a part is needed, a distributor uses the system to order the part and arrange for its delivery. To ensure distributor participation, Dunlop-Enerka guaranteed 24-hour delivery of each part to each distributor—if a part was not in stock, Dunlop-Enerka custom manufactured and shipped it within the available time window. This guarantee reassured distributors enough that they committed to the system, and over time, inventory throughout the system dropped by 20 percent.

5.6 SUMMARY

In this chapter we examined various types of partnerships that can be used to manage the supply chain more effectively. We started off by discussing the different paths a firm can take to ensure that particular supply chain–related issues are addressed, including performing them internally or outsourcing them completely. Obviously, many different strategic and tactical issues play a part in the selection of the most appropriate strategy. We discussed a framework that can help in selecting the most appropriate way to address a particular logistics issue.

Increasingly, 3PL providers are taking over some of a firm's logistics responsibilities. There are both advantages and disadvantages to outsourcing the logistics function, as well as many important issues to consider once the decision has been made and a 3PL agreement is being implemented.

RSPs, in which the supplier manages a portion of the retailer's business—typically retail inventories—are also becoming common. There is a spectrum of possible types of RSP, ranging from agreements that cover only information sharing to agreements in which the supplier has complete control over the retailer's inventory policy. We considered various issues and concerns relating to the implementation of these types of arrangement.

Finally, we discussed a class of alliances, called DI, in which manufacturers coordinate the efforts of their (potentially competing) distributors to create risk-pooling opportunities across the various distributors and to enable different distributors to develop different areas of expertise.

CHAPTER 6

Outsourcing, Procurement, and Supply Contracts

6.1 INTRODUCTION

In the 1990s, outsourcing was the focus of many industrial manufacturers; firms considered outsourcing everything from the procurement function to production and manufacturing. Executives were focused on stock value, and huge pressure was placed on the organization to increase profits. Of course, one "easy" way to increase profit is by reducing costs through outsourcing. Indeed, in the mid-1990s there was a significant increase in purchasing volume as a percentage of the firm's total sales. More recently, between 1998 and 2000, outsourcing in the electronics industry has increased from 15 percent of all components to 40 percent.[1]

Consider, for instance, the athletic shoe industry, a fashion industry with products that require significant investment in technology. No company in this industry has been as successful as Nike, a company that outsources almost all its manufacturing activities. Nike, the largest supplier of athletic shoes in the world, focuses mainly on research and development on the one hand and marketing, sales, and distribution on the other. Indeed, this strategy allowed Nike to grow in the 1990s at an annual rate of about 20 percent.[2]

Cisco's success story is even more striking. According to Peter Solvik, CIO of Cisco, "Cisco's Internet-based business model was instrumental in its ability to quadruple in size from 1994 to 1998

($1.3 billion to over $8 billion), hire approximately 1000 new employees per quarter while increasing their productivity, and save $560 mil-
lion annually in business expenses." Specializing in enterprise network
solutions, Cisco used, according to John Chambers, Cisco CEO, a
"global virtual manufacturing strategy." As he explained, "First, we
have established manufacturing plants all over the world. We have also
developed close arrangements with major suppliers. So when we work
together with our suppliers, and if we do our job right, the customer
cannot tell the difference between my own plants and my suppliers in
Taiwan and elsewhere."[3] This approach was enabled by Cisco's single-
enterprise system, which provides the backbone for all activities in the
company and connects not only customers and employees but also
chip manufacturers, component distributors, contract manufacturers,
logistics companies, and systems integrators. These participants can
perform like one company because they all rely on the same Web-
based data sources. All its suppliers see the same demand and do not
rely on their own forecasts based on information flowing from multiple points in the supply chain. Cisco also built a dynamic replenishment system to help reduce supplier inventory. Cisco's average inventory turns in 1999 were 10 compared with an average of 4 for
competitors. Inventory turns for commodity items are even more impressive; they reach 25 to 35 turns a year.

Apple Computers also outsources most of its manufacturing activities; in fact, the company outsources 70 percent of its components.
As Quinn and Hilmer point out, "Apple focused its internal resources
on its own disk operating system and the supporting macro software
to give Apple products their unique look and feel."[2]

Unfortunately, the landscape has changed for Nike, Cisco, Apple, and other companies who rely heavily on outsourcing, particularly
for manufacturing.

- In 2001, Nike reported an unexpected profit shortfall due to
  inventory buildup in some products, shortages for others, and
  late deliveries.[4] The company blamed both the weak U.S.
  economy and complications with the implementation of a
  supply planning system.
- In 1999, Apple's ability to satisfy customer demand was
  reduced significantly due to shortages in the G4 chip supplied
  by Motorola.[3]

- In 2000, Cisco was forced to announce a $2.25 billion write-down for obsolete inventory. This was the result of a significant reduction in demand for telecommunication infrastructure to which Cisco was not able to respond effectively.

What went wrong? Are these problems merely a reflection of supply chain strategies that need fine-tuning or do they reflect a need for more effective information technology? Perhaps these problems uncover fundamental difficulties with outsourcing. Clearly, Nike, Apple, and Cisco represent industries with short-life-cycle products, where technologies change rapidly and uncertainty in customer demand is enormous. Can these characteristics explain the problems that these companies are facing, or are there more fundamental principles that need to be considered?

To answer these questions, we first discuss the buy/make decision process. We will identify the advantages and the risks associated with outsourcing and present a framework for optimizing buy/make decisions.

After presenting this framework, we will discuss the procurement process, which can be a very expensive process for many buyers. Since 1995, when the first online marketplace was established, the procurement landscape has changed considerably with the introduction of independent (also referred to as public), private, and consortium-based e-marketplaces. These developments increase both the opportunities and challenges faced by many buyers. Specifically, executives are faced with an important question: Should the firm invest in a costly private marketplace, use a public marketplace that provides data standards and spreads cost investment among many buyers, or perhaps use a hybrid approach in which certain types of goods are purchased in a public marketplace and others are purchased in a private marketplace? To answer this question, we develop a framework for selecting the correct procurement strategy. As we shall see, this framework implies that the procurement strategy is tightly linked to the firm's outsourcing strategy.

Finally, we conclude with a discussion of supply contracts. In many cases firms use supply contracts to establish the parameters of their relationships with their suppliers. As we will see, the proper use of supply contracts can ensure that both supplier and buyer benefit.

6.2 OUTSOURCING BENEFITS AND RISKS

Throughout the 1990s, strategic outsourcing, i.e., outsourcing the manufacturing of key components, was used as a tool to rapidly cut costs. In a recent study, Lakenan, Boyd, and Frey[3] reviewed eight major contract equipment manufacturers (CEMs)—Solectron, Flextronics, SCI Systems, Jabil Circuit, Celestica, ACT Manufacturing, Plexus, and Sanmina—that were the main suppliers to companies such as Dell, Marconi, NEC Computers, Nortel, and Silcon Graphics. The aggregated revenue for the eight CEMs quadrupled between 1996 and 2000, whereas their capital expenditure grew 11-fold.[3]

Some of the motivations for outsourcing are[2,3]

Economies of scale. An important objective in outsourcing is to reduce manufacturing costs through the aggregation of orders from many different buyers. Indeed, the aggregation allows suppliers to take advantage of economies of scale both in purchasing and in manufacturing.

Risk pooling. Outsourcing allows buyers to transfer demand uncertainty to the CEM. One advantage that the CEMs have is that they aggregate demand from many buying companies and thus reduce uncertainty through the risk-pooling effect. The CEMs thus can reduce component inventory levels while maintaining or even increasing service level.

Reduce capital investment. Another important objective in outsourcing is to transfer not only demand uncertainty to the CEM but also capital investment. Of course, the CEM can make this investment because it is implicitly shared between many of the CEM's customers.

Focus on core competency. By carefully choosing what to outsource, the buyer is able to focus on its core strength, i.e., the specific talent, skills, and knowledge sets that differentiate the company from its competitors and give it an advantage in the eye of the customers. For instance, Nike focuses on innovation, marketing, distribution, and sales, not on manufacturing.[2]

Increased flexibility. Here we refer to three issues: (1) the ability to better react to changes in customer demand, (2) the ability to use the supplier's technical knowledge to accelerate product development cycle time, and (3) the ability to gain access to new technologies and innovation. These are critical issues in industries where technologies change very frequently, e.g., high-tech, or where products have a short life cycle, e.g., fashion products.

These benefits come with new and considerable risks. Consider how IBM benefited and was hurt by outsourcing.

EXAMPLE 6-1

When IBM decided to enter the personal computer (PC) market, in late 1981, the company did not have the infrastructure in place to design and build a PC. Rather than take the time to develop these capabilities, IBM outsourced almost all the major components of the PC. For example, the microprocessor was designed and built by Intel, and the operating system was provided by a small company in Seattle called Microsoft. IBM was able to get this computer to market within 15 months of starting the design by tapping into the expertise and resources of these companies. Furthermore, within 3 years, IBM replaced Apple as the number-one supplier of PCs, and by 1985, IBM had over 40 percent of market share. However, the downside to IBM's strategy soon became clear as competitors such as Compaq were able to enter the market *by using the same suppliers as IBM*. Furthermore, when IBM tried to regain control of the market by introducing its PS/2 line of computers, featuring a new, proprietary design and an operating system called OS/2, other companies did not follow IBM's lead, and the original architecture remained dominant in the market. By the end of 1995, IBM's market share had fallen to less than 8 percent, behind market leader Compaq's 10 percent.[5]

The IBM personal computer example and the more recent Cisco example reveal two substantial risks associated with outsourcing. These include[2,3,6]

Loss of competitive knowledge. Outsourcing critical components to suppliers may open up opportunities for competitors (as in the IBM PC example). Similarly, outsourcing implies that companies lose their ability to introduce new designs based on their own agenda rather than the supplier's agenda.[2] Finally, outsourcing the manufacturing of various components to different suppliers may prevent the development of new insights, innovations, and solutions that typically require cross-functional teamwork.[2]

Conflicting objectives. Suppliers and buyers typically have different and conflicting objectives. For instance, increased flexibility is a key objective when buyers outsource the manufacturing of various components. This implies an ability to better match supply and demand by adjusting production rates as needed. Unfortunately, this objective is in direct conflict with the suppliers' objectives of long-term, firm, and stable commitment from the buyer. Indeed, this is an important issue for suppliers because unlike the buyers, their profit margins are relatively small, and hence they have to focus on cost reduction rather than flexibility. In good times, when demand is high, this conflict can be addressed by buyers who are willing to make long-term commitments to purchase minimum quantities specified by a contract. However, in a slow economy, when there is a significant decline in demand, these long-term commitments entail huge financial risks for the buyers.[3]

Similarly, product design issues are affected by the conflicting objectives of suppliers and buyers. Again, buyers, insisting on flexibility, would like to solve design problems as fast as possible, whereas suppliers focus on cost reduction that typically implies slow responsiveness to design changes.

6.3   A FRAMEWORK FOR BUY/MAKE DECISIONS

How can a firm decide on which component to manufacture and which to outsource? Consultants and supply chain pundits typically suggest focusing on core competencies, but how can the firm identify what is in the core, and hence should be made internally, and what is outside the core, and hence should be purchased from outside suppliers?

Below we introduce a framework developed by Fine and Whitney.[6] To introduce the framework, they classify the reasons for outsourcing into two major categories:

Dependency on capacity. In this case the firm has the knowledge and the skills required to produce the component but for various reasons decides to outsource.

Dependency on knowledge. In this type of dependency the company does not have the people, skills, and knowledge required to produce the component and outsources in order to have access to these capabilities. Of course, the company has to have the knowledge and skills to evaluate customer needs and convert these into key requirements and characteristics that the component should have.

To illustrate these two concepts, Fine and Whitney consider outsourcing decisions at Toyota. As a successful Japanese car manufacturer, the company designs and makes about 30 percent of its car components. The details are quite revealing:

- Toyota has both the knowledge and the capacity to produce its engines, and indeed, 100 percent of its engines are produced internally.
- For transmissions, the company has the knowledge and indeed designs all the components but depends on its suppliers' capacities, since 70 percent of the components are outsourced.
- Vehicle electronic systems are designed and produced by Toyota's suppliers. Thus in this case the firm has a dependency on both capacity and knowledge.

Fine and Whitney observe that "Toyota seems to vary its outsourcing practice depending on the strategic role of the components and subsystems." The more strategically important the component is, the smaller the dependency on knowledge or capacity. This suggests the need for a better understanding of product architecture when considering what to outsource.

For this purpose, and following Ulrich[7] and Swaminathan,[8] we distinguish between integral and modular products. A modular product can be made by combining different components. A PC is an excellent example of a modular product in which the customers specify memory and hard-drive sizes, monitor, software, and so forth. Other examples that are cited frequently include home stereo equipment and high-end bicycles. The definition of modular products implies that[9]

- Components are independent of each other.
- Components are interchangeable.
- Standard interfaces are used.

- A component can be designed or upgraded with little or no regard to other components.
- Customer preference determines the product configuration.

An integral product, on the other hand, is a product made up from components whose functionalities are tightly related. Thus

- Integral products are not made from off-the-shelf components.
- Integral products are designed as a system by taking a top-down design approach.
- Integral products are evaluated based on system performance not component performance.
- Components in integral products perform multiple functions.

Of course, in real life, very few products are either modular or integral. Indeed, the degree of modularity or integrality may vary, with PCs being on one end of the spectrum, i.e., highly modular products, and airplanes being on the other end of the spectrum, i.e., highly integral products. For instance, a car is a product that includes many modular components, e.g., the stereo system or other electronic systems, and many integral components, e.g., the engine.

Table 6-1 presents a simple framework for make/buy decisions developed in Fine[9] and Fine and Whitney.[6] This framework considers both modular and integral products and the firm's dependence on knowledge and capacity. For modular products, capturing knowledge is important, whereas having the production capacity in-house is less

Table 6-1   A Framework for Make/Buy Decisions

Product	Dependent on Knowledge and Capacity	Independent of Knowledge, Dependent on Capacity	Independent of Knowledge and Capacity
Modular	Outsourcing is risky	Outsourcing is an opportunity	Opportunity to reduce cost through outsourcing
Integral	Outsourcing is very risky	Outsourcing is an option	Keep production internal

critical. For example, for a PC manufacturer, capturing knowledge may refer to the design of the various components. Thus, if the firm has the knowledge, outsourcing the manufacturing process provides an opportunity to reduce cost. On the other hand, if the firm has neither knowledge nor capacity, outsourcing may be a risky strategy because the knowledge developed by the supplier may be transferred to a competitor's products. For integral products, capturing both knowledge and capacity is important as long as it is possible to have both. This implies that if the firm has both the knowledge and the capacity, then in-house production is appropriate. On the other hand, if the firm does not have both, perhaps it is in the wrong business.

6.4 e-PROCUREMENT

In the middle to late 1990s, business-to-business (B2B) automation was considered a trend that would have a profound impact on supply chain performance. Between 1998 and 2000, hundreds of e-markets were established in dozens of industries, from chemicals and steel to utilities and human resources. These marketplaces promised, among other things, increased market reach for both buyers and suppliers, reduced procurement costs, and paperless transactions. Indeed, companies such as Ariba and CommerceOne were founded on the premise that e-procurement software that automates the requisitioning process would be able to reduce processing cost per order from as high as $150 to as low as $5.[10]

To better understand the huge expectations from e-procurement, as well as the need for a new business model that would allow manufacturers and suppliers to improve supply chain performance, consider the business environment in the mid-1990s. At that time, many manufacturers were desperately looking to outsource their procurement functions. These companies recognized that the procurement process is highly complex, requires significant expertise, and is very costly. Indeed, B2B transactions represent an enormous portion of the economy [much larger than business-to-consumer (B2C) transactions], and the B2B marketplace is frequently highly fragmented, with a large number of suppliers competing in the same marketplace and offering similar products.

Of course, a fragmented marketplace provides both opportunities and challenges. Indeed, buyers recognize that by forcing many suppliers that offer similar products to compete against each other, procurement costs can be reduced significantly. Unfortunately, to achieve these lower costs, buyers need significant expertise in the procurement process, which many of them do not have.

It is this environment that led to the initial offering of independent e-marketplaces with either a vertical industry focus or a horizontal business process or functional focus. Companies such as FreeMarkets or VerticalNet offered both expertise in the procurement process and the ability to force competition between a large number of suppliers. In particular, the value proposition offered to buyers by many of the startup e-markets included

- Serving as an intermediary between buyers and suppliers
- Identifying saving opportunities
- Increasing the number of suppliers involved in the bidding event
- Identifying, qualifying, and supporting suppliers
- Conducting the auction

Thus between 1996 and 1999 the focus was on reducing procurement cost. Indeed, depending on the industry, e-markets were reported to reduce procurement cost by a few percentage points to as much as 40 percent and, on average, about 15 percent. Clearly, this business model is appropriate when buyers are focused on the spot market and long-term relationships with suppliers are not important. Indeed, if long-term relationships are important, selecting a supplier based on an online bidding event may be a risky proposition.

The problem, of course, was that the value proposition for the suppliers was not as clear. e-Markets allow relatively small suppliers to expand their market horizon and reach buyers that they could not have reached otherwise. e-Markets allow suppliers, particularly in fragmented industries, to access spot markets where buyers are looking not for long-term relationships but rather for a great price at an acceptable quality. Equally important, these markets allow suppliers to reduce marketing and sales costs and thus increase their ability to compete on price. Finally, e-markets allow suppliers to better use their available capacities and inventories. The natural question to ask is whether these benefits compensate for a reduction in revenue by on average 15 percent and sometimes as high as 40 percent. At the same time, it is not clear that many suppliers feel comfortable competing on price alone. Thus suppliers, especially those with brand-name recognition, may resist selling their services through e-markets.

What about the e-markets themselves? How do they generate revenue? Initially, many of the markets charged a *transaction fee* paid by either the buyer, the suppliers, or both. This fee was typically a percentage of the price paid by the buyer and varied from 1 to 5 percent.[11] However, transaction fees pose serious challenges to the market maker because

1. Sellers resist paying a fee to the company whose main objective is to reduce the purchase price.
2. The revenue model needs to be flexible enough so that transaction fees are charged to the party that is more motivated to secure the engagement. For instance, if demand is much larger than supply, buyers are more motivated than sellers, and hence the transaction fee should be paid by the buyers.
3. Buyers also resist paying a fee in addition to the purchase price.

Finally, low barriers to entry created a fragmented industry flooded with participants. For instance, just in the chemical industry there were about 30 e-markets, including CheMatch, e-Chemicals, ChemB2B.com, ChemCross, OneChem, ChemicalDesk, Chem-Round, and Chemdex.[12] Low margins and inability to build scale resulted in a major shakeup in this industry.

These challenges have motivated a continuous evolution of the e-markets' business model. To start, many exchanges have changed the way they charge their clients. Indeed, two other types of charge mechanisms have been used by some e-markets. These include a *licensing fee* and a *subscription fee*. In the former case, the market maker licenses its software so that the company can automate access to the marketplace. In the latter case, the marketplace charges a membership fee that depends on the size of the company, the number of employees who use the system, and the number of purchase orders.[11]

At the same time, many e-markets have completely modified their value proposition. Initially, the focus of the value proposition was on market reach for buyers and sellers, as well as lower purchase cost. The landscape has changed completely in the last few years with the introduction of four types of markets:

Value-added independent (public) e-markets. Independent e-markets have expanded their value proposition by offering additional services such as inventory management, supply chain planning, and financial services.[13] For instance, Instill.com focuses on the food service industry and provides an infrastructure that links together operators, i.e., restaurants, distributors, and manufacturers. This e-marketplace provides value to its customers by offering not only procurement services but also forecasting, collaboration, and replenishment tools.

Private e-markets. Private e-markets have been established by Dell Computers, Sun Microsystems, Wal-Mart, and IBM, among others. These companies are not using the e-market to force suppliers to compete on price. Rather, they see the e-market as a way to improve supply chain collaboration by providing demand information and production data to their suppliers. Other companies use their private e-market to consolidate their purchasing power across the entire corporation. For instance, the Subway restaurant franchise with 16,000 members in over 70 countries has a private e-market that allows the different restaurants to purchase from over 100 suppliers.

Consortia-based e-markets. These e-markets are very similar to public e-markets except that they are established by a number of companies within the same industry. Examples include Covisint in the automotive industry, Exostar in the aerospace industry, Trade-Ranger in the oil industry, and Converge and E2Open in the electronics industry. The objective of these consortia-based e-markets is not only to aggregate activities and use the buying power of consortia members but, more important, to provide suppliers with a standard system that supports all the consortia's buyers and hence allows suppliers to reduce cost and become more efficient.

Content-based e-markets. These include two types of markets. The first focuses on maintenance, repair, and operations

(MRO) goods, whereas the second focuses on industry-specific products. As its name suggests, the focus of the e-marketplace is on content, which is achieved by integrating catalogs from many industrial suppliers. To achieve scale and increase efficiencies, content-based e-markets unify suppliers' catalogs and provide effective tools for searching and comparing suppliers' products. For example, Aspect Development offers electronics parts catalogs that integrate with computer-aided design (CAD) systems.

To emphasize the difference between private and consortia-based e-markets, consider the automotive industry.

EXAMPLE 6-2

Covisint was established in early 2000 by Detroit's big-three automakers. In April 2000, Renault and Nissan joined the marketplace. More recently, Mitsubishi and Peugeot have signed on. Interestingly, not all automakers have joined. For example, focusing on its own suppliers and processes, Volkswagen established its own private e-market, VWgroup-supply.com. Volkswagen's e-market provides not only similar capabilities to that of Covisint but also provides suppliers with real-time information on production plans so that suppliers can better use their production capacities and other resources. In both cases the e-marketplaces do not focus on reducing purchase costs but rather on improving supply chain processes and thus supply chain efficiencies. For instance, both are integrating design activities within the marketplace so that if an automaker's engineer changes the design of a component, the relevant suppliers are involved in the process and can respond quickly to the design change, cutting cycle time and effectively reducing cost. Of course, one important challenge faced by Covisint is whether competing automakers will be willing to risk their most sensitive procurement standards and processes by using the consortium.[14]

These issues are not unique to the automotive industry, as is illustrated by the following example from the electronics industry.

EXAMPLE 6-3

Celestica and Solectron are competitors with similar products and customers but different procurement strategies. In 1999, Celestica estab-

(continued)

lished a private e-marketplace for its 10,000 suppliers. The company uses its private marketplace to provide its suppliers with production data. Demand forecast data received by Celestica from its customers are transferred to its suppliers through the private portal so that suppliers can coordinate the back end of Celestica's supply chain, i.e., the suppliers' production activities, with the front end of Celestica's supply chain, i.e., its customer demand forecast. Unlike Celestica, Solectron is using a public e-marketplace. According to Bud Mathaisel, CIO of Solectron, it could cost more than $80 million to build and support an integrated private marketplace for its 8000 suppliers. By focusing on a public marketplace, Solectron can take advantage of standard data and standard business processes provided by the exchange and thus reduce cost.[15]

Table 6-2 compares public/consortia and private e-marketplace; see [16] for a similar comparison.

Finally, it is appropriate to point out that the boundaries between the different types of e-markets are blurred. Indeed, many consortium-based e-markets provide content-based services. For instance, the Covisint custom catalog provides detailed MRO information to buyers. In addition, Covisint recognizes the potential of the exchange in improving communication between trading partners and hence provides collaborative tools used by buyers and suppliers in a secure environment. Thus this consortium-based marketplace provides services similar to those provided by private exchanges.

6.5 A FRAMEWORK FOR e-PROCUREMENT

The changes in the B2B marketplace described in the preceding section provide both opportunities and challenges. e-Markets allow buyers to increase market reach, better collaborate with suppliers, and remove inefficiencies from their supply chains. However, with the introduction of different types of e-marketplaces, it is unclear whether the firm should build a private marketplace, use independent markets, or perhaps participate in a consortium-based market. Below we provide a framework that allows executives and managers to better match procurement strategies with products. For this purpose, we distinguish between the different types of goods purchased by the firm:[17]

Strategic components. These are components that are part of the finished goods and are not only industry-specific but also

Table 6-2 Private and Public Marketplaces

	Private Marketplace	Public/Consortium Marketplace
Owner	A single buyer	Independent owner or a group of companies from the same industry
Objectives	1. Share proprietary data including product design, demand forecast, and production plans 2. Allow for logistics and supply chain collaboration	1. Buying and selling commodities by focusing on price 2. Finding new suppliers 3. Buying and selling excess inventory and capacity
Participants	Select group of suppliers	Open market
Buyer cost	Building and maintaining the site	1. Subscription fee 2. Licensing fee 3. Transaction fee
Supplier cost	No fee	1. Transaction fee 2. Subscription fee
Main problems	1. Initial investment 2. Data normalization and uploading	1. Recent collapse of many marketplaces 2. Objections by preferred suppliers because of price focus 3. Sharing of proprietary information 4. Data normalization and uploading

company-specific. These are typically integral products, such as a PC motherboard and chassis, that are specific for every computer.

Commodity products. These are products that can be purchased from a variety of vendors and whose price is determined by market forces. These are typically the modular components that go directly into the finished product, such as the memory unit in a PC. Also inclued here are commodities that do not go directly into the finished product, i.e., electricity.

Indirect materials. Indirect materials are often referred to as *maintenance, repair, and operations* (MRO) and include components that are not part of the finished product or the manufacturing process but are essential for the business. Examples include lighting, janitorial supplies, office supplies, fasteners, and generators.

The appropriate procurement strategy clearly depends on the *type of product* the firm is purchasing as well as the *level of risk* the firm is willing to take. This risk is associated with[18]

- *Uncertain demand,* implying inventory risk
- *Volatile market price,* implying price risk
- *Component availability,* implying a shortage risk with an impact on the firm's ability to satisfy customer demand

To illustrate the various types of risks, consider the purchase of commodity products, i.e., components that go directly into the finished good. By their nature, these can be purchased either in the open market through online auctions or through the use of long-term contracts. Long-term contracts guarantee a certain level of supply but may be risky for the buyer if realized demand is either lower or higher than the demand forecast. In the former case, the buyer faces huge inventory holding costs; in the latter case, the buyer faces either shortage risk or price risk. This price risk is associated with the need to purchase additional components in the open market at a time of shortage, which typically implies higher prices. It is also completely possible that components are not available in the open market, thus the shortage risk.

Consider the following framework:

Indirect material. The risk associated with indirect material is typically low, and hence the focus is on using *content-based* hubs. Specifically, here the firm should use MRO hubs that specialize in unifying catalogs from many suppliers.

Strategic components. These are high-risk components that can be purchased from a small number of suppliers. Thus our analysis suggests that a private or consortium-based e-marketplace is appropriate. In this case the focus of the organization is on a marketplace that allows for better *collaboration* with the suppliers. That is, the focus is on using the marketplace to provide suppliers with real-time demand information as well as the buyer's production plans so that

suppliers can better use their capacities and resources. Of course, the decision whether to establish a private marketplace or to use a consortium-based e-market depends on
- Transaction volume
- Number of suppliers
- Cost to build and maintain a private site
- The importance of protecting proprietry business practices
- Technology and product life cycles

The last item needs some explanation: Clearly, the shorter the technology and product life cycles, the closer is the required collaboration with key suppliers. With current exchange technology, a private exchange, controlled by the buyer, better facilitates this type of relationship, which allows buyers and suppliers to cut design cost and development cycle time using the features of this private exchange.

Commodity products. This is the most challenging product category because, on the one hand, many of these products go directly into finished goods, so the risk is quite high, whereas on the other hand, the firm has a variety of potential options to choose from. These include selecting from many potential suppliers offering long-term, sometimes flexible contracts and/or using the spot market for short-term purchasing. The high risk and the available options suggest that in this case the focus should be on both price and risk management. This is achieved by using a *portfolio approach* focused on the appropriate tradeoffs between risk and cost.[18,19] To implement a portfolio approach, the firm should use a combination of

1. Long-term contracts where the buyer and supplier commit to a certain volume, and the supplier guarantees a level of supply for a committed price; we refer to the committed level of supply as the *base commitment* level.
2. Flexible, or option, contracts, in which the buyer prepays a relatively small fraction of the product price up front, in return for a commitment from the supplier to satisfy demand up to a certain level. We refer to this level as the *option* level. If the buyer does not exercise the option, the initial payment is lost. The buyer can purchase any amount up to the option level by paying an additional price (agreed to at the time the contract is signed) for each unit purchased.

Of course, the total price (prepayment plus the exercise price) paid by the buyer for each purchased unit is higher than the unit price in a long-term contract.
3. Spot purchasing, in which buyers look for additional supply in the open market. In this case the firm should use an independent e-marketplace to select a supplier. The focus at this stage is on using the marketplace to find new suppliers and on forcing *competition* between suppliers to reduce product price.

How does this portfolio approach address risk? If demand is much higher than anticipated and the base commitment level plus the option level do not provide enough protection, the firm must use the spot market for additional supply. Unfortunately, this is typically the worst time to buy in the spot market because prices are high due to shortages. Thus the buyer can select a tradeoff level between price risk, shortage risk, and inventory risk by carefully selecting the level of long-term commitment and the option level. For instance, for the same option level, the higher the initial contract commitment, the smaller is the price risk but the higher is the inventory risk taken by the buyer. On the other hand, the smaller the level of the base commitment, the higher are the price and shortage risks due to the likelihood of using the spot market. Similarly, for the same level of base commitment, the higher the option level, the higher is the risk assumed by the supplier because the buyer may exercise only a small fraction of the option level. These tradeoffs are summarized in Table 6-3, where in parentheses we identify the party that takes on most of the risk.

Table 6-3 Risk Tradeoff in Portfolio Contracts

Option level		Low	High
	High	Inventory risk (supplier)	N/A*
	Low	Price and shortage risks (buyer)	Inventory risk (buyer)
		Low	High
		Base commitment level	

*For a given situation, either the option level or the base commitment level may be high, but not both.

6.6   SUPPLY CONTRACTS

The preceding discussion of procurement strategies emphasized the need, in many cases, to develop relationships with suppliers. These relationships can take many forms, both formal and informal, but often, to ensure adequate supplies and timely deliveries, buyers and suppliers agree on supply contracts. These contracts address issues that arise between a buyer and a supplier, whether the buyer is a manufacturer purchasing raw materials from a supplier or a retailer purchasing manufactured goods from a manufacturer. In a supply contract, the buyer and supplier may agree on

- Pricing and volume discounts
- Minimum and maximum purchase quantities
- Delivery lead times
- Product or material quality
- Product return policies

In most cases, each party, i.e., the buyer or the supplier, makes decisions with very little regard to the impact of its decisions on the other party or on supply chain performance. For instance, distributors focus on their own costs and risks and will try to reduce those as much as possible. For these reasons, distributors order small quantities and concentrate on selling what they have in their distribution centers (DCs), rather than on what the manufacturer offers.

Interestingly, in the last few years many academic researchers and industry practitioners have recognized that supply contracts are a powerful method that can be used for far more than to ensure adequate supply of and demand for goods. Indeed, recently, new contracts have been designed and used to enable supply chain parties not only to ensure adequate supply and demand for goods, but also to improve supply chain performance. This is achieved by a variety of contracts that allow risk sharing between suppliers and distributors and hence increases profit for both.

To illustrate the importance and impact of different types of supply contracts on supply chain performance, consider a typical two-stage supply chain consisting of a retailer and a supplier. The sequence of events in such a supply chain is as follows. The retailer starts by generating a forecast, determines how many units to order from the supplier, and places an order to the manufacturer so as to optimize its own profit; the manufacturer reacts to the order placed by the retailer. Recall that this process is referred to as a *sequential supply chain optimization* because decisions are made sequentially. Thus in a sequential supply chain each party determines its own course of action independent of the impact of its decisions on other parties. As we observed in Chapter 1, this cannot be an effective strategy for supply chain partners.

It is natural to look for mechanisms that enable supply chain entities to move beyond this sequential process and toward *global optimization*. More specifically, are there mechanisms that the supply chain parties can use to improve each participant's profits? To answer this question, observe that in typical sequential supply chains such as the one described previously, the retailer assumes all the risk of having more inventory than sales, whereas the manufacturer takes no risk. Indeed, since the manufacturer takes no risk, the manufacturer would like the retailer to order as much as possible, whereas the retailer limits its order quantity because of the financial risk. *Of course, since the retailer limits its order quantity, there is a significant increase in the likelihood of stockouts.* If the manufacturer is willing and able to share some of the risk with the retailer, it may be profitable for the retailer to order more items, thereby reducing the likelihood of stocking out and increasing profit for both the manufacturer and the retailer.

It turns out that a number of supply contracts enable this risk sharing and therefore increase profits for both supply chain entities.

> *Buy-back contracts.* In a buy-back contract, the seller agrees to buy back unsold goods from the buyer for some agreed-on price. Clearly, this gives the retailer incentive to order more units, since the risk associated with unsold units is decreased. On the other hand, the supplier's risk clearly increases. Thus the contract is designed such that the increase in order quantity placed by the retailer, and hence the decrease in the likelihood of out of stock, more than compensates the manufacturer for the increase in risk.
>
> *Revenue-sharing contracts.* Observe that in the sequential supply chain one important reason for the retailer to order a limited number of units is the high wholesale price. If somehow the retailer can convince the manufacturer to reduce the wholesale price, then clearly the retailer will have an incentive to order more units. Of course, a reduction in wholesale price will decrease the manufacturer's profit if it is unable to sell more units. This is addressed by revenue-sharing contracts. In a

revenue-sharing contract, the buyer shares some of its revenue with the seller in return for a discount on the wholesale price. That is, in this contract the retailer transfers a portion of the revenue from each unit sold to the end customer.

Quantity-flexibility contracts. Quantity-flexibility contracts are contracts in which the supplier provides full refund for returned (unsold) items as long as the number of returns is no larger than a certain quantity. Thus this contract gives a full refund for a portion of the returned items, whereas a buy-back contract provides partial refund for all returned items.[20]

Sales rebate contracts. Sales rebate contracts provide a direct incentive to the retailer to increase sales by means of a rebate paid by the supplier for any item sold above a certain quantity.

Global optimization. The various contracts just described raise an important question: What is the most profit both the supplier and the buyer can hope to achieve? To answer this question, we take a completely different approach. What if an unbiased decision maker is allowed to identify the best strategy for the entire supply chain? This unbiased decision maker would consider the two supply chain partners, the manufacturer and the retailer, as two members of the same organization. That is, the transfer of money between the parties is ignored, and the unbiased decision maker will maximize supply chain profit.

Of course, this kind of unbiased decision maker does not usually exist. However, effective supply contracts provide incentives for supply chain partners to replace traditional strategies, in which each partner optimizes its own profit, with global optimization, where supply chain profit is maximized. The difficulty with global optimization is that it requires the firm to surrender decision-making power to an unbiased decision maker.

This is precisely why supply contracts are so important. *They help firms achieve global optimization, without the need for an unbiased decision maker, by allowing buyers and suppliers to share the risk* and the potential benefit. Indeed, it can be shown that *carefully designed supply contracts achieve the exact same profit as global optimization.*

In addition, from an implementation point of view, the main drawback of global optimization is that it does not provide a mechanism to allocate supply chain profit between the partners. It only provides information on the best, or optimal, set of actions that need to be taken by the supply chain to improve profit. Supply contracts allocate this profit among supply chain members.

More important, effective supply contracts allocate profit to each partner in a way that no partner can improve its profit by deciding to deviate from the optimal set of decisions. That is, there is no incentive for either the buyer or the seller to deviate from the set of actions that will achieve the global optimal solution.

The following example illustrates the impact of supply contracts in practice.

E X A M P L E   6-4

> Until 1998, video rental stores used to purchase copies of newly released movies from the movie studios for about $65 and rent them to customers for $3. Because of the high purchase price, rental stores did not buy enough copies to cover peak demand, which typically occurs during the first 10 weeks after a movie is released on video. The result was low customer service level; in a 1998 survey, about 20 percent of customers could not get their first choice of movie. Then, in 1998, Blockbuster Video entered into a revenue-sharing contract with the movie studios in which the wholesale price was reduced from $65 to $8 per copy, and in return, the studios were paid about 30 to 45 percent of the rental price of every rental. This revenue-sharing contract had a huge impact on Blockbuster revenue and market share. Today, revenue sharing is used by most large video rental stores.[21]

Thus, if these types of supply contracts are so effective, why do we not see more and more companies applying them in practice? The answer, of course, has to do with the various implementation drawbacks and challenges. For example, buy-back contracts

- Require *the supplier to have an effective reverse logistics system* that may increase the supplier logistics cost.
- Provide *retailers with an incentive to push competing products from suppliers with whom the buyer does not have a buy-back contract*. Indeed, a buy-back contract implies that the marginal loss encountered by the buyer from not selling a unit under the buy-back contract is smaller than that under no contract; thus the retailer has an incentive to push competing products that have no buy-back agreement.

Revenue-sharing contracts have a different set of drawbacks. These include

- *The cost of administrating the program.* This cost is associated with the ability of the supplier to monitor the retailer's revenue.
- *The retailers have an incentive to push competing products with higher profit margins.* That is, revenue-sharing contracts typically reduce the retailer profit margin (since some of the revenue is transferred to the supplier). Thus the retailer has an incentive to focus on selling other products, in particular similar products from competing suppliers with whom the retailer has no revenue-sharing agreement.

Thus, both revenue-sharing and buy-back contracts have a serious drawback that make them inappropriate when distributors (or retailers) have an ability to divert demand in the direction of certain products. In this case, a more appropriate strategy is the so-called sales rebate contract in which the manufacturer provides a direct incentive to the distributor to increase sales by applying a rebate paid by the manufacturer for items sold above a certain quantity.

6.7 SUMMARY

In this chapter we examined outsourcing and procurement strategies. Outsourcing has both benefits and risks, and we considered a framework for making buy/make decisions. These decisions should depend on whether a particular component is modular or integral and whether or not a firm has the expertise and capacity to manufacture a particular component or product.

We also considered the growth of e-markets and their impact on business strategies. A number of e-markets have appeared, and each of these types addresses a different business need. Depending on the type of component being procured, a different type of e-market is appropriate. For commodity products, a portfolio of procurement strategies may be most appropriate.

Finally, we saw that well-designed supply contracts enable independent firms in a supply chain to make purchasing and inventory decisions in a globally optimal way.

CHAPTER 7

Product Design and Supply Chain Management

7.1 INTRODUCTION

For many years manufacturing engineering was the last stop in the product engineering process. The researchers and design engineers worked on developing a product that worked and perhaps one that used materials as inexpensively as possible. Then manufacturing engineers were charged with determining how to make this design efficiently. In the 1980s this paradigm began to change. Management began to realize that product and process design were key product cost drivers and that taking the manufacturing process into account early in the design process was the only way to make the manufacturing process efficient. Thus the concept of *design for manufacturing* (DFM) was born.

Recently, a similar transformation has begun in the area of supply chain management. We have discussed appropriate strategies for supply chain design and operation, assuming that *product design decisions were already made* by the time the supply chain is designed. Designing the supply chain, we have assumed, involves determining the best way to supply existing products using existing manufacturing processes. In the last few years, however, managers have started to realize that by taking supply chain concerns into account in the product and process design phase, it becomes possible to operate a much more efficient supply chain. Obviously, this is analogous to the DFM practice of taking manufacturing into account during the product design phase. In the following sections we discuss various approaches that leverage product design in order to manage the supply chain more effectively.

In the next section we discuss a series of concepts introduced by Professor Hau Lee[1] and known collectively as *design for logistics* (DFL). These concepts suggest product and process design approaches that help to control logistics costs and increase customer service levels.

Following that, we discuss the advantages of including suppliers in the product design process. This discussion is based on an extensive report issued by the Global Procurement and Supply Chain Benchmarking Initiative at Michigan State University, which is titled *Executive Summary: Supplier Integration into New Product Development: A Strategy for Competitive Advantage*.

Finally, we discuss the concept of mass customization, developed by Joseph Pine II with several coauthors. In particular, we focus on the ways in which advanced logistics and supply chain practices help to enable this exciting new business model.

7.2 DESIGN FOR LOGISTICS

7.2.1 Overview

Transportation and inventory costs, as we have seen, are often critical supply chain cost drivers, particularly when inventory levels must be kept fairly high to ensure high service levels. These are exactly the issues that DFL addresses, using the following three key components:[1]

- Economic packaging and transportation
- Concurrent and parallel processing
- Standardization

Each of these components addresses the issue of inventory or transportation costs and service levels in complementary ways. They are discussed in detail in the following subsections.

7.2.2 Economic Packaging and Transportation

Of the various DFL concepts, perhaps the most obvious involves designing products so that they can be packed and stored efficiently. Products that can be packed more compactly are cheaper to transport, particularly if delivery trucks "cube out" before they "weigh out." In other words, if the space taken up by a product and not its weight constrain how much can fit in a delivery vehicle, products that can be stored more compactly can be transported less expensively.

EXAMPLE 7-1

Swedish furniture retailer Ikea, with $9.6 billion in sales, is the world's largest furniture retailer. Started in Sweden by Ingvar Kamprad, Ikea currently has 143 stores in 35 countries.[2] It has grown so dramatically by "reinventing the furniture business."[3] Traditionally, furniture sales were split between department stores and small, locally owned shops. Typically, customers would place an order, and delivery could take place up to 2 months after the order was placed. Ikea changed this formula by displaying all its 10,000 products in large warehouse-like spaces in out-of-town stores and keeping all of these items in the warehouse. This was accomplished by designing products so that they can be packed compactly and efficiently in kits, which customers take from the stores and assemble at home. These kits are easy and cheap to transport, so products can be manufactured efficiently in a small number of factories and then shipped relatively cheaply to stores all over the world. Since Ikea has so many stores, each of which is very large, the company is able to take advantage of vast economies of scale. This has enabled the firm to sell good-quality furniture at prices lower than that of its competitors.[3] Ikea continues to work toward improved design and packaging to continue its dramatic growth—"recently the company figured out how to shave one-third off the width of bookcase packing boxes by making the back panels a separate assembly piece."[4]

There are other reasons to design products to pack compactly. For example, many major retailers favor products that take up less storage space and stack easily. Efficient storage reduces certain components of inventory cost because handling costs typically decrease, space per product (and thus rent per product) decreases, and revenue per square foot can increase. For example, many of the large plastic items available in discount stores, such as garbage pails, are designed to stack so that they take up less shelf (or floor) space in the store. Thus, while it might not be enough to design packaging efficiently after the product design is completed, it may be valuable to redesign the product itself in order to take these issues into account.

EXAMPLE 7-2

Recently Rubbermaid won several design awards from *BusinessWeek* magazine. When describing why the Clear Classics food storage containers won an award, the writers mention that "Wal-Mart loves products designed to fit 14 by 14-inch shelves," which is one of the reasons these products were so successful. In addition, when describing the children's Icy Rider sled designed by Rubbermaid (which also won the award), the writers state, "Of course, not all products sold in Wal-Mart can fit into 14-by-14 shelving. But if designers create them to stack and save space, they have a shot of selling toWal-Mart. . . . After researching Wal-Mart's needs, Rubbermaid made the Icy Rider thin and stackable."[5]

Similarly, it is often possible to ship goods in bulk and only complete final packaging at the warehouse or even at the retailer. This may save on transportation costs because bulk goods tend to be shipped more efficiently.

EXAMPLE 7-3

The Hawaiian sugar industry switched over to bulk transportation after World War II, when costs began to increase. They estimate that the cost of transporting a bulk ton of sugar is about $0.77 today, whereas the cost of transporting the same quantity of sugar in bags would be about $20.00.[6]

In some cases, final packaging can even be delayed until the goods are actually sold. For example, many grocery stores now sell flour, cereal, and many other goods in bulk, allowing consumers to package as much as they want.

Recall that cross-docking (discussed in Chap. 3) involves moving goods from one truck (e.g., from the supplier) to another set of trucks (e.g., perhaps going to individual retail stores). In some cases boxes or pallets are taken off an incoming truck and moved directly to an outgoing one. However, it is often necessary to repackage some of the products. In many cases bulk pallets of single items come in from suppliers, but mixed pallets with many different items have to go out to individual retailers. In this case goods must be repacked at the cross-dock point, so more identification or labeling also might be needed if packages are broken up.[7] In general, packaging and products that are designed to facilitate this type of cross-docking operation by making repacking easier clearly will help to lower logistics costs.

7.2.3 Concurrent and Parallel Processing

In the preceding subsection we focused on simple ways that redesign of the product and packaging could help to control logistics costs. In this subsection we will focus on modifying the manufacturing *process*—which also may require modification of the product design.

We have seen that many difficulties in operating supply chains are due to long manufacturing lead times. Most manufacturing processes consist of manufacturing steps performed in sequence. The requirements of short startup times and ever-shorter product life cycles often dictate that certain manufacturing steps be performed in different locations to take advantage of existing equipment or expertise. *Concurrent and parallel processing* involves modifying the manufacturing process so that steps that were previously performed in a sequence can be completed at the same time. This obviously helps to reduce manufacturing lead time, lower inventory costs through improved forecasting, and reduce safety stock requirements, among other benefits.

A key to keeping the manufacturing process parallel is the concept of decoupling. If many of the components of the product can be *decoupled*, or physically separated, during manufacturing, it is possible that these components can be manufactured in parallel. If manufacturing each of the individual components takes the same amount of time in the newly decoupled design, but the manufacturing steps are performed in parallel, lead time will decrease. Even if some of these modular components take slightly more time to manufacture, the overall lead time still may decrease because various components are being manufactured in parallel. An added advantage of this manufacturing strategy of decoupling is that it may be possible to design different inventory strategies for the various decoupled components. If the supply of raw materials or manufacturing yield is uncertain for a particular component, a higher inventory level can be held of that single component rather than for the entire end product.

EXAMPLE 7-4

A European manufacturer produces network printers for the European market in alliance with a manufacturer in the Far East. The main printer PC board is designed and assembled in Europe. It is then

(continued)

shipped to Asia, where it is integrated with the main printer housing in a process that involves building the printer, including the motor, print head, housing, and so forth, around the board. The finished product is then shipped to Europe. The manufacturer is concerned with the long production and transportation lead times, which make it essential to maintain a large safety stock in Europe. However, much of the long manufacturing lead time is due to the sequential manufacturing process. Redesigning the printer manufacturing process and product so that the board can be integrated with the rest of the printer at the end of the manufacturing process will decrease lead times by allowing parallel manufacturing in Europe and the Far East. In addition, moving final assembly to Europe can serve to further increase responsiveness and decrease lead times. The two manufacturing processes are diagrammed in Figure 7-1.[1]

7.2.4 Standardization

As we discussed earlier, it is possible in some cases to shorten lead times (e.g., by taking advantage of parallel processing) in order to reduce inventory levels and increase forecast accuracy. Sometimes, however, it is impossible to reduce the lead time beyond a certain point. In these cases it may be possible to achieve the same objectives by taking advantage of standardization.

Recall the third principle of forecasting described in Chapter 2: Aggregate demand information is always more accurate than

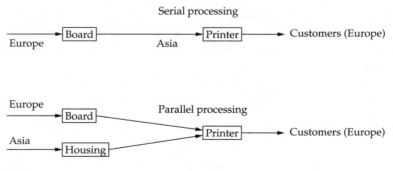

Figure 7-1 Concurrent processing.

disaggregate data. Thus we can better forecast demand for a continent than for a country or for a product family (e.g., ski jackets) than for a specific product (or style). Unfortunately, in a traditional manufacturing environment, aggregate forecasts are not of much use—the manufacturing manager has to know exactly what needs to be made before starting the process. However, by effectively using standardization, it may be possible to make effective use of the information in aggregate forecasts. Specifically, approaches based on product and process commonality make it possible to delay decisions about which specific product will be manufactured until after some of the manufacturing or purchasing decisions have been made. Thus these decisions can be made on an aggregate level using the more accurate aggregate forecasts.

Professor Jayashankar Swaminathan has developed a wide-ranging framework for effective implementation of standardization through the use of the correct operational strategy.[8] Swaminathan suggests that product modularity and process modularity are the key drivers that enable a standardization strategy that lowers inventory costs and increases forecast accuracy.

Following Swaminathan, we define the following concepts:

A *modular product* is a product assembled from a variety of modules such that for each module there are a number of options. The classic example of a modular product is the personal computer (PC), which can be customized by combining different video cards, hard drives, memory chips, and so forth. Recall that this concept of modularity is also important for the implementation of *concurrent and parallel processing*, which was described in the preceding subsection.

A *modular process* is a manufacturing process consisting of discrete operations so that inventory can be stored in partially manufactured form between operations. Products are differentiated by completing a different subset of operations during the manufacturing process. Observe that modular products are not necessarily made of modular processes because it may not be possible to store intermediate, or semifinished, inventories.

Swaminathan identifies four different approaches to standardization:

- Part standardization
- Process standardization

- Product standardization
- Procurement standardization

In *part standardization,* common parts are used across many products. Common parts reduce required part inventories due to risk pooling and reduce part costs due to economies of scale. Of course, excessive part commonality can reduce product differentiation so that less expensive customization options might cannibalize sales of more expensive parts. Sometimes it is necessary to redesign product lines or families to achieve commonality.

Process standardization involves standardizing as much of the process as possible for different products and then customizing the products as late as possible. In this case products and manufacturing processes are designed so that decisions about which specific product is manufactured—differentiation—can be delayed until after manufacturing is under way. The manufacturing process starts by making a *generic* or *family* product that is later differentiated into a specific end product. For this reason, this approach is also known as *postponement* or *delayed product differentiation.*[1] By delaying differentiation, production starts can be based on aggregate forecasts. Thus design for delayed product differentiation can be used effectively to address the uncertainty in final demand even if forecasts cannot be improved.

It is usually necessary to redesign products specifically for delayed differentiation. For example, it may be necessary to resequence the manufacturing process to take advantage of process standardization. *Resequencing* refers to modifying the order of product manufacturing steps so that those operations which result in the differentiation of specific items or products are postponed as much as possible. One famous and dramatic example of a firm using resequencing to improve its supply chain operation is Benetton Corporation.

EXAMPLE 7-5

Benetton is a major supplier of knitwear, at one point (in 1982) the largest consumer of wool in the world, supplying hundreds of shops. The nature of the fashion industry is that consumer preferences change rapidly. However, because of the long manufacturing lead time, store owners frequently had to place orders for wool sweaters up to 7 months in advance before the sweaters would appear in their stores. The wool sweater manufacturing process typically consists of acquiring yarn, dyeing it, finishing it, manufacturing the garment parts, and then joining those parts into a completed sweater. Unfortunately, this left little flexibility to respond to the changing tastes of consumers.

To address this issue, Benetton revised the manufacturing process, postponing the dyeing of the garments until *after* the sweater was completely assembled. Thus color choices could be delayed until after more forecasting and sales information were received. Hence, because of the postponement of the dyeing process, yarn purchasing and manufacturing plans could be based on aggregate forecasts for product families rather than on forecasts for specific sweater/color combinations. This revised process made sweater manufacturing about 10 percent more expensive and required the purchasing of new equipment and the retraining of employees. However, Benetton was more than adequately compensated by improved forecasts, lower surplus inventories, and in many cases higher sales.[8]

A U.S. disk drive manufacturer provides another notable example. Notice in this example that although lower levels of inventory need to be held to achieve specific service levels, the per-unit inventory cost tends to be more expensive.

EXAMPLE 7-6

A major U.S. manufacturer of mass storage devices makes different unique hard-drive products for each of a variety of customers. Orders are placed to be delivered by a certain time, and since lead times are very long, the manufacturer has to keep a variety of products in process in order to meet promised delivery dates. Since variability of demand is high and each product is unique, the manufacturer has to maintain high levels of in-process inventory to meet demand reliably.

The manufacturing process involves a brief generic segment, through which products intended for all customers must go, and then an extensive customization portion. Clearly, the ideal point to hold inventory is before customization begins. Unfortunately, however, the majority of manufacturing time, due particularly to time-consuming testing, occurs after differentiation has started. This testing has to take place after differentiation starts because a particular circuit board has to be added to the assembly for the testing to take place, and this circuit board is different for each customer. In order to delay differentiation, it is possible

(continued)

to insert a generic circuit board into the assembly, complete much of the testing, remove the generic circuit board, and add the customer-specific boards later. In this way, disk drive differentiation can be delayed until more order information is available. Clearly, this will decrease the level of required in-process inventory needed to meet demand reliably. However, this will add some additional manufacturing steps. In particular, the generic board has to be added and removed. Thus it is necessary to compare the manufacturing inefficiencies caused by adding and removing this circuit board with the gains in inventory savings. The manufacturing processes are illustrated in Figure 7-2.[1]

Part and process standardization are frequently connected. Sometimes part standardization is necessary for implementing process standardization.

EXAMPLE 7-7

A major printer manufacturer was preparing to introduce a new color printer into the market. Demand for the new printer and an existing printer was expected to be highly variable and negatively correlated. The manufacturing processes for the two products were similar, except that different circuit boards and printhead assemblies were used. Differences in head assemblies and circuit boards led to very different manufacturing processes. To implement process standardization, i.e., delayed differentiation, it is necessary to ensure that the manufacturing processes are similar until the final step. To do this, the printers have been redesigned so that both products share a common circuit board and printhead. This ensures that differentiation can be delayed as much as possible. Thus part standardization enables process standardization in this case.[1]

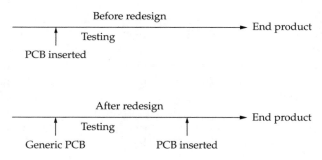

Figure 7-2 Delaying differentiation.

In some cases the concepts of resequencing and commonality allow the final manufacturing steps to be completed at distribution centers (DCs) or warehouses instead of at the factory. One of the advantages of this approach is that if DCs are much closer to the demand than the factories, products can be differentiated closer to the demand, thus increasing the firm's ability to respond to rapidly changing markets. A dramatic example of this is given next.

EXAMPLE 7-8

In the early 1990s, Hewlett-Packard (HP) faced an inventory and service level crisis in Europe with its DeskJet printer line. At that time, the DeskJet was manufactured exclusively in a plant in Vancouver. At the time of its manufacture, the printer was "localized" for a particular market. The localization of the printer involved assembling the correct power supply and plug and packaging the printer with the appropriate manual and labeling. The printer was then shipped to a regional distribution center (DC); for European printers, the DC was located in Germany, and it took 4 to 5 weeks for the printer to travel from Vancouver to the European DC. Unfortunately, the European DC typically had too many printers localized for some European markets and not enough printers localized for other European markets. After considering a variety of options, HP decided to redesign the DeskJet printer so that localization could be completed in the DC in Germany rather than at the Vancouver plant. Although this redesign was fairly expensive, it was very successful. Indeed, inventory level declined significantly even as service level improved, leading to significant cost savings and increased profitability.

Sometimes processes can be redesigned so that the differentiating steps do not have to be performed in a manufacturing facility or DC at all but can take place at the retailer facility after the sale is made. Often this is accomplished by focusing on modularity during the design phase, placing functionality in *modules* that can be easily added to a product. For example, some printers are sold in generic Macintosh/PC versions. Along with the printer, each retail store stocks separately packaged modules that differentiate the product for the Mac or PC. Obviously, this can greatly lower required inventory because only modules have to be stocked in Mac and PC versions instead of entire printers. Similarly, many color ink-jet printers are black-and-white printers with added "color kits."

In *product standardization*, a large variety of products may be offered but only a few kept in inventory. When a product not kept in stock is ordered, the order may be filled by a product that offers a superset of the features required by a customer. This process, known as *downward substitution*, is common in many industries. For example, in the semiconductor industry, it is quite common to sell a higher-speed or a higher-functionality chip as a lower-speed/functionality chip when the low-end chip is out of stock. Similarly, car rental agencies and hotels frequently fill reservations with higher-end vehicles or rooms when the lower-end vehicles or rooms are not available. Sometimes it may be possible to redesign products so that one product can be adjusted to meet several end-customer requirements. For example, as we have seen previously, many products are similar, except that power supplies have to be different for different markets. Instead of manufacturing two versions of a product, however, manufacturers can use a standardized product with a switchable power supply. We discuss this issue further in the case at the end of this chapter.

Finally, *procurement standardization* involves standardizing processing equipment and approaches even when the product itself is not standardized. This is particularly valuable when processing equipment is very expensive. In the production of application specific integrated circuits (ASICs), for example, very expensive equipment is required. Although end products are highly customized and demand is unpredictable, the same equipment is used to produce each of the possible end products. Thus equipment procurement can be managed independent of the final demand.

7.2.5 Selecting a Standardization Strategy

To help with the selection of an appropriate standardization strategy, Jayashankar Swaminathan[8] proposed a framework based on the observation that the firm's choice of standardization strategy is a function of the firm's ability to modularize its products and processes. Table 7-1 illustrates the proposed strategic choices under different conditions.

- If process and product are modular, process standardization will help to maximize effective forecast accuracy and minimize inventory costs.
- If the product is modular but the process is not, it is not possible to delay differentiation. However, part standardization is likely to be effective.

Table 7-1 Operational Strategies for Standardization

		Process	
		Nonmodular	*Modular*
Product	*Modular*	Part standardization	Process standardization
	Nonmodular	Product standardization	Procurement standardization

- If the process is modular but the product is not, procurement standardization may decrease equipment expenses.
- If neither the process nor the product is modular, some benefits may still result from focusing on product standardization.

7.2.6 Important Considerations

The various strategies just described are designed to deal with inaccurate forecasts and product variety; frequently, it may not be possible or cost-effective to implement these strategies in the context of a particular product or a specific supply chain. Even if implementing a particular strategy is theoretically possible, in many cases the expenses resulting from product and packaging redesign will exceed the savings under the new system. In addition, capital expenditures are likely to be required to retool assembly lines. Sometimes, as we discussed earlier, it may even be necessary to add manufacturing capability at distribution centers. Typically, the value of these types of changes is higher at the start of the product life cycle, when expenditures can be amortized over the entire life of the product. It is possible that DFL initiatives that make a great deal of sense at the start of the product life cycle do not pay for themselves when implemented later.[1] It also may be more expensive to manufacture a product with a new process. In many of the examples mentioned earlier, the products and manufacturing processes became more expensive. It is therefore necessary to estimate the savings produced by a more effectively designed product or process and compare these savings with the increased cost of manufacturing. Many of the benefits of implementing such a system are very difficult to quantify; increased flexibility, more efficient customer service, and decreased market response times may be hard to place a value on, which only serves to make the analysis more difficult. To add to the difficulty, engineers often are forced to take a broader perspective than they have been trained to take when they are making these kinds of decisions.

To add to these complications, process modifications such as resequencing will cause the level of inventory in many cases to go down, but the per-unit value of inventory being held will be higher. In Example 7-5, it may be possible to hold less wool in inventory because it does not have to be dyed before it is assembled. However, much of this wool will be held in the form of sweaters, which have a higher value than dyed wool. Of course, if manufacturing or customizing steps are postponed, the generic products may have a lower value than customized products, so value is added later in the supply chain than it would be otherwise.

Finally, in some cases tariffs and duties are lower for semifinished or nonconfigured goods than for final products.[1] Thus, implementing a strategy of completing the manufacturing process in a local DC may help to lower costs associated with tariffs and duties.

All these issues have to be taken into consideration when implementing a specific DFL strategy. Nevertheless, it is clear that in many cases DFL can help to improve customer service and greatly reduce the costs of operating the supply chain.

7.2.7   The Push-Pull Boundary

Recall our discussion of the push-pull boundary in Chapter 3. In push-based systems, production decisions are based on long-term forecasts, whereas in pull-based supply chains, production is driven by demand. We listed many advantages of pull-based systems and concluded that compared with push-based systems, pull-based systems typically lead to a reduction in supply chain lead times, inventory levels, and system costs while simultaneously making it easier to manage system resources.

Unfortunately, it is not always practical to implement a pull-based system throughout the entire supply chain. Lead times may be too long, or it may be necessary to take advantage of economies of scale in production or transportation. The standardization strategies we have been discussing in this section can be viewed as a method to combine push and pull systems within a single supply chain into what we called in Chapter 3 a *push-pull system*. Indeed, that portion of the supply chain prior to product differentiation is typically a push-based supply chain. That is, the undifferentiated product is built and transported based on long-term forecasts. In contrast, differentiation occurs as a response to market demand. Thus the portion of the supply chain starting from the time of differentiation is a pull-based supply chain.

For instance, in the Benetton example, uncolored sweaters are made to forecast, but dyeing takes place as a reaction to customer demand. We call the point of differentiation the *push-pull boundary* because this is the point where the system changes from a push-based system to a pull-based system.

One way to view the push-pull boundary concept is through the third rule of forecasting discussed in Chapter 2. Since aggregate demand information is more accurate than disaggregate data, the push portion of the supply chain includes only activities and decisions made prior to product differentiation. These activities and decisions are based on aggregate demand data.

Clearly, then, an additional advantage of postponement is that it allows firms to realize many of the advantages of pull-based systems while at the same time allowing for the economies of scale inherent in push-based systems. Often, when implementing a standardization strategy, if there is more than one possible differentiation point, it may be useful to think in terms of locating the push-pull boundary in order to achieve a balance between the advantages of the push- and the pull-based systems.

7.3 SUPPLIER INTEGRATION INTO NEW PRODUCT DEVELOPMENT

Another key supply chain issue involves the selection of appropriate suppliers for components of the new product. Traditionally, this has been done after design and manufacturing engineers have determined the final design for a product. Recently, a study in *The Global Procurement and Supply Chain Benchmarking Initiative* at Michigan State University[10] found that firms often realize tremendous benefits from involving suppliers in the design process. Benefits include a decline in purchased material costs, an increase in purchased material quality, a decline in development time and cost and in manufacturing cost, and an increase in final product technology levels.

In addition to the competitive forces that drive managers to seek out all types of supply chain efficiencies, several competitive forces are specifically encouraging managers to find opportunities to work with suppliers during the product design process. These forces include the continuing focus on strategies that encourage companies to focus on their core competencies and outsource other business capabilities and to continually reduce the length of product life cycles. Both these forces encourage companies to develop processes that make the design process more efficient. Taking advantage of supplier competencies is certainly one way to do this.

7.3.1   The Spectrum of Supplier Integration

The supplier integration study[10] notes that there is no single "appropriate level" of supplier integration. Instead, the authors develop the notion of a *spectrum of supplier integration*. In particular, they identify a series of steps from least to most supplier responsibility as follows:

> *None.* The supplier is not involved in design. Materials and subassemblies are supplied according to customer specifications and design.
>
> *White box.* This level of integration is informal. The buyer "consults" with the supplier informally when designing products and specifications, although there is no formal collaboration.
>
> *Gray box.* This represents formal supplier integration. Collaborative teams are formed between the buyer's and the supplier's engineers, and joint development occurs.
>
> *Black box.* The buyer gives the supplier a set of interface requirements, and the supplier independently designs and develops the required component.

Of course, just because the black-box approach is at one end of the continuum does not mean that it is the best approach in all cases. Instead, firms must develop a strategy that helps them to determine the appropriate level of supplier integration for different situations.

The Global Procurement and Supply Chain Benchmarking Initiative has developed a strategic planning process to help firms make this determination.[10] The first several steps of the process are as follows:

- Determine internal core competencies.

- Determine current and future new product developments.
- Identify external development and manufacturing needs.

These three steps help management determine what is going to be procured from suppliers and what level of supplier expertise is appropriate. If future products have components that require expertise that the firm does not possess, and if development of these components can be separated from other phases of product development, then taking a black-box approach makes sense. If this separation is not possible, then it makes more sense to use the gray-box development. If the buyer has some design expertise but wants to ensure that the supplier can adequately manufacture the component, perhaps a white-box approach is appropriate.

7.3.2 Keys to Effective Supplier Integration

Simply selecting an appropriate level of supplier integration is not sufficient. Much work goes into ensuring that the relationship is a success. The next steps of the strategic planning process[10] help to ensure this success:

- Select suppliers and build relationships with them.
- Align objectives with selected suppliers.

Selecting suppliers in general involves various considerations, such as manufacturing capacity and response time. Since supplier integration partners typically supply components (in addition to cooperating in their design), all the traditional considerations still apply. In addition, the special nature of supplier integration presents an additional set of supplier requirements.

The same study[10] identifies many of these, including

- The capability to participate in the design process
- The willingness to participate in the design process, including the ability to reach agreements on intellectual property and confidentiality issues
- The ability to commit sufficient personnel and time to the process, including collocating personnel if appropriate
- Sufficient resources to commit to the supplier integration process

Of course, the relative importance of these requirements depends on the particular project and type of integration. Once suppliers are identified, it is critical to work on building relationships with them. For example, firms have found it useful to involve suppliers early in the design process. Companies that do so report greater gains than those which involve suppliers only after design concepts have been generated. Sharing future plans and technologies with suppliers helps to build this relationship, as does a joint continuous improvement goal. Separate organizational groups dedicated to managing the relationship are also useful. In all these cases, the goals of the purchasing firm revolve around building long-term, effective relationships with trusted suppliers. These naturally will lead to the alignment of buyer and supplier objectives, which will result in more effective integration.

7.3.3   A "Bookshelf" of Technologies and Suppliers

"The global procurement and supply chain benchmarking initiative"[10] also developed the idea of a "bookshelf" of technologies and suppliers within the context of supplier integration. This involves monitoring the development of relevant new technologies and following the suppliers that have demonstrated expertise in these technologies. Then, when appropriate, a buyer firm can quickly introduce these technologies into new products by integrating the supplier design team with its own. This enables a firm to balance the advantages and disadvantages of being on the cutting edge of new technology. On the one hand, there is no need to use the technology immediately in order to gain experience with it; suppliers are developing this knowledge with other customers. On the other hand, the danger of being slow to introduce cutting-edge technology and concepts is lessened. The bookshelf concept is a dramatic example of the power of supplier integration.

7.4 MASS CUSTOMIZATION

7.4.1 What Is Mass Customization?

In his book *Mass Customization*,[11] Joseph Pine II introduced a concept that is becoming important to more and more businesses—*mass customization*. In this section we will first review the concept and then discuss how logistics and supply chain networks play an important role in the implementation of related ideas.

Mass customization has evolved from the two prevailing manufacturing paradigms of the twentieth century—craft production and mass production. Mass production involves the efficient production of a large quantity of a small variety of goods. Spurred by the industrial revolution, so-called mechanistic firms developed in which management put a high priority on automating and measuring tasks. A very bureaucratic management structure, with rigid, functionally defined groups and tasks and tightly supervised employees, is common. This kind of organization enables tight control and predictability, which tends to lead to high degrees of efficiency. The quality of a small number of items can be quite high, and prices can be kept relatively low. This is particularly critical for commodity products, where firms typically have competed on price and, more recently, on quality.

Craft production, on the other hand, involves highly skilled and flexible workers, often craftsmen in the manufacturing setting, who are governed by personal or professional standards and motivated by the desire to create unique and interesting products or services. These workers, found in so-called organic organizations, typically are trained through apprenticeships and experience; the organization is flexible and continually changing. This type of organization is able to produce highly differentiated and specialized goods, but it is very difficult to regulate and control. As a consequence, the quality and production rates of these goods are hard to measure and reproduce, and they are typically much more expensive to manufacture.[12]

In the past, managers often had to make a decision between these two types of organizations with their inherent tradeoffs. For some products, a low-cost, low-variety strategy was appropriate, whereas for others, a higher-cost, higher-variety, more adaptable strategy was more effective. The development of mass customization demonstrates that it is not always necessary to make this tradeoff.

Mass customization involves the delivery of a wide variety of customized goods or services quickly and efficiently at low cost. Thus it captures many of the advantages of both the mass production and craft production systems described earlier. Although not appropriate for all products (e.g., commodity products may not benefit from differentiation), mass customization gives firms important competitive advantages and helps to drive new business models.

7.4.2   Making Mass Customization Work

Pine[12] points out that the key to making mass customization work is highly skilled and autonomous workers, processes, and modular units so that managers can coordinate and reconfigure these modules to meet specific customer requests and demands.

Each module continually strives to upgrade its capabilities; a module's success depends on how effectively, quickly, and efficiently it completes its task and how good it is at expanding its capabilities. Managers are charged with determining how these capabilities "fit together" efficiently. Thus management's success depends on how effectively it can develop, maintain, and creatively combine the links between modules in different ways to meet different customer requests and on the creation of a work environment that encourages the development of a variety of different modules.

Since each unit has highly specialized skills, workers can develop expertise and efficiency in the manner of mass production. Since these units or modules can be assembled in many ways, the differentiation of craft production is achievable. Pine calls this type of organization a *dynamic network*.

There are several key attributes that a company or, more specifically, the *systems within a company that link different modules* must possess to implement mass customization successfully.[12] They are

Instantaneousness. Modules and processes must be linked together very quickly. This allows rapid response to various customer demands.

Costless. The linkages must add little, if any, cost to the processes. This attribute allows mass customization to be a low-cost alternative.

Seamless. The linkages and individual modules should be invisible to the customer so that customer service does not suffer.

Frictionless. Networks or collections of modules must be formed with little overhead. Communication must work instantly, without taking time for the team building that is necessary in so many other types of environments.

With these attributes in place, it becomes possible to design and implement a dynamic, flexible firm that can respond to varying customer needs quickly and efficiently.

EXAMPLE 7-9

National Bicycle is a subsidiary of Matsushita that sells bicycles under the Panasonic and National brand names in Japan. Several years ago management found that sales were not at acceptable levels primarily because the company was unable to predict and satisfy varying customer demand. In the year before beginning the mass customization efforts, 20 percent of bicycles from the previous year remained in inventory. Rather than market to a particular niche or try to improve forecasts, National became a mass customizer.

The company developed a highly flexible bicycle frame manufacturing facility, noting that painting and the installation and tuning of components were separate functions that could be performed by other "modules" in its manufacturing facility. Next, the company installed a sophisticated custom-order system called the *Panasonic Order System* at retailers. This system includes a unique machine that measures customer weight and size and the appropriate dimensions of the frame, position of the seat, and extension of the bar stem. The customers also can select model type, color patterns, and various components. Information from the dealer is transmitted instantaneously to the factory, where a computer-aided design (CAD) system produces technical details in 3 minutes. The information is transmitted automatically to the appropriate modules, where manufacturing is completed. The bike is then delivered to the consumer 2 weeks later.

Thus, by noting that the production process could be separated into independent production modules in a seamless and essentially costless manner, and by installing sophisticated information systems, National Bicycle was able to increase sales and customer satisfaction without significantly increasing manufacturing costs.[13]

7.4.3 Mass Customization and Supply Chain Management

Clearly, many of the advanced supply chain management approaches and techniques that we have discussed in this and earlier chapters are essential if mass customization is to be implemented successfully. This is particularly true if the components in the network stretch across several companies.

The same information technology that is so critical for effective supply chain management is also critical for coordinating the different modules in the dynamic network and ensuring that together they meet customer requirements. The required system attributes listed earlier make effective information systems mandatory. Similarly, in many cases the modules in the dynamic network exist across different firms. This makes concepts such as strategic partnerships and supplier integration essential for the success of mass customization. Finally, as many of the printer-related examples indicate, postponement can play a key role in implementing mass customization. For instance, postponing regional differentiation until products have reached regional distribution centers facilitates regional customization. As the following example illustrates, postponing differentiation until orders have been received allows customer-specific customization.

EXAMPLE 7-10

Dell Computer has become one of the dominant players in the PC industry—in 1998 it was the second largest manufacturer of PCs for business—by adopting a unique strategy based on mass customization. Dell never builds a PC for a customer until the customer's order has been placed. This allows the customer to specify unique requirements, and Dell builds the computer to these requirements. A growing number of orders come in over the Internet. The order-taking system interfaces with Dell's own supply chain control system, which ensures that inventory is where it needs to be for the computer to be manufactured quickly. In addition, Dell stores very little inventory. Instead, Dell's suppliers have built warehouses close to Dell's facilities, and Dell orders parts on a just-in-time basis. By implementing these strategies, Dell has been able to provide customers with exactly what they want very quickly. In addition, inventory costs are low, and Dell minimizes the danger of parts obsolescence in the rapidly changing computer industry. In this way, Dell has become one of the dominant players in the desktop PC market and is well on its way to doing so in the laptop and server markets.

Dell has used many of the important concepts we have discussed to achieve its goals. The company is driven by advanced information systems that do everything from taking many of the orders (over the Web) to managing inventory in the supply chain. Strategic partnerships have been established with many of Dell's suppliers. Dell is even establishing supplier integration partnerships with some of its key suppliers (e.g., 3Com, the network equipment supplier) to ensure that new computers and networking devices are compatible. Finally, Dell has used the concept of postponement, deferring final assembly of computers until orders have been received, to achieve mass customization.[14]

7.5 SUMMARY

In this chapter we focused on various ways that product design inter-acts with supply chain management. First, we considered various de-sign for logistics (DFL) concepts, in which product design is used to lower the costs of logistics. Products designed for efficient packaging and storage obviously cost less to transport and store. Designing prod-ucts so that certain manufacturing steps can be completed in parallel can cut down on manufacturing lead time, leading to a reduction in safety stocks and increased responsiveness to market changes. Finally, standardization enables risk pooling across products, leading to lower inventories, and allows firms to use the information contained in ag-gregate forecasts more effectively.

Another critical design–supply chain interaction involves inte-grating suppliers into the product design and development process. We discussed different approaches for integrating suppliers into the development process and considered guidelines for managing this in-tegration effectively.

Finally, advanced supply chain management helps to facilitate mass customization. Mass customization involves the delivery of a wide variety of customized goods or services quickly and efficiently at low cost. Obviously, this approach helps to provide firms with impor-tant competitive advantages, and just as obviously, effective supply chain management is critical if mass customization is to be successful.

CHAPTER 8

Customer Value

8.1 INTRODUCTION

In today's customer-driven market it is not the product or service it-self that matters most but the perceived value to the customer of the entire relationship with a company. The approach used by companies to measure the quality of their product and services has evolved from internal quality assurance to external customer satisfaction and from there to *customer value*. Internal quality measures, such as the number of production defects, dominated company goals in the era of supply-driven manufacturing. The ability to provide customers with quality product was the main goal. External customer satisfaction measures were focused on developing an understanding of the company's cur-rent customers, their use of a company's products, and their impres-sion of its service. This provided valuable information about current customers and generated ideas for areas of improvement within the company. The current emphasis on customer value goes a step further; it tries to establish the reasons a customer chooses one company's product over another's and looks at the entire range of product, ser-vices, and intangibles that constitute the company's image.

Thinking in terms of customer value promotes a broader look at a company's offerings and its customers. It requires learning why cus-tomers purchase, continue to purchase, or defect from a company. What are their preferences and needs, and how can they be satisfied?

Which customers are profitable and have potential for revenue growth, and which customers may lead to losses? Assumptions about customer value need to be examined carefully to make sure that the tradeoffs made are the correct ones. Some examples include

- Does the customer value low prices more than superior customer support services?
- Does the customer prefer next-day delivery or lower prices?
- Does the customer prefer to purchase the item in a store that specializes in this type of item or from a large megastore that provides one-stop shopping opportunities?

These are critical questions for any business and should be the driving force behind business strategy and performance measures.

Indeed, *logistics*, previously considered a back-office function, has evolved into the highly visible discipline of supply chain management partly because of this change in perspective. Supply chain management is naturally an important component of fulfilling customer needs and providing value. Equally important, supply chain management determines the availability of products, how fast they will arrive in the market, and at what cost. Our definition of *supply chain management* (see Chap. 1) implies that the ability to respond to customer requirements is the most basic function of this discipline. This function includes not only the physical attributes of product distribution but also related information, such as production or delivery status, and the ability to access this information.

Supply chain management also can affect the important customer value of price by significantly reducing costs. As we have seen in previous chapters, Dell's strategy to reduce its supply chain costs by postponing the final product assembly until after the purchase (i.e., by building to order) has allowed Dell to underprice its competitors in the personal computer (PC) industry. Wal-Mart has been able to lower costs by introducing the cross-docking strategy and by engaging in strategic partnering with its suppliers. Finally, the policy of everyday low prices applied by Wal-Mart and other retailers is also motivated in large part by supply chain efficiencies.

EXAMPLE 8-1

The recent downfall of Kmart is attributed in part to its strategy of competing on price with Wal-Mart. As observed in Chapter 1,

Wal-Mart's goal since the early 1980s was to provide customers with access to goods when and where they want them and to develop cost structures that enable competitive pricing. The key to achieving this goal was to make supply chain efficiencies the centerpiece of its strategy. On the other hand, Kmart's strong desire to keep up earnings discouraged investments in supply chain efficiencies and, in particular, in information technology. By the late 1990s, it became clear that Kmart's supply chain was not as efficient as that of Wal-Mart.[1]

This example suggests the importance of linking pricing strategies with supply chain efficiencies. We discuss this issue in Section 8.3.

Customer value drives changes and improvements in the supply chain, some forced by customer and competitor activities and others undertaken to achieve competitive advantage. Furthermore, large manufacturers, distributors, or retailers place certain requirements on their suppliers that force them to adopt supply chains that will make these requests feasible. Specifically, Wal-Mart requires many of its suppliers to practice vendor-managed inventory. Large manufacturers such as Hewlett-Packard and Lucent Technologies require that their parts manufacturers have 100 percent availability of stock for the parts they use. In return, they are willing to commit to a single supplier for the product or service or at least commit to a minimum volume of purchases from a primary supplier.

Finally, customer value is also important for determining the type of supply chain required to serve the customer and what services are required to retain customers. A company's supply chain strategy is determined by the type of products or services it offers and the value of various elements of this offering to the customer. For example, if customers value one-stop shopping, this would entail carrying a large number of products and options, even if this is costly in terms of inventory management. If customers value innovative products, then companies who produce them need to apply their supply chain to supply these products efficiently while demand lasts. If a company offers personal customization of its products, then its supply chain needs to be flexible enough to provide the infrastructure for this offering. Thus the supply chain needs to be considered in any product and sales strategy and could, in itself, provide competitive advantages leading to increased customer value.

8.2 DIMENSIONS

We have defined *customer value* as the way the customer perceives the entire company's offerings, including products, services, and other intangibles. The customer's perception can be broken into several dimensions:

- Conformance to requirements
- Product selection
- Price and brand
- Value-added services
- Relationships and experiences

The list of dimensions starts with the essentials—the first three items above—and goes on to more sophisticated types of features that may not always be critical. However, the less critical features can be mined for ideas to create a unique way to add value and differentiation to a company's offering. In this section we suggest how each dimension is affected by supply chain management and how, in turn, it needs to take into account the customer values inherent in each dimension.

8.2.1 Conformance to Requirements

The ability to offer what the customer wants and needs is a basic requirement to which supply chain management contributes by creating availability and selection. Marshall Fisher calls it the *market mediation* function of the supply chain.[2] This function is distinct from the supply chain physical function of converting raw materials into goods and shipping them through the chain to the customer. The costs associated with the market mediation function occur when there are differences between supply and demand. If the supply exceeds demand, there are inventory costs throughout the supply chain; if demand exceeds supply, there are lost sales and possibly lost market share.

If product demand is predictable, as in *functional items* such as diapers, soup, or milk, market mediation is not a major issue. Clearly, efficient supply chains for functional items can reduce costs by focusing on reducing inventory, transportation, and other costs. This is the strategy Campbell Soup and Procter & Gamble employ for their supply chains.

However, when dealing with fashion items or other high-variability items, the nature of demand can create large costs due to lost sales or excess inventory. These high-variability products require responsive supply chains that stress short lead times, flexibility, and speed over cost efficiencies. When the supply chain strategy does not match the product characteristics, there are major implications in the ability to conform to the market, as illustrated in the following example.

EXAMPLE 8-2

Consider a Korean company that manufactures electronic relays. Since competition is intense in this industry, customers can pick and choose their supplier. Thus, if the manufacturer does not have the right products at the right time, it will lose customers to the competition. To make matters worse, forecasting customer demand is a challenge because variation in monthly demand is very high. To reduce cost, the manufacturer ships products from a number of manufacturing facilities in the Far East by sea. Unfortunately, by the time the product has arrived at the U.S. warehouse, the demand has changed, and there is a shortage of one type of component and obsolete inventory of another. Therefore, the manufacturer is considering shipping the products by air, which would reduce lead times and hence inventory levels and costs, as well as improve customer sales and retention.

Conformance to requirements is also achieved through attention to *customer access*, the ability to easily find and purchase a product. For companies such as McDonald's, Starbucks, and Walgreens, access involves prime real estate. Providing mail, phone, and Web access in addition to or instead of retail stores can enhance the customer's ability to purchase the product conveniently. Finally, *access* includes the perception of providing the consumers with a store or Web site layout that makes it easy to find and purchase the product they are seeking.[3] Grainger's success in integrating the Web with its older business channels is a good example of the ability to provide customers with the access they need to a company's services.

EXAMPLE 8-3

The business that William W. Grainger founded in 1927 has been one of the success stories of the Internet. Grainger wanted to provide an efficient solution to the need for a speedy and consistent supply of

(continued)

electric motors. The *MotorBook*, as it was originally called, was the basis for today's *Grainger Catalog*. The product line has since expanded to over 220,000 MRO supplies and parts. Grainger is the largest firm in the market for industrial products, with 1999 revenues of $4.5 billion. In 1995 Grainger started its Web initiative with a variety of goals:

- Provide customers with access to all the products Grainger makes available, over 220,000, and not just the 86,500 that could be presented in the paper catalog.
- Provide customers with much better tools for searching, locating, and selecting the product that best suits their needs.
- Deliver products the same day from the branch closest to the customer who placed the order, or ship them from one of Grainger's five regional distribution centers and have them delivered the next day.

Grainger faces a variety of challenges:

- Grainger offers 65 million different price points, so no "one price fits all," and the Internet needs to honor each business account's unique pricing structure.
- Servicing business accounts requires checking credit and establishing payment guidelines.
- Real-time inventory availability—many customers looking for parts cannot wait and need immediate service.
- Compensating the sales force—Grainger decided to pay commissions on Internet orders, thus getting a buy-in from their sales reps, who have relationships with the customers and can encourage customers to use the Web, which is more cost-effective than other channels.

The initiative had a huge impact on Grainger. In 1999, Grainger spent $20 million for the development, marketing, and customer service of Grainger.com, which led to $100 million worth of orders. In the first half of 2000, Grainger generated $120 million in revenue, with the size of the average order on the Web site being $250, compared with $140 for branch and phone orders.[4]

8.2.2 Product Selection

Many products come in a large variety of options, styles, colors, and shapes. For instance, a car may come in 5 styles, 10 different exterior colors, and 10 interior colors, as well as with automatic or manual transmission—a total of 1000 configurations. The difficulty is that distributors and retailers need to stock most of the various configurations and combinations of products. As explained in Chapter 2, this proliferation of options makes it difficult to predict customer demand for a specific model, thus forcing retailers and distributors to build large and diverse inventories.

The contribution of product proliferation to customer value is difficult to analyze and understand. Three successful business trends exist:

- *Specializing in offering one type of product.* Examples include companies such as Starbucks and Subway.
- *Megastores that allow one-stop shopping for a large variety of products.* Examples include Wal-Mart and Target.
- *Megastores that specialize in one product area.* Examples include Home Depot, Office Max, and Sportmart.

These trends also have emerged on the Internet, where some sites have been successful in offering a large variety of different products and others specialize in a single offering. For instance, www.BlueDenimShirts.com is touted as the "World's only factory outlet for Blue Denim Shirts. Whether you are shopping for 1 shirt for yourself or 1000 shirts with your company's logo, you can buy them here—directly from the factory. And, by the way, we guarantee The World's lowest prices." Along similar lines, consider Black-LeatherBags.com and WhiteTowels.com.

The PC industry has seen significant changes in the way products are sold. In the mid-1980s, PCs were sold through specialized stores such as Egghead. At the beginning of the 1990s, PCs were sold in department stores such as Sears. More recently, however, the direct business model has caught on. Finally, Gateway, one of the leaders in the direct business model, has opened its own retail stores. This suggests that there may be a need for a company to sell its products through various outlets to reach the largest number of customers. In fact, companies such as Circuit City enable customers to shop on the Web and pick up at the store.

As observed earlier, the proliferation of products and the difficulty in predicting demand for a specific model force retailers and distributors to hold large inventories. There are several ways to control inventory of a large variety of configurations or products.

1. The approach pioneered by Dell is the *build-to-order model*, where the configuration is determined only when the order comes in. This is an effective way to implement the push-pull strategy discussed in Chapter 3 by employing the concept of postponement introduced in Chapter 7. An interesting way to implement this strategy is described in the following example.

EXAMPLE 8-4

Amazon.com is the most famous and successful e-tailer. It started in 1995 by selling a huge variety of books, and later added music and videos. More recently, Amazon started selling toys, electronics, and other merchandise. Amazon's fulfillment strategy has evolved over time. Initially, the company did not hold any inventory. When a customer ordered a book, Amazon would transfer the order to Ingram Books. Recently, however, Amazon established its own seven large warehouses (one warehouse was later closed) and started shipping directly to the customers. In 2001, Amazon.com shifted its focus to improving its distribution operations in a push toward profit. It has improved its fulfillment costs, which include costs associated with six warehouses, customer service, and credit card fees, to 9.8 percent in the fourth quarter of 2001, down from 13.5 percent of sales in the fourth quarter of 2000. Amazon did this by

- Improving sorting order and utilization of sophisticated packing machines, which allowed Amazon to ship 35 percent more units with the same number of workers as the previous year.
- Using software to forecast purchasing patterns, which allowed Amazon to slash inventory levels by 18 percent in the fourth quarter.
- Consolidated shipping of 40 percent of goods into full trucks driven directly into major cities, bypassing regional postal sorting facilities and cutting transportation costs significantly.
- Partnering to sell goods for other companies such as Toys 'R' Us and Target, who pay Amazon for handling distribution and customer service. These partnerships brought in $225 million in revenue with gross profit margins double Amazon's overall 25 percent margins.
- Allowing other sellers to offer used books, which increased sales during the holiday season by 38 percent. For these products, Amazon's gross margins were about 85 percent—a business model similar to that of eBay.

Amazon.com also has had challenges on the pricing front. Amazon discounts nearly all books over $20 by 30 percent. Amazon once offered discounts of as much as 50 percent on best sellers and 20 percent discounts on other books. Early in 2001, the company started to raise book prices—with 5 to 10 percent discounts more common—only to reverse the increases as sales fell. In the book business, few other retailers have offered discounts, other than for best sellers. There is good reason Amazon can afford to cut book prices: The average book may sit on the shelf of a store for 6 months or a year before it is bought. The cost of this inventory in a chain of hundreds of stores is huge. Amazon, on the other hand, can keep just one or two copies in its warehouse—and still make the title available to the whole country—and restock as quickly as customers buy books.[4]

2. A different strategy, suitable for products with long manufacturing lead times, such as vehicles, is to keep *larger inventories at major distribution centers (DCs)*. These DCs allow the manufacturer to reduce inventory levels by taking advantage of risk pooling (see Chap. 3) and delivering the vehicles quickly to customers. General Motors has initiated this approach with its Cadillac unit in Florida. Dealers can order cars that they do not have on their lot from a regional warehouse that can ship the car out in a day. Of course, two major issues need to be raised when considering this strategy:

- *Inventory costs of cars at the regional warehouse.* Is the manufacturer (i.e., General Motors) going to pay for the inventory at the regional warehouse? If it is, then there is an incentive for the dealers to reduce inventory in their lots and reduce their cost while increasing that of the manufacturer.
- *Equalizing small and large dealers.* If all dealers have access to the regional warehouse, then there is no difference between the different dealers. Thus it is difficult to see why large dealers would be interested in participating in such an arrangement, especially if they are going to pay for inventory at the regional warehouse.

3. Another possibility is to offer *a fixed set of options that cover most customer requirements*. For instance, Honda offers a limited number of options on its cars. Dell offers a few options for modems or software that can be installed on its machines, although the overall number of possible configurations remains quite high. Indeed, large product variety is not required in all cases. For example, a dysfunctional level of variety exists in many grocery products—28 varieties of toothpaste, to give one example.[2] It is not clear whether this variety actually adds any customer value.

8.2.3 Price and Brand

Price of products and the level of service are essential parts of customer value. Although the price may not be the only factor a customer considers, there may be a narrow price range that is acceptable for certain products. For instance, for commodity products (and even sophisticated items such as PC's are commodities), there is very little flexibility in price. Therefore, companies achieve cost advantages through innovations in their supply chains. As we have seen in Dell's direct business model, allowing clients to configure their own systems and building a supporting supply chain not only improve customer value but also reduce costs.

Wal-Mart has been a supply chain innovator, which has enabled it to provide low-cost merchandise and undercut its competition (see Example 8-1). In addition, we have seen that the "everyday low pricing" policy applied by retailers such as Wal-Mart and manufacturers such as Procter & Gamble is an important tool in reducing the bullwhip effect (see Chap. 2). This policy appeals to customers who do not have to worry about buying at the wrong time and to the retailer and manufacturer who do not need to plan for demand variations as a result of promotions.

An important factor affecting the product price is its brand. In today's market, there are fewer salespeople and more customers looking for supermarket-style shopping.[6] This is true across a wide variety of retail environments, from auto superstores to e-tailers.

EXAMPLE 8-5

Consider prices for books and CDs sold on the Internet. A recent study found "substantial and systematic differences in price across retailers on the Internet. Prices posted on the Internet differ by an average of 33 percent for books and 25 percent for CDs." More important, Internet retailers with the lowest price do not necessarily sell more. For instance,

> the research found that Books.com had a lower price than Amazon.com
> in 99 percent of the cases, yet Amazon had about 80 percent of the mar-
> ket at the time of the study, whereas Books.com had about 2 percent.
> One way to explain this behavior is through "trust consumers have for
> the various Internet retailers and the associated value of branding."[7]

The Internet and its impact on consumer behavior have increased the importance of brand names because a brand name is a
guarantee of quality in the buyer's mind. Brand names such as Mer-
cedes cars, Rolex watches, and Coach purses can be promoted for high
quality and prestige and command much higher prices than products
that lack this aura. Furthermore, the higher price in itself may be a
large part of the prestige and perceived quality. The product's high
margins will require a focus on service level, and hence the supply
chain needs to be more responsive; the increase in supply chain cost
will be offset by the higher margin.

EXAMPLE 8-6

> One of the key elements in the rise of Federal Express as the most suc-
> cessful small package carrier is that it was the first carrier to narrow its
> focus to overnight delivery, thereby owning the word *overnight* in the
> market. Even though there are cheaper alternatives, customers are will-
> ing to pay a premium to ship by Federal Express because of the brand
> name and the perception of dependability it conveys.[6]

In many industries, *product* typically means both the "physical
product" and associated "services." Typically, pricing the physical
product is not as difficult as pricing services. At the same time, it is
quite difficult to compare different services, and as a result, variability
in pricing increases. This suggests opportunities for companies that
develop new offerings and services that are more difficult to turn into
commodities. As we will see below, there is a challenge in turning
these opportunities into offerings that customers are actually willing
to pay for.

In Section 8.3 we examine strategic pricing, where companies
can employ sophisticated analyses to align customer service preferences with supply chain costs.

8.2.4   Value-Added Services

Many companies cannot compete on product price alone in an economy that has an overabundance of supply. Therefore, they need to consider other sources of income. This drives companies toward value-added offerings that differentiate them from competitors and provide them with more profitable pricing structures.

Value-added services, such as support and maintenance, can be a major factor in the purchase of some products, especially technical products. Indeed, many companies are adding more services around their products.[8] This is due in part to

1. The commoditization of products, where only the price matters and all other features are identical, reducing profitability and competitive advantage from the sale of products alone.
2. The need to get closer to the customer.
3. The increase in information technology capabilities that make this offering possible.

A sophisticated service offering is illustrated in the following example.

EXAMPLE 8-7

> Goodyear Tire & Rubber Co. provides truck manufacturer Navistar International Transportation Corp. with an automated supply chain service that includes delivering mounted tires sequenced for just-in-time use on automated assembly lines. Goodyear has a 13-person information technology group dedicated to the tire maker's materials management division. This division acts as systems integrator on supply chain projects it takes on with wheel manufacturer Accuride, Inc., in Henderson, Kentucky. Under a joint venture called AOT, Inc., Goodyear and Accuride furnish entire wheel assemblies, painted and ready for use, to Mitsubishi Motor Co. and Ford Motor Co. as well as Navistar. Those assemblies include Goodyear's or competitors' tires, depending on customer specifications.[8]

A recent example of a market with a low entry barrier and many companies initially competing mostly on price is the business-to-business (B2B) e-marketplace. It only took a few years for many of these market makers to realize that they needed to extend their service offerings; they now provide a variety of additional services, including financial, logistics, and supply chain services (see Chap. 6 for more detail).

As observed in the preceding section, pricing services is not an easy task. For many years companies such as IBM did not charge for their services, although the company's slogan was "IBM Means Service." Today, service provides most of IBM's income. Companies that have not stressed customer support, such as Microsoft, are enhancing their capabilities in this area. In many cases there is a charge associated with receiving support, such as a one-time call fee or a service agreement. Service and support not only can generate additional revenue but, more important, also can bring the company closer to the customer and provide it with insight on how to improve its offerings, tailor support, and find the next idea to add value to its products and services.

An important value-added service is information access. Allowing customers access to their own data—such as pending orders, payment history, and typical orders—enhances their experience with the company. For example, it is well known that customers value the ability to know the status of an order, sometimes even more than the actual turnaround time. This capability provides reliability and enables planning. Federal Express pioneered the package tracking systems that are now standard in this industry. As we will see below, this not only enhances service but also can result in large savings for the provider of the information by handing over to its customers some of the data entry and inquiry functions.

The ability of customers to access information is becoming an essential requirement in supply chain management because visibility of information is what an increasing number of customers expect. The Internet enables these capabilities, and companies will need to invest in information systems that support it. In Chapter 10 we consider these issues in more detail.

8.2.5 Relationships and Experiences

The final level of customer value is an increased connection between the firm and its customers through development of a relationship. This makes it more difficult for customers to switch to another provider because a relationship requires an investment of time from both the customer and the provider. For example, Dell configures PCs and supports them for large customers. When Dell manages the entire PC purchase for a large customer, including special custom features, it becomes more difficult for the customer to switch to another vendor.

The learning relationship, where companies build specific user profiles and use this information to enhance sales as well as retain customers,[9] is another example of a relationship providing customer value. Companies such as Individual, Inc., which builds tailored information services, and USAA, which uses its databases to offer customers other services and products, are examples of this kind of organization.

EXAMPLE 8-8

Founded in 1989 by brothers Andrew and Thomas Parkinson, Peapod, Inc., has grown to be one of America's leading Internet grocers. Peapod is a wholly owned subsidiary of international food provider Royal Ahold and works in partnership with Ahold USA supermarket companies, including Stop & Shop and Giant Food. The company, which operates in Boston, southern Connecticut, Washington, Chicago, and Long Island, New York, serves over 103,000 members. Shoppers browse through Peapod's offerings on its Internet site through a personalized interface based on their location. Peapod's computers are linked directly to the databases of the supermarkets from which it purchases the groceries. The shoppers can create their own virtual supermarket by accessing the information according to category and creating customized shopping lists that can be saved for repeated use. At the end of each shopping session, Peapod has the opportunity to learn about its service by asking, "How did we do on the last order?" and using the relatively high response rate of its customers (35 percent) to institute requested changes to its services.[9]

The approach used by Peapod, Inc. is an example of the *one-to-one enterprise* concept suggested by Don Peppers and Martha Rogers.[10] Companies learn about each customer through databases and interactive communications and sell to one customer as many products and services as possible throughout the lifetime of the customer's patronage. Indeed, Peapod is using its databases to suggest new offerings to customers, tracking the customer's preferences and needs, and further tailoring the company's offering to the customer.

The learning process can take time, but this will make it difficult for competitors to emulate the strategy. In addition, it typically ensures that a customer who considers switching to another provider will have to take into account the investment in time and money required to make the switch.

Indeed, some Internet sites, such as Amazon.com, are applying new modes of learning, with suggestions to customers based on their own previous purchases or those of customers who make similar purchases. Of course, one issue with an Internet service that provides customer reviews and suggestions is that a customer can distinguish between a Web site where he or she purchases the product and the Web site on which he or she receives information about the product. That is, it is not clear that a service offering in which a Web site provides suggestion tools and customer reviews may convince the consumer to purchase the product at that site. The consumer may well receive information from one site and make the purchase on another.[7]

A different approach, tailored toward large customers and designed to make it difficult to switch to another vendor, was introduced by Dell. It offers large corporations custom PC configurations loaded with specific software, tags, and other special requirements. Dell also has tailored its Web site so that different types of users can access it according to their needs. In many ways this approach is a more extensive application of mass customization, which we discussed in Chapter 7.

Beyond relationships, some companies are also designing, promoting, and selling unique experiences to their customers, which, according to Pine and Gilmore,[11] is a way to differentiate and thrive in a customer-driven economy. These authors define *experience* as an offering distinct from customer service: "An experience occurs when a company intentionally uses services as the stage, and goods as props, to engage individual customers in a way that creates memorable events."[11] Examples include airline frequent flyer programs, theme parks, Saturn owner gatherings, and Lexus weekend brunch with car wash events.

EXAMPLE 8-9

Silicon Graphics opened the Visionarium Reality Center in June 1996. The Visionarium was a virtual reality center intended for use as a sales and marketing tool. The idea was that designers who develop products using Silicon Graphics technology can simulate the experience achieved with new products. The virtual reality center was used for the

(continued)

design of automobiles, airplanes, and architecture. It allowed the developers, or potential customers, to view, hear, touch, and even drive, walk, or fly various prototype product configurations. This enabled customers to know what their products would look, feel, and sound like before manufacturing.[11]

The Internet provides other opportunities for creating experiences that have not yet been fully explored. One of the strengths of the Internet is the creation of collaborative communities that can be used to develop relationships between people with similar interests or desire to collaborate. One such technology is eRoom, which is a virtual workspace in which multiple parties can view and work with almost any form of unstructured data, such as drawings and presentations that are far too big for e-mail. These can be placed in an eRoom and discussed and walked through with clients or prospects via teleconference and Web demo. In addition, participants can trade comments within eRoom with no phone contact at all. Since the room is always there, it works for everyone's schedule. Companies use the same technology to create "communities of interest," some of which involve only their own employees and others a mix of internal staff and outside partners.[12]

As with the initial introduction of services, companies do not yet charge for experiences. Before a company can charge for this offering, experiences must be seen by the customer as worth the price. This requires a large investment in making the experience valuable in itself. Disney's theme parks are the prime example of a successful experience that many are willing to pay for. The parks also can be viewed as a means of selling Disney's products—movies and various spin-off toys and accessories.

The ability to provide sophisticated customer interactions (e.g., relationships and experiences) is very different from the ability to manufacture and distribute products. Patricia Seybold, in *The Customer Revolution*,[4] states that thriving when a customer is in control requires that businesses transform into completely customercentric entities. She outlines eight steps to delivering a great total customer experience:

1. Create a compelling brand personality—a distinct offering that customers can identify with.
2. Deliver a seamless experience across channels and touch points. In other words, make sure that customers' experience

and information are the same no matter what access method they choose to use at a certain point.

3. Care about customers and their outcomes.
4. Measure what matters to customers: the quality of the customer's experience as opposed to internal company measures.
5. Hone operational excellence.
6. Value customers' time.
7. Place customers' information requirements and needs at the core. This requires the ability to be proactive, e.g., reminding customers of maintenance requirements and training opportunities.
8. Design to morph—the ability to change practices based on customer requirements.

Supply chain performance is critical in most of these points. It can play a role in the branding as well as the seamless experience and operational excellence required to deliver leading customer experience.

8.2.6 Dimensions and Achieving Excellence

Our analysis of customer value dimensions clearly shows that companies need to select their customer value goals because the supply chain, market segmentation, and skill sets required to succeed depend on this choice. In *The Myth of Excellence*,[3] the authors analyze many companies along the lines of how they rank on price, product, service, access, and relationship. Their conclusion is that companies cannot excel along all these dimensions (thus the name of the book). They show that in order to succeed, a company needs to be dominating in one attribute, differentiate itself on another, and be adequate in all the rest. Some of their examples:

1. Wal-Mart stands out on price, as in its motto "Always low prices, Always," and secondarily in large brand selection.
2. Target competes by emphasizing brand selection before price.
3. Nike Stores emphasize experience first and product second.
4. McDonald's provides access first (they have stores almost everywhere) and service second.

5. American Express emphasizes service first and access as a second attribute.

8.3 STRATEGIC PRICING

We have mentioned the tight connection between pricing and supply chain strategy. In this section we explore some more sophisticated pricing issues that could influence supply chain strategy. No company underscores the impact of the Internet on product pricing strategies more than Dell Computers. The exact same product is sold at different prices on Dell's Web site depending on whether the purchase is made by a private consumer; a small, medium-sized, or large business; the federal government; or an education or health care provider. A more careful review of Dell's strategy[13] suggests that even the price of the same product for the same industry is not fixed; it may change significantly over time.

Dell is not alone in its use of a sophisticated pricing strategy. Consider the following:

- IBM and Compaq say that they have begun investigating software that will allow them to adjust their prices according to demand for certain machines.[14]
- The Nikon Coolpix Digital Camera is sold either online or in stores for about $600. The manufacturer provides a rebate of $100 independently of where the camera is purchased.
- The Sharp VL-WD255U Digital Camcorder is sold for about $500 at retail or virtual stores. Sharp provides a rebate to the customer of $100 independently of where the product was purchased.
- Boise Cascade Office Products sells many products online. Boise Cascade states that prices for the 12,000 items ordered most frequently online might change as often as daily.[15]

Thus the question is, What are these companies doing? Why does Dell charge a different price for different consumers? If Dell can do it, why not other companies? What is the impact of the mail-in rebate? In fact, shouldn't Nikon and Sharp just reduce the wholesale price paid by the retailers instead of asking the consumer to mail in the coupon? More important, if rebates work, shouldn't the retailer give the rebate to the consumer? And finally, what is wrong with a traditional fixed-price policy?

A careful review of these companies suggests that they have one thing in common: They are trying to boost profit by using revenue management techniques, techniques that have been applied very successfully in the airline, hotel, and rental car industries. In the airline industry, revenue management increased revenue significantly; American Airlines estimates that revenue management provides incremental revenue of $1 billion annually.[16] In fact, if it were not for the combined contributions of revenue management and airline schedule planning systems, American Airlines would have been profitable only one year in the last decade.[17]

In the next subsection we review the fundamentals of revenue management, and in the following subsection we identify effective pricing strategies and their impact on supply chain performance.

8.3.1 Revenue Management

Revenue management techniques have received significant attention in recent years from companies trying to improve profitability. These methods, which integrate pricing and inventory strategies to influence market demand, provide controls for companies to improve the bottom line. Revenue management has been described as "selling the right inventory unit to the right type of customer, at the right time, and for the right price."[18]

As observed earlier, revenue management techniques traditionally have been applied in the airline, hotel, and rental car industries. A number of characteristics are common to all these applications. These include[18] (1) the existence of perishable products, i.e., products that expire or are irrelevant after a certain date, (2) fixed capacity of the system, and (3) segmentation of the market based, for instance, on sensitivity to price or service time.

To understand revenue management, we proceed with the following example.

EXAMPLE 8-10

Consider an exclusive resort with 400 identical rooms. Management is focusing on pricing rooms for the next 5-day holiday. The goal is to price rooms so as to maximize revenue. Based on past experience, management estimates the relationship between demand D and price p by the linear function

$$D = 1000 - 0.5\,p$$

(continued)

This implies that when the price is $1600, there is demand for 200 rooms, whereas if the price is $1200, there is demand for 400 rooms. Notice that revenue equals price times demand at that price. Thus, when rooms for the holiday season are priced at a level of $1200, revenue equals

$$1200 \times 400 = 480,000$$

Figure 8-1 depicts the demand-price curve, where the shaded area represents total revenue. Since supply is 400 rooms, at first glance it seems that this is the best pricing strategy. However, observe that according to the demand-price curve, the resort charges many customers who are willing to pay a higher price only $1200. In fact, there are about 200 customers among the 400 who are willing to pay $1600 per room. Of these 200 customers, there are about 100 who are willing to pay $1800. All these customers are charged the same price, $1200.

This simple analysis illustrates that by charging a single price, management is leaving a large amount of money on the table. In fact, the amount of money left on the table is represented by the upper triangle in Figure 8-1, and it is equal to

$$(2000 - 1200) \times 400/2$$

The question therefore is, How can management increase revenue by taking advantage of the amount of money left on the table?

For this purpose, consider a more sophisticated pricing strategy in which the hotel introduces a *differential* or *customized* pricing strategy. In differential pricing, the firm tailors its pricing to different market segments: those who can pay the higher price and those who are willing to pay only the lower price. For instance, consider a two-price strategy in which the hotel introduces two fare classes, $1600 and $1200. Observe that at a price of $1600 there is demand for 200 rooms, whereas at a price of $1200 there is demand for 400 rooms, out of which 200 customers pay the higher price. Thus total revenue in this case is

$$1600 \times 200 + 1200 \times (400 - 200) = 560,000$$

Hence, using this strategy, the hotel was able to increase its revenue by $80,000 by capturing 50 percent of the money left on the table.

Can the hotel increase revenue even more? Observe that a three-tier pricing strategy can do even better. Indeed, consider a strategy in which the hotel introduces three classes of fare: $1800, $1600, and $1200. At a price of $1800, there is demand for 100 rooms. At a price of $1600, there is demand for 200 rooms, out of which 100 customers pay the higher price. Finally, at a price of $1200, there is demand for 400 rooms, out of which 200 customers pay higher prices. Thus total revenue equals

$$1800 \times 100 + 1600 \times (200 - 100) + 1200 \times (400 - 200) = 580,000$$

an increase of $20,000 relative to the two-tier strategy.

This example illustrates the opportunities and challenges of revenue management. By increasing the number of price fares, the firm can increase total revenue and, in fact, can capture the entire amount left on the table. Of course, the main challenge is ensuring that those who can pay the higher price do not pay a lower one. This is achieved by building fences between the various classes of customers, fences that make it difficult for customers in one class to switch and pay the lower price.

To illustrate this, consider the airline industry.[19] Airline passengers can be classified into two segments: leisure and business travelers. Leisure customers are highly sensitive to price but not that sensitive to the duration of the trip. On the other hand, business travelers are highly sensitive to the duration of the trip but not that sensitive to price. Similarly, business travelers need high flexibility so that they can adjust their travel plans as needed, whereas leisure travelers typically do not need that level of flexibility. This suggests the framework developed by Duadel and Vialle,[19] which we introduce in Table 8-1.

Thus the airlines build fences to prevent business travelers from moving from the top-left box to the bottom-right box. This is done by requiring weekend stays and early booking. Of course, the more fare

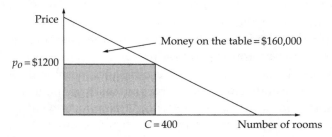

Figure 8-1 Revenue-sharing contract.

Table 8-1   Market Segmentation in the Airline Industry

		Sensitivity to price	
		Low	*High*
Sensitivity to duration; **need for flexibility**	*High*	Business travelers	No offer
	Low	No demand	Leisure travelers

classes, the more fences need to be built between the different market segments.

8.3.2   Smart Pricing

The pricing strategies applied by Dell, Nikon, Sharp, and Boise Cascade Office Products have one thing in common. These companies use price as a tool to influence customer demand, and hence they apply the principles of revenue management techniques to their respective industries. Two different but complementary approaches are used.

Customized Pricing In customized pricing, the objective is to distinguish between customers according to their price sensitivity. Dell does this by distinguishing between private consumers, small or large businesses, government agencies, and health care providers. Sharp and Nikon use mail-in rebates to differentiate between customers based on their sensitivity to price. This is done by adding a significant hurdle to the buying process; to receive the rebate, you have to complete and mail the coupon to the manufacturer. The assumption is that customers willing to pay the higher price will not necessarily send the coupon. Of course, the problem with this assumption is that unlike traditional revenue management techniques, mail-in rebates do not incorporate fences that will prevent customers willing and able to pay the higher price from sending their coupon back and claiming the discount. Thus mail-in rebates require a more detailed analysis.

- With no rebate, each retailer decides on the price and the amount to order from the manufacturer so as to maximize its profit. The retailer tradeoffs are clear: the higher the price, the smaller the demand. Thus the retailer needs to find a price and an order quantity so as to maximize its expected profit. The manufacturer, on the other hand, would like the retailer to order as much as possible. Its profit is proportional to the wholesale price, not to the price paid by the customers.

- With mail-in rebates, the manufacturer influences customer demand and provides an upside incentive to the retailer to increase its order quantity. Indeed, by introducing the rebate, the effective price paid by (some of) the customers to the retailer is reduced, and hence the retailer faces a higher demand level. Thus the retailer's profit increases. Of course, the increase in demand forces the retailer to order more from the manufacturer. By selecting the rebate appropriately, this increase in order quantity more than compensates for the rebate, and hence it implies an increase in the manufacturer's expected profit.

- From the manufacturer's point of view, the question, of course, is, Why not discount the wholesale price? Various answers may be given. First, the rebate strategy has the advantage that not every consumer will mail the coupon to the manufacturer. Second, if the manufacturer merely reduces the wholesale price, the retailer may keep the discount and not transfer it to the customers. Finally, and most important, even if the retailer uses the discounted wholesale price to optimize its pricing and ordering decisions, and even if every consumer mails back the rebate, the mail-in rebate strategy is a better strategy for the manufacturer. That is, it increases the manufacturer's profit more than a discounted wholesale price. To understand this issue, suppose that the retailer orders the same amount in both strategies, i.e., in the mail-in rebate strategy and in the discounted wholesale price strategy. Consider two situations: one in which the order quantity is smaller than realized demand and another in which the order quantity is larger than realized demand. If the order quantity is smaller than realized demand, the two strategies provide the manufacturer with exactly the same profit. On the other hand, if the order quantity is larger than demand, the manufacturer's profit with rebate is larger than its profit under discounted wholesale price.

Dynamic Pricing Dynamic pricing, or changing prices over time without necessarily distinguishing between different types of customers, has been employed for ages but traditionally has been used only for sales or promotions. For example, fashion clothing retailers may offer discounts later in the season to reduce inventory, and this discount is the same for all customers at a given time. The current wave of smart pricing applies this strategy to the manufacturing environment by using price as a tool to better match demand and supply. This, of course, requires executives in the front end of the supply chain, i.e., those who make pricing decisions, to have complete visibility into the back end of the supply chain—to suppliers' inventory—as well as into their own production schedule.

The key challenge when considering dynamic pricing strategies is to identify conditions under which this strategy provides significant profit benefit over (the best) fixed-price strategy:

- *Available capacity.* Assuming that everything else is equal, the smaller the production capacity relative to average demand, the larger is the benefit from dynamic pricing.[21]
- *Demand variability.* The benefit of dynamic pricing increases as the degree of demand uncertainty, measured by the coefficient of variation, increases.[20]
- *Seasonality in demand pattern.* The benefit of dynamic pricing increases as the level of demand seasonality increases.[20,21]
- *Length of the planning horizon.* The longer the planning horizon, the smaller is the benefit from dynamic pricing.[20]

All in all, research[20,21] indicates that depending on the data and the model assumptions, dynamic pricing may increase profit by 2 to 6 percent. This increase in profit due to dynamic pricing is very significant for industries with low profit margins, e.g., retail and computer industries.

The Internet has made these developments possible:

1. *Menu cost*, the cost that retailers incur when changing the posted price,[7] is much lower on the Internet than in the offline world. This allows online sellers such as Dell and

Boise Cascade Office Products to update their prices on a daily basis.

2. *Lower buyer search price*, which is the cost that buyers incur when looking for a product, forces competition between sellers[7,22] and hence leads to a focus on smart pricing strategies.

3. *Visibility* to the back end of the supply chain, such as that provided to Dell by its private e-marketplace (see Chap. 7), makes it possible to coordinate pricing, inventory, and production decisions.

4. *Customer segmentation* using buyers' historical data is possible on the Internet and very difficult in conventional stores.[23]

5. *Testing* capability—because of its low menu cost, the Internet can be used to test pricing strategies in real time. As suggested by Baker, Marn, and Zawada,[23] an online seller may test a higher price on a small group of the site visitors and use those data to determine a pricing strategy.

A word of caution is in order. Recent experiments by a number of companies reveal that anyone who considers using smart pricing strategies must avoid the appearance of unfair treatment of their customers.

- Amazon.com experimented with a pricing strategy in which customers were paying different amounts for the same DVD based on demographics or even the browser they used.

  "Amazon was trying to figure out how much their loyal customers would pay," said Barrett Ladd, a retail analyst with Gomez Advisors. "And the customers found out." A number of DVDTalk.com visitors were particularly distressed to find that prices seemed to be higher for the best customers. "They must figure that with repeat Amazon customers they have 'won' them over and they can charge them slightly higher prices since they are loyal and don't mind and/or don't notice that they are being charged 3 percent to 5 percent more for some items," wrote a user whose online handle is Deep Sleep.[24]

  Customers responded negatively to the strategy, and Amazon.com stopped the pricing tests.

- Doug Ivester, the former chairman of Coca-Cola Co., had considered a dynamic pricing strategy in which price would vary by season. Rumors have it that Ivester left Coca-Cola in part due to customer dissatisfaction over the pricing strategy.

- Online sites such as Priceline and San Francisco–based Hotwire.com provide an outlet for last-minute, unsold seats and hotel rooms through what are called *opaque fares*. This means that travel providers can cut their losses by offering unsold tickets and rooms at deep discounts without identifying which airline or hotel, for example, is selling the ticket or room. This "protects" the published fares promoted by the airlines and hotels themselves. Opaque fares are like the store-brand merchandise in grocery stores that sells for much less than the same goods with a brand name attached. However, opaque fares are supposed to be ancillary sources of income, and finding the right balance can be tricky. In an unstable economy, when many published fares are about as good as the opaque fares, it is harder to attract customers to the Priceline and Hotwire sites.[25]

8.4 CUSTOMER VALUE MEASURES

Because customer value is based on customer perceptions, it requires measures that start with the customer. Typical measures include service level and customer satisfaction. Patricia Seybold[4] goes a step further and suggests managing companies by additional customer value measures such as growth in number of active customers, customer retention, defections, referrals, acquisition costs, and share of customer's spending.

Our objective in this section is to introduce various basic measures of customer value, as well as supply chain performance measures. The latter are important because supply chain performance is an important contributor to customer value.

1. *Service level.* Service level is the typical measure used to quantify a company's market conformance. In practice, the definition of service level can vary from company to company, but *service level* is usually related to the ability to satisfy a customer's delivery date, e.g., the percentage of all orders sent on or before the promised delivery date. Many companies consider this measure so critical to their ability to succeed in today's markets that they invest heavily in decision-support systems that allow them to quote delivery dates accurately by analyzing information from the entire supply chain.

There is a direct relationship between the ability to achieve a certain level of service and supply chain cost and performance. For instance, demand variability and manufacturing and information lead times determine the amount of inventory that needs to be kept in the supply chain. Clearly, when setting the level of service that should be used for a particular offering, it is important to understand customer value. For instance, customers may value low cost, information about the delivery date, and the ability to customize the product more than they value immediate delivery itself. This is definitely the case for PC buyers, where Dell's direct business model, with the additional time it takes to build and deliver the PC, seems to be winning over off-the-shelf store purchases.

2. *Customer satisfaction.* Customer satisfaction surveys are used to measure sales department and personnel performance as well as to provide feedback for necessary improvements in products and services. In addition, as in the Peapod example, there are other innovative ways to receive information about customer satisfaction. However, customer surveys may not be the best way to learn about customer value. As Reichheld[26] points out, relying on customer satisfaction surveys often can be misleading. These surveys are easy to manipulate and typically are measured at the selling point, while nothing is said about retaining the customer.

Indeed, more important than what customers say about their satisfaction is *customer loyalty*, which is easier to measure than customer satisfaction. This can be accomplished by analyzing customer repurchase patterns based on internal databases.

E X A M P L E   8-11

Lexus is a consistent winner of automobile satisfaction awards, but it refuses to consider surveys as the best measure of satisfaction. To Lexus, the only meaningful measure of satisfaction is repurchase loyalty. Lexus considers the repurchase activities of cars and services as the only measure for its dealers' success. Each Lexus dealership has a satellite dish that keeps information flowing back and forth to headquarters, where these measures are tracked constantly.[26]

An additional option is to learn from customer defections. Unfortunately, identifying such customers is not an easy task because dissatisfied customers seldom cancel an account completely. Instead, they gradually shift their spending, making a partial defection. However, if this type of tracking is possible, it may provide the key to increasing customer value.

Another example is Charles Schwab.[4] The online broker tracks customer asset accumulation, customer satisfaction, customer retention, and employee retention. These are the measures on which managers and employees receive incentives.

3. *Supply chain performance measures.* As we have seen, supply chain performance affects the ability to provide customer value, especially in the most basic dimension of availability of products. Therefore, there is a need to develop independent criteria to measure supply chain performance. The need for well-defined measures in the supply chain stems from the presence of many partners in the process and the requirement of a common language. This is precisely the motivation behind standardization initiatives such as the Supply Chain Council's Supply Chain Operations Reference (SCOR) Model.

The SCOR Model uses a *process reference model* that includes analyzing the current state of a company's processes and its goals, quantifying operational performance and comparing it with benchmark data. For this purpose, the Supply Chain Council has developed a set of metrics for supply chain performance; its members are in the process of forming industry groups to collect best-practice information that companies can use to evaluate their supply chain performance. Table 8-2 lists examples of metrics used to evaluate supply chain performance in the SCOR Model.[27]

Once a specific company's metrics are calculated, they are compared with those of industry benchmarks such as average and best in class. This enables identifying the company's advantages as well as opportunities for supply chain improvement.

Examples of these metrics are reported in the "Overall Business Performance" survey conducted by Pittiglio, Rabin, Todd & McGrath (PRTM):[28]

- *Total supply chain management cost.* This includes the total cost to manage order processing, acquire materials, manage inventory, and manage supply chain finance and information systems. The survey found that leading companies have total costs between 4 and 5 percent of sales. Median performers spend 5 to 6 percent more.

Table 8-2   SCOR Level 1 Metrics

Perspectives	Metrics	Measure
Supply chain reliability	On-time delivery Order fulfillment lead time Fill rate Perfect order fulfillment	Percentage Days Percentage Percentage
Flexibility and responsiveness	Supply chain response time Upside production flexibility	Days Days
Expenses	Supply chain management cost Warranty cost as percentage of revenue Value added per employee	Percentage Percentage Dollars
Assets/utilization	Total inventory days of supply Cash-to-cash cycle time Net asset turns	Days Days Turns

- *Cash-to-cash cycle time.* The number of days between paying for raw materials and getting paid for product, as calculated by inventory days of supply plus days of sales outstanding minus average payment period for material. The survey shows that best in class have less than 30 days of cycle time, whereas median performers can have up to 100 days.
- *Upside production flexibility.* The number of days required to achieve an unplanned, sustainable 20 percent increase in production. This measure is now under 2 weeks for best in class and even less than a week for some industries. The main constraint is material availability and not internal manufacturing or labor constraints.
- *Delivery performance to request.* The percentage of orders that are fulfilled on or before the customer's requested date. The survey indicated that best-in-class performance is at least 94 percent and in some industries approaches 100 percent. The median performance ranges from 69 to 81 percent.

The SCOR Model is a good example of a set of supply chain metrics and is an effective way to compare performance with that of other companies in the same industry or in others. It has the additional advantage of possibly becoming an industry standard. However, every company needs to understand its own unique environment and determine its measures based on this insight. For instance, Dell measures inventory velocity and not the more standard inventory turns (see Ex. 8-13).

8.5 INFORMATION TECHNOLOGY AND CUSTOMER VALUE

Information technology has produced many valuable benefits for customers and businesses. We will briefly review three aspects below. The first is exchange of information between customers and businesses, the second is the use of information by companies to learn more about their customers so that they can better tailor their services, and the third is enhanced business-to-business (B2B) capabilities.

  1. *Customer benefits.* Customer service has changed for many reasons. One of the most dramatic is the opening of corporate, government, and educational databases to the customer. This started with kiosks and voice mail and has accelerated significantly with the uniform data access tools of the Internet. These innovations have had the effect of increasing customer value while reducing costs for the supplier of the information. Banks were the first to realize that by installing automated teller machines (ATMs), they could reduce their workforce. Voice mail was at first derided as dehumanizing, preventing interactions with a live person, but it actually allowed unmediated access to a user's accounts at any time of the day from almost anywhere. The Internet has expanded these capabilities and allows users to access their accounts and perform transactions from any location at any time. This opening of the information boundaries between customer and company is part of the new customer value equation, where the information is part of the product.

  The Internet has also had some less obvious effects[29]:

  - *Increased importance of intangibles.* Customers have become accustomed to ordering even high-priced products from unseen salespeople over the phone or Internet. This increases the importance of brand names and other intangibles, such as service capabilities or community experience in purchasing decisions.

- *Increased ability to connect and disconnect.* The Internet makes it easier not only to identify business partners and connect to them but also to disconnect and find new partners. Increasing availability of information, including performance measures and data, reduces the need to develop long-term trust relationships. Companies can rely on accessible, published track records to make decisions on quality of service. This ability is mainly important when there is not a considerable initial investment in setting up the partnership. If there is, then frequent changes of partners may have a major impact on cost and available resources.

- *Increased customer expectations.* The ability to compare and the ease of performing various transactions over the phone and the Internet have raised expectations of similar services from every type of business as well as for B2B interactions.

- *Tailored experience.* The ability to provide each customer with an individual experience is an important part of the Internet. Amazon.com saves the customer's information and recommends books and other items based on previous purchases. Mass customization can allow users to store their individual preferences or sizes and order custom-fit clothes and shoes from various vendors without having to reenter the information.

2. *Business benefits.* One way to enhance customer value is to use the information captured in the supply chain to create new offerings for customers. The information now available allows companies to "sense and respond" to customers' desires rather than simply to make and sell products and services. Indeed, as we have seen, learning about customers takes time, requires some of the customers' time, and eventually makes switching vendors more difficult. The learning process takes many forms from sophisticated data mining methods used to correlate purchasing patterns to learning about each individual customer by keeping detailed data of preferences and purchases. The method applied depends on the industry and business model. Retailers would use the first method, whereas service companies, as in the following example, would be more likely to track individual customer preferences and requirements.

E X A M P L E   8-12

In the 1930s it was difficult for military personnel to obtain reasonably priced insurance, so a group of officers formed United Services Automobile Association (USAA) to provide insurance for military officers. USAA still offers services only to active and former military officers and their families and handles all transactions by mail and phone. USAA has used its extensive databases to expand into financial and shopping services for its members. When a customer calls USAA, the information about him or her can be accessed and updated, and the customer can be offered a variety of services to match his or her needs. For instance, if a customer owns a boat purchased or financed through USAA, he or she could receive an offer to acquire insurance.[8]

3. *Business-to-business benefits.* The Dell Computer example 8-13 illustrates how information technology allows companies to improve the performance of their suppliers and service providers. More recently, with the establishment of its private e-marketplace (see Chap. 6), Dell is using the Internet to improve supply chain collaboration by providing demand information and production data to its suppliers. Thus these developments make it possible to outsource important parts of a company's business but still keep close control over what it produces or services. For instance, strategic partnering relies heavily on information sharing and enables the partners to achieve supply chain efficiencies (see Chap. 5).

Narus and Anderson[30] describe various arrangements between manufacturers such as Volvo, GM and Okuma America and their distributors for sharing information on inventory that results in cost reduction. These arrangements, motivated by the risk-pooling concept introduced in Chapter 4, allow manufacturers and distributors to reduce overall inventory by sharing information about inventory in all locations and allowing any member of the channel to share the inventory.

E X A M P L E   8-13

Michael Dell started a computer business in his dormitory room in 1984 with this simple insight: He could bypass the dealer channel through which PCs were being sold and instead sell directly to customers and build their PCs to order. This idea, now called the *direct business model*, eliminated the cost of inventory and the reselling expenses. The model had other benefits that were not apparent when Dell founded his company, Dell Computer Corporation. "You actually get to have a relationship with the customer," Michael Dell explains, "and this creates valuable information which, in turn, allows us to leverage our relationships with both suppliers and customers. Couple that information with technology, and you have the infrastructure to revolutionize the fundamental business models of major global companies."

Dell Computer's model involves building computers based on components that are available in the market. The decision not to manufacture the computer components has relieved Dell of the burden of owning assets, research and development risks, and managing a large number of employees. Spreading the development and manufacturing risk among several suppliers allowed Dell to grow much faster than if these functions were performed inside the company.

Dell's use of technology and information to blur the traditional boundaries in the supply chain between suppliers, manufacturers, and end users has been named *virtual integration*. In a traditional computer company, such as Digital Computer, processes were *vertically integrated*, with all the research, development, manufacturing, and distribution capabilities in-house. This allowed for a high level of communication and ability to develop products based on the company's interaction with its clients. The disadvantage was the high risk and costs of development and the ownership of assets in a volatile industry. To achieve the advantages of an integrated company, Dell treats suppliers and service providers as if they were inside the company. Their systems are linked in real time to Dell's system, and their employees participate in design teams and product launches. Technology enhances the economic incentives to collaborate because it makes it possible to share design databases and methodologies and speed the time to market.

Dell measures *inventory velocity*, the reciprocal of the average amount of time a product spends in inventory. For this purpose, each component is marked with a date stamp. Accumulating inventory in the fast-moving PC industry is a high-risk proposition because the components can become obsolete very quickly. In some cases, such as Sony monitors, Dell does not keep any inventory but has UPS or Airborne Express pick up the monitors from Sony's Mexican factory, the computer from Dell's Austin, Texas, facility, and then match and deliver them to the customers. Dell suppliers benefit from the real-time information about demand and a commitment from Dell for a certain level of pur-

(*continued*)

chases. The results are impressive. While Compaq, IBM, and Hewlett-Packard all announced plans in late 1998 to emulate portions of Dell's business model, with various build-to-order plans, all have had difficulty in making the transition. Most are moving to a target inventory level of 4 weeks, whereas Dell maintains just 8 days of inventory, allowing it to turn over inventory 46 times a year.

On the customer side, Dell has segmented its customer base so that it can offer value-added services to different customers. Dell configures PCs and supports them for large customers. It also will load standard software and place asset stickers on the machines based on customer requests. For some clients, Dell has an on-site team that assists in PC purchasing and servicing. "The whole idea behind virtual integration is that it lets you meet customers' needs faster and more efficiently than any other model." Furthermore, it allows Dell to be efficient and responsive to change at the same time. By spending time with customers and following technological trends, Dell tries to be a few steps ahead of the change and even create and shape it.[31]

8.6 SUMMARY

Creating customer value is the driving force behind a company's goals, and supply chain management is one of the means of achieving customer value. The Dell example illustrates many of the concepts in this chapter. Supply chain management strategy affects customer value; its considerations affect every aspect of customer value and must be part of any strategy or plan, not an afterthought. It is important to choose the appropriate supply chain strategy to match customer value with the company's market. Excellence in supply chain management translates into customer value in many dimensions, from availability and selection to influencing the price at which a product can be sold.

The supply chain strategy in the Dell example was the business model, and it created the customer value of low prices. Customer access to information about the availability of products and the status of orders and deliveries is becoming an essential capability. This also creates opportunities to learn about customers and their preferences and to create new modes of interaction. Dell uses this information to enhance its services.

Adding services, relationships, and experiences is a way for companies to differentiate their offerings in the market and learn about their customers. It also makes it difficult for the customers to switch to another service provider. Dell has added excellent customer support to its capabilities. Larger companies find that it provides more extensive options, from custom preloaded PCs to in-house service and support.

Measuring customer value is at the heart of company goals and objectives, but identifying the appropriate measure is not an easy task. Dell measures inventory velocity, the reciprocal of the average amount of time a product spends in inventory, and not the traditional inventory turns.

The ability to provide sophisticated customer interactions (e.g., relationships and experiences) is very different from the ability to manufacture and distribute products. Because a distinctive expertise is required for each function, companies will gain by specializing. This concept has been applied successfully by Dell through virtual integration. Dell has relationships with many of the suppliers that provide the components of its product.

We also observe this trend in consumer product industries, where firms such as Nike and Sara Lee lend their name to products produced by many manufacturing companies.

A virtually integrated company can lose some of its ability to innovate and collaborate if it does not pay close attention to its relationships with suppliers. This is also true for other third-party providers performing tasks for the company. Communication systems, methods of sharing information and resources, and proper incentives need to be in place to make these relationships work. Dell, a company built on outsourcing, has been working on this type of collaboration for many years. It has practices in place to make sure that the quality of work performed by its partners meets its own standards.

There is no real customer value without a close relationship with customers. Today this is possible not only through direct interaction but also through information and communications technology. By allowing customers to state their preferences and learning from them—a true two-way interaction—a firm can develop the means to achieve greater customer value and therefore loyalty. Dell has inadvertently been able to achieve this because of its direct supply chain model. The company has taken full advantage of its close relationships with its customers to become the largest PC seller in the world.

CHAPTER 9

Global Issues in Supply Chain Management

9.1 INTRODUCTION

It is readily apparent that global operations and supply chains are becoming increasingly significant. Philippe-Pierre Dornier and colleagues[1] collected the following statistics, which help to indicate the magnitude of this trend:

- About one-fifth of the output of U.S. firms is produced overseas.
- One-quarter of U.S. imports are between foreign affiliates and U.S. parent companies.
- Since the late 1980s, over half of U.S. companies increased the number of countries in which they operate.

In many ways international supply chain management is the same as domestic supply chain management spread over a larger geographic area. However, as we will discuss in this chapter, international supply chain networks can provide a wealth of additional opportunities if they are managed effectively. At the same time, there are many additional potential problems and pitfalls of which to be aware.

International supply chains can run the gamut from a primarily domestic business with some international suppliers to a truly integrated global supply chain. Some of the advantages and disadvantages that we will discuss apply equally to all the systems in the following list, whereas others apply only to the most complex integrated systems.

International distribution systems. In this type of system, manufacturing still occurs domestically, but distribution and typically some marketing take place overseas.

International suppliers. In this system, raw materials and components are furnished by foreign suppliers, but final assembly is performed domestically. In some cases the final product is then shipped to foreign markets.

Offshore manufacturing. In this type of system, the product is typically sourced and manufactured in a single foreign location and then shipped back to domestic warehouses for sale and distribution.

Fully integrated global supply chain. Here products are supplied, manufactured, and distributed from various facilities located throughout the world. In a truly global supply chain, it may appear that the supply chain was designed without regard to national boundaries. Of course, this is far from the truth! As we shall see, the true value of a global supply chain is realized by taking advantage of these national boundaries.

Clearly, a supply chain can fit more than one of these categories. Throughout the following discussion, consider how each of the issues discussed applies differently to firms depending on their position in this global supply chain spectrum.

In any event, many firms cannot help but become involved in global supply chain issues. Dornier and colleagues[1] identified the following forces that collectively drive the trend toward globalization:

- Global market forces
- Technological forces
- Global cost forces
- Political and economic forces

9.1.1 Global Market Forces

Global market forces involve the pressures created by foreign competitors, as well as the opportunities created by foreign customers. Even if companies do not do business overseas, the presence of foreign competitors in home markets can affect their business significantly. To defend domestic markets successfully, companies may find it necessary to move into foreign markets. Sometimes the threat of a presence is sufficient, as in the dry breakfast cereal business, dominated by Kellogg Co. in the United States and Nestlé in Europe. Apparently, failed attempts in the past to penetrate each other's home markets, combined with the threat of retaliation, are enough to maintain the status quo. In addition, much of the demand growth available to companies is in foreign and emerging markets. Recently, companies have made great sacrifices (particularly in terms of proprietary technology) and taken on considerable business risk to become involved in ventures in mainland China. Indeed, the United States is accounting for less and less of the total consumption of goods in the world.

One cause of this increasing demand for products throughout the world is the global proliferation of information. Television introduces products to Europeans. Japanese vacation abroad. Businesses send overnight mail between continents. More recently, the Internet provides instant international exposure, as well as the ability to purchase goods in one country that will be delivered in another without leaving home or office.

EXAMPLE 9-1

In Brazil, thousands of people move from preindustrial villages to rapidly growing cities. Once there, their first goal is to install television sets, even as they continue to "make sacrificial offerings of fruit and fresh-killed chickens to Macumban spirits by the candlelight."[2]

As Kenichi Ohmae, head of management consulting firm McKinsey's Japanese office, points out, people have "all become global citizens, and so must the companies that want to sell us things."[3] Products are universally desired, and many companies are willing to sell them globally. This is clearly a self-amplifying trend for an industry because, as companies become global, their competitors also must become global in order to compete. Thus many companies are becoming global citizens with universal products and the opportunity to hire talented employees worldwide.

Along similar lines, particular markets often serve to drive technological advances in some areas. By participating in these competitive markets, companies are forced to develop and enhance leading-edge technologies and products. These products then can be used to increase or maintain market position in other areas or regions where the markets are not as competitive. To be a leader in software, for example, you have to compete in the U.S. market. Similarly, the German machine tools market and the Japanese consumer electronics market are hotly contested.

9.1.2 Technological Forces

Technological forces are related to the products themselves. Various subcomponents and technologies are available in different regions and locations around the world, and many successful firms need to have the ability to use these resources quickly and effectively. To achieve this, it may be necessary for firms to locate research, design, and production facilities close to these regions. This is often particularly useful if suppliers are involved in the design process, as discussed in Chapter 7. The same logic applies to collaborations and interfirm development projects. To gain access to markets or technology, companies in different regions frequently collaborate, resulting in the location of joint facilities close to one of the partners.

Along similar lines, global location of research and development facilities is becoming more common primarily for two reasons. First, as product cycles become shorter and time more important, companies have discovered how useful it is to locate research facilities close to manufacturing facilities. This helps transfer technology from research facilities to manufacturing facilities and speeds up the resolution of problems that inevitably arise during this transfer. In addition, specific technical expertise may be available in certain areas or regions. For example, Microsoft recently opened a research lab in Cambridge, England, to take advantage of the expertise available in Europe.

9.1.3 Global Cost Forces

Cost forces often dictate global location decisions. In the past, the low cost of unskilled labor was a decisive factor in determining factory location. Recently, studies have found that in many cases the costs of cheaper unskilled labor were more than offset by the increase in other costs associated with operating facilities in remote locations. In some cases, of course, cheaper labor is sufficient justification for overseas manufacturing.

More recently, however, other global cost forces have become more significant. For example, cheaper *skilled labor* is drawing an increasing number of companies overseas. Many of the analyses and programs that U.S. consulting firms undertook to address the year 2000 problem (in which computer programs might fail when the year changed from 1999 to 2000) were done in India, where programming skills are much cheaper.

We have discussed how a supplier and the customer supply chain often must be tightly integrated to deliver certain products effectively. Often this can be accomplished most cost-effectively if the various participants are located close together. This may necessitate establishing integrated supply chains in different markets.

Finally, the capital costs of building a new facility often dominate labor costs. Many governments are willing to provide tax breaks or cost-sharing arrangements to lower the cost of the new facility. In addition, supplier price breaks and cost-sharing joint ventures may dictate these types of decisions.

9.1.4 Political and Economic Forces

Political and economic forces may greatly affect the drive toward globalization. In Section 9.2 we will discuss exchange-rate fluctuation and the operational approaches to dealing with this issue. There are also several other political and economic factors. For example, regional trade agreements may drive companies to expand into one of the countries in the regional group. It may be to a company's advantage to obtain raw materials from or to manufacture within European, Pacific Rim, or North American trading blocks. In some cases production processes may even be redesigned to avoid tariffs; for example, almost-finished goods may be shipped into a trading block to avoid tariffs on finished goods.

Similarly, various trade protection mechanisms can affect international supply chain decisions. Tariffs and quotas affect what can be imported and may lead a company to decide to manufacture within the market country or region. More subtle regulations, including local content requirements, affect supply chains. To address local content requirements, for example, TI and Intel, both U.S. firms, make microprocessors in Europe, and various Japanese automakers produce cars in Europe. Even voluntary export restrictions can affect the supply chain: Japanese manufacturers began to manufacture more expensive cars after agreeing voluntarily to limit exports to the United States. Recall that this is why brands such as Infiniti and Lexus came into existence.

Government procurement policies can affect the ability of international companies to be successful in various markets. In the United States, for example, the Department of Defense gives as much as a 50 percent advantage to U.S. companies in the bidding on contracts.

9.2 RISKS AND ADVANTAGES OF INTERNATIONAL SUPPLY CHAINS

We have looked at the various forces that drive companies to develop international supply chains. In this section we take a slightly different perspective by examining the various advantages and risks inherent in different types of international supply chains. Certain advantages of sourcing, manufacturing, and selling globally are immediately obvious.

Clearly, the world is converging in many instances toward standardized products. This means that more and more, vast markets have opened up for products—far greater than anything managers in the past could have imagined. By taking advantage of this trend, companies can realize vast economies of scale in terms of production, management, distribution, marketing, and so forth.[2]

Indeed, as we discussed in the preceding section, costs can be lowered with greater potential raw material, labor, and outsourcing sources and a greater number of potential manufacturing sites. At the same time, the increase in potential markets allows for an increase in sales and profits. These advantages are due to the increase in the size and scope of the supply chain—they are independent of the specific characteristics of the global supply chain.

To use these advantages, it is essential that management understand the different *demand characteristics* and *cost advantages* of different regions. We will discuss this issue in more depth in the next section. This discussion is greatly influenced by Bruce Kogut's "Designing Global Strategies: Profiting from Operational Flexibility."[4]

Most important, the global supply chain can provide a firm with the *flexibility* to address the uncertainty in international markets. In particular, this flexibility can be used to counteract the inherent risks from various factors that are particularly relevant to global companies.

9.2.1 Risks

So what are these risks? First, fluctuating exchange rates change the relative value of production and the relative profit of selling a product in a particular country. Relative costs change so that manufacturing, storing, distributing, or selling in a particular region at a particular price can change from being extremely profitable to a total loss.

The same is true domestically. In many cases certain regions within the same country may be less expensive for storage or manufacturing than others. However, the cost differences between domestic regions are not typically as dramatic as those across countries, and more important, they do not change as frequently.

It should be stressed that although managers typically think of exchange rates as affecting the dollar value of assets and liabilities denominated in foreign currencies, it is the *operating exposure* described in preceding paragraphs that can have the most dramatic effect on annual operating profit. This operating exposure reflects the fact that in the short run, changes in currency exchange rates do not necessarily reflect changes in relative inflation rates between countries. Thus, over the short term, regional operations can become relatively more or less expensive in terms of dollars. Note that this operating exposure is a function not only of a firm's global supply chain but also of its competition's global supply chain. If a competitor's relative costs decrease more, a firm can be underpriced in the market.[5]

Indeed, Philippe-Pierre Dornier and colleagues[1] identified several factors that affect the impact of operating exposure on a firm. *Customer reactions* influence how a firm adjusts prices in various markets in response to changes in operating expenses. As discussed earlier, *competitor reactions* also influence how a firm can react to changes in the relative cost of doing business. Competitors can react to price increases by raising their own prices to increase profitability or gain market share. As we discuss in the next section, *supplier reaction*—the ability of suppliers to respond with flexibility to varying demands—is a strong factor in the effectiveness of certain strategies that help firms address the risk of operating exposure. Finally, *government reactions* play a large role on the global stage. Governments can intervene to stabilize currencies or even directly support endangered firms by providing subsidies or tariffs. In addition, other political instabilities also can affect multinational companies. Tax situations can change rapidly because political factors dictate different treatment of corporations, particularly foreign corporations, in various regions.

Likewise, foreign companies can enter domestic markets. These companies may even use domestic profits to subsidize low-priced goods in foreign markets. This could even affect companies that have decided not to compete on the global stage.

9.2.2 Addressing Global Risks

Bruce Kogut[4] identified three ways a global supply chain can be employed to address global risks: speculative, hedge, and flexible strategies.

> *Speculative strategies.* Using *speculative strategies*, a company bets on a single scenario, with often spectacular results if the scenario is realized and dismal ones if it is not. For example, in the late 1970s and early 1980s, Japanese automakers bet that if they did all their manufacturing in Japan, rising labor costs would be more than offset by exchange rate benefits, rising productivity, and increased levels of investment and productivity. For a while these bets paid off, but then rising labor costs and unfavorable exchange rates began to hurt manufacturers, and it became necessary to build plants overseas. Of course, if it had remained favorable to do all the manufacturing in Japan, the Japanese manufacturers would have "won the bet" because building new facilities is time-consuming and expensive.
>
> *Hedge strategies.* Using *hedge strategies*, a company designs the supply chain in such a way that any losses in part of the supply chain will be offset by gains in another part. For example, Volkswagen operates plants in the United States, Brazil, Mexico, and Germany, all of which are important markets for Volkswagen products. Depending on macroeconomic conditions, certain plants may be more profitable at various times than others. Hedge strategies, *by design*, are simultaneously successful in some locations and unsuccessful in others.
>
> *Flexible strategies.* When employed properly, *flexible strategies* enable a company to take advantage of different scenarios. Typically, flexible supply chains are designed with multiple suppliers and excess manufacturing capacity in different

countries. In addition, factories are designed to be flexible so that products can be moved at minimal cost from region to region as economic conditions demand.

When considering the implementation of a flexible strategy, managers have to answer several questions:

1. Is there enough variability in the system to justify the use of flexible strategies? Clearly, the more variability in international conditions, the more a company can benefit from using flexible strategies.

2. Do the benefits of spreading production over various facilities justify the costs, which may include loss of economies of scale in terms of manufacturing and supply?

3. Does the company have the appropriate coordination and management mechanisms in place to take rapid advantage of flexible strategies?

If the supply chain is designed appropriately, several approaches can be used to implement flexible strategies effectively:

Production shifting. Flexible factories and excess capacity and suppliers can be used to shift production from region to region to take advantage of current circumstances. As exchange rates, labor cost, and so on change, manufacturing can be relocated.

Information sharing. Having an increased presence in many regions and markets often will increase the availability of information, which can be used to anticipate market changes and find new opportunities.

Global coordination. Having multiple facilities worldwide provides a firm with a certain amount of market leverage that it might otherwise lack. If a foreign competitor attacks one of your main markets, you can attack back. Of course, various international laws and political pressures place limits on this type of retaliation.

EXAMPLE 9-2

When Michelin began to target North American markets aggressively, Goodyear was able to drop its tire prices in Europe. This forced Michelin to slow its overseas investment program.

Political leverage. The opportunity to move operations rapidly gives firms a measure of political leverage in overseas operations. For example, if governments are lax in enforcing contracts or international law or present expensive tax alternatives, firms can move their operations. In many cases the implicit threat of movement is sufficient to prevent local politicians from taking unfavorable actions.

9.2.3 Requirements for Global Strategy Implementation

Any company, even a huge global company, is not immediately ready for integrated global supply chain management on this scale. Michael McGrath and Richard Hoole[6] discuss important developments that are necessary to set the stage for this kind of massive global integration. These developments are outlined below for each of the *five basic functions of firms:* product development, purchasing, production, demand management, and order fulfillment.

1. *Product development.* It is important to design products that can be modified easily for major markets and which can be manufactured in various facilities. As we discuss in the next section, this is not always possible, but it is certainly helpful in those cases where it is achievable. While it is dangerous to design a product to be the "average" of what several markets require, it may be possible to design a base product or products that can be adapted more easily to several different markets. An international design team may be helpful in this regard.

2. *Purchasing.* A company will find it useful to have management teams responsible for the purchase of important materials from many vendors around the world. In this way it is much easier to ensure that the quality and delivery options from various suppliers are compatible and that a qualified team is present to compare the pricing of various suppliers. Also, these teams can work to guarantee that sufficient suppliers in different regions are at hand to ensure the flexibility necessary to take full advantage of the global supply chain.

3. *Production.* As we discussed earlier, excess capacity and plants in several regions are essential if firms are to take full advantage

of the global supply chain by shifting production as conditions warrant. To use this kind of strategy, however, effective communications systems must be in place so that this global supply chain can be managed effectively. Centralized management is thus essential to this system, which implies that centralized information must be available. Indeed, knowledge of the current status of factories, supplies, and inventory is essential when making the types of decisions described earlier. In addition, since factories are typically supplying each other in a complex supply chain, it is important that interfactory communication is solid and that centralized management makes each factory aware of the system status.

4. *Demand management.* Often demand management, which involves setting marketing and sales plans based on projected demand and available product, is carried out on a regional basis. For the supply chain to be managed in an integrated way, demand management clearly has to have at least some centralized component. On the other hand, much of this sensitive, market-based information is best supplied by analysts located in each region. Thus, once again, communication is a critical component of the success of global supply chain management.

5. *Order fulfillment.* To successfully implement a truly flexible supply chain management system, a centralized system must be in place so that regional customers can receive deliveries from the global supply chain with the same efficiency as they do from local or regionally based supply chains. All the flexibility in the world is of little use if it makes the system so cumbersome and unpleasant that customers turn elsewhere. We discuss the kinds of advanced information systems that this centralized order fulfillment requires in Chapter 10.

Only when a company is sufficiently prepared to implement flexible strategies can it take advantage of all that the global supply chain has to offer.

9.3 ISSUES IN INTERNATIONAL SUPPLY CHAIN MANAGEMENT

In this section we will discuss other important issues of international supply chains that were not appropriate for the preceding sections.

9.3.1   International versus Regional Products

The preceding discussion suggests that the ideal company builds "universal products" that can be sold in many markets. In many cases, however, this is not simple. Kenichi Ohmae[3] pointed out that there are several categories of products, each of which has different "international requirements."

> *Region-specific products.* Some products have to be designed and manufactured specifically for certain regions. For example, automobile designs are often region-specific. The 1998 Honda Accord has two basic body styles: a smaller body style tailored to European and Japanese tastes and a larger body style catering to American tastes. Of course, even if regional designs are different, effective supply chain management can take advantage of common components or subassemblies within the different designs.

EXAMPLE 9-3

Nissan designates "lead country" status to each of its car models. For example, the Maxima and Pathfinder are designed for American tastes, often by American design studios. Similar designs are developed primarily for Japanese and European markets. Once regional product managers ensure that vehicles meet lead-country requirements, other regional product managers suggest slight changes that might promote local sales. But the focus is on developing cars for regions. Otherwise, Nissan fears "the trap of pleasing no one well by pleasing everyone half way." There is no effective way to average size, color, and other aesthetic and substantive differences in cars across regions without ending up with a model that no customers in that region particularly like. Of course, if models can be modified slightly to increase sales in other regions, it helps, but that isn't the primary focus.[3]

> *True global products.* These products are truly global, in the sense that no modification is necessary for global sales. For example, Coca-Cola is essentially the same throughout the world, as are Levi's jeans and McDonald's burgers. Similarly, luxury brands such as Coach and Gucci are essentially the same worldwide. It should be noted, however, that some of these brands and

products, such as Coke and McDonald's, depend on very specific regional manufacturing and bottling facilities and distribution networks, whereas others are essentially distributed and sold in the same way throughout the world.[2]

The difference between region-specific products and global products does not imply that one is inherently better than the other. However, it is important to consider carefully which of the two product types is more appropriate for a particular situation because employing strategies for regional products that are designed for global products, or vice versa, can lead to disastrous results.

9.3.2 Local Autonomy versus Central Control

Centralized control can be important in taking advantage of some of the strategies we have discussed, but in many cases it makes sense to allow local autonomy in the supply chain. Sometimes, after independent regional operations have proven to be successful, headquarters cannot resist the temptation to tamper with the system, and performance suffers.

In addition, it is important to temper expectations for regional business depending on the characteristics of the region involved. For example, companies typically experience, in the short term, relatively low returns in Japan, medium returns in Germany, and higher returns in the United States. Indeed, those companies which are successful in Japan often had settled initially for low returns.[3]

However, managers may be tempted to follow local conventional wisdom and thus miss some of the opportunities derived from the knowledge acquired in the operation of a global supply chain.

EXAMPLE 9-4

When it first introduced the decongestant Contac 600 to Japanese markets, SmithKline Corporation was advised to use the traditional approach, involving more than 1000 distributors with which the firm would have little contact. Rather than accept this advice, SmithKline used 35 wholesalers, with whom it remained in close contact. SmithKline had used this approach successfully elsewhere. Despite the naysayers, the introduction was highly successful.[2]

9.3.3 Miscellaneous Dangers

To be sure, there are many potential dangers that firms must face as they expand their supply chains globally. Exchange-rate fluctuations, discussed earlier as an opportunity, can just as easily be a risk if not managed properly. It may be harder to administer offshore facilities, especially in less-developed countries. Similarly, the promise of cheap labor may mask the threat of reduced productivity.[7] Expensive training may be required, but even then productivity may not reach domestic levels.

Often local collaboration occurs in the global supply chain. In this case, collaborators ultimately can become competitors:

- Hitachi, which used to manufacture under license from Motorola, now makes its own microprocessors.
- Toshiba, which manufactured copiers for 3M, is now a major supplier of copiers under the Toshiba brand name.
- Sunrise Plywood and Furniture of Taiwan was for many years a partner of Mission Furniture in California. Now it is one of Mission's major competitors.[7]

Similar dangers exist with foreign governments. To deal with China and gain access to that country's huge markets, many companies are handing over critical manufacturing and engineering expertise to the Chinese government or to Chinese partners. It is only a matter of time until these Chinese companies or other companies selected by the government begin to compete under favorable terms with their original partners. The only question is whether the overseas firms that gave away their technology will still be able to compete successfully in the Chinese market, or if they will lose this opportunity even as Chinese companies begin to compete on the world stage.

Indeed, this serves to highlight only one of the dangers that foreign governments pose to the international supply chain. Although world markets are becoming more open all the time, the world is far from becoming a giant free trade zone. At any time the threat of *protectionism* might appear, and if the global supply chain is not set up with some kind of counter to this threat, companies will not be able to do much about it. Sometimes the threat comes not from the foreign government, but from the domestic government dealing with the concerns of smaller local firms.

EXAMPLE 9-5

In 1986, Taiwan had a $15.7 billion trade surplus with the United States, heightening domestic pressure on the U.S. government to impose trade restrictions on Taiwanese products. This occurred despite the fact that the vast majority of Taiwanese imports were parts to supply American companies, such as GE, IBM, Hewlett-Packard, and Mattel, which had moved manufacturing offshore to take advantage of lower costs. In response, Taiwan was forced to increase the value of its currency relative to the U.S. dollar, thus effectively removing much of the cost advantage of manufacturing in Taiwan.[7]

9.4 REGIONAL DIFFERENCES IN LOGISTICS

In preceding sections we discussed the general advantages, disadvantages, and strategies for using global supply chains effectively. Of course, it is important to be aware of the cultural, infrastructural, and economic differences between regions when decisions are made about particular foreign links in the global supply chain. Donald Wood and colleagues[8] identified several categories of differences that managers must consider when designing international supply chains. In particular, major differences can be highlighted between the so-called triad, or first world, nations, Japan, the United States, and the nations of western Europe; emerging nations such as Thailand, Taiwan, China, Brazil, Argentina, and the countries of eastern Europe; and the third world nations. These differences are summarized in Table 9-1 and analyzed below.

9.4.1 Cultural Differences

Cultural differences can critically affect the way international subsidiaries interpret the goals and pronouncements of management. Wood and colleagues[8] highlighted beliefs and values, customs, and language, all of which play a big role in global business and can strongly affect negotiation and communication.

Language consists not only of words but also of expressions, gestures, and context. Many times the words appear to be translated correctly, but the meaning is not. We have all heard stories of American businesspeople using the wrong gestures in Asia, leading to disastrous

Table 9-1   Major Differences Between Different Regions

	First World	Emerging	Third World
Infrastructure	Highly developed	Under development	Insufficient to support advanced logistics
Supplier operating standards	High	Variable	Typically not considered
Information system availability	Generally available	Support system not available	Not available
Human resources	Available	Available with some searching	Often difficult to find

consequences. It is important to use appropriate resources to make sure that communication is effective.

Beliefs, or specific values about something, can differ widely from culture to culture. The belief that effective communication is important, for instance, can vary from culture to culture. Similarly, values, or more general conceptions, can vary. For example, American manufacturers value "efficiency" in ways that some other cultures do not.[8] Also, some cultures may value time more than others, so a late delivery may be viewed in some places as a serious problem, whereas in others it is not particularly important.

Customs, of course, vary greatly from country to country. In many cases it is important for the businessperson to adhere to local customs to avoid offending anyone. For example, the practice of gift giving varies greatly from country to country.

9.4.2   Infrastructure

In first world countries, the manufacturing and logistics infrastructure is highly developed. Highway systems, ports, communication and information systems, and advanced manufacturing techniques allow the development of advanced supply chains. Regional differences do exist, primarily for geographic, political, or historical reasons. For example, road widths, bridge heights, and communications protocols may differ from region to region, but in general, techniques have been developed to overcome these differences.

Regardless of the infrastructure, geography also affects supply chain decisions, even within first world countries. In the United States, for example, where large distances often exist between major cities, more inventory might be held than in countries such as Belgium, where the distance between cities is small.

Similarly, relative economic conditions have affected the mix of logistics and supply chain components in many first world countries. For example, countries with relatively cheap land and cheap labor, such as France, have built many large, "low-tech" warehouses, whereas the Scandinavian countries have developed warehouse automation because labor in those countries is so expensive.[9]

In the emerging nations, the supply chain infrastructure is usually not fully in place. Most domestic companies in emerging nations see logistics as a necessary expense and not a strategic advantage, so they limit investments in logistics infrastructure. In many cases, gross national income in an emerging nation may not yet be sufficient to fully implement an advanced logistics infrastructure. In addition, the focus of infrastructure development may have been on exports instead of building a system appropriate for imports and exports. This is true in China.[8] Nonetheless, these nations are "emerging" because they have begun to address these issues. For example, many countries have national transportation policies in place and are beginning or continuing to implement them.

In the third world, the infrastructure is generally insufficient to support advanced logistics operations. Roads are often in poor shape. Warehousing facilities are frequently unavailable. Distribution systems may be nonexistent. In general, specific supply chain decisions have to be considered carefully because many of the things taken for granted in the triad or emerging nations may not exist here.

9.4.3 Performance Expectation and Evaluation

Although regional differences remain among first world nations, operating standards are generally uniform and high. For example, overnight carriers are expected to make deliveries overnight. Contracts are legally binding documents. Environmental regulations and constraints are typically present, and companies are expected to obey them. However, the approaches to developing and enforcing relationships do differ from region to region. For example, European and American companies use formal partnership contracts more frequently than Japanese firms, which tend to favor informal partnership agreements built over time.[10]

In emerging nations, operating standards typically vary greatly. Some firms may have—and meet—high expectations and place great value on contracts and agreements. Others, however, might not be so scrupulous. Research and negotiation are essential to successful deal making in the emerging nations. In addition, the government typically plays a large role in business, so foreign partners and corporations often must be ready to respond to the government's changing whims.

In the third world, traditional performance measures have no meaning. Shortages are common, and customer service measures that are used in the West (e.g., stock availability, speed of service, and service consistency) are irrelevant; given this situation, a firm has little control over the timing and availability of inventory.[8]

9.4.4 Information System Availability

Within the triad nations, computer technology has increased at more or less the same rate across different nations. In most cases, point-of-sale (POS) data, automation tools, personal computers, and other information system tools are just as available in Spain as in California. Of course, there may be incompatibilities in various systems. For example, European electronic data interchange (EDI) standards may vary from country to country and industry to industry. In addition, legal standards relating to data protection and document authentication vary from country to country. Nevertheless, efforts are underway to overcome these hurdles, and technology exists to overcome the technical incompatibilities.[11]

Support systems in the emerging nations may not be in place to implement efficient information systems. Communications networks may be incomplete and not reliable enough to support the traffic. Technical support expertise may not be available to use and maintain the equipment. However, governments in these nations typically have plans or programs in place to address these issues.

Advanced information technology is simply not available in third world countries. Systems such as EDI and bar coding cannot be supported in this type of environment. Even the value of a personal computer is limited because of inefficient communications systems. In addition, data on the economy and population typically are unavailable.

9.4.5 Human Resources

Within most first world countries, technically and managerially competent workers are available. As Donald Wood and colleagues[8] pointed out, "Cultural differences aside, a logistics manager from Japan would be functionally at home in a counterpart's position in America." Unskilled labor, however, is relatively expensive in these regions. While it may be true that skilled managerial and technical personnel are frequently not available in emerging nations, sometimes this is not the case. It might take some searching, but employees with the appropriate skills often can be found. In particular, the eastern European countries generally have well-educated populations.[12] In addition, the wages of skilled workers in emerging nations generally are competitive on the world market. On the other hand, many Chinese managers have been selected for political reasons rather than technical or managerial expertise, so experience in this case may not be an appropriate indicator of ability.[12]

Although it may be possible to find employees who are appropriate to the available technology level, it is often difficult to find trained logistics professionals and managers familiar with modern management techniques in third world countries. Thus training becomes especially important in this type of environment.

9.5 SUMMARY

In this chapter we examined issues specific to *global* supply chain management. First, we discussed various types of international supply chains, covering the spectrum from primarily domestic supply chains with some international product distribution all the way to fully integrated global supply chains. We then examined the various forces compelling companies to develop international supply chains. Both advantages and risks are inherent in global supply chains. Besides the obvious cost advantages, we discussed the advantages of having a truly flexible global supply chain to address the inherent risks in operating a global company. However, even with a flexible supply chain, the strategies and approaches used to address these risks will work only if the appropriate infrastructure is in place.

We next surveyed some of the many issues in global supply chain management, including the concepts of international and regional products and the issue of centralized versus decentralized control in an international context. We concluded with a discussion of regional logistics differences that influence the design of effective supply chains in different parts of the world.

CHAPTER 10

Information Technology

10.1 INTRODUCTION

Information technology (IT) is an important enabler of effective supply chain management. Supply chain management spans the entire enterprise and beyond, encompassing suppliers on the one end to customers on the other. Therefore, our discussion of IT for supply chains will include both systems that are internal to an individual company and external systems, which facilitate information transfer *between* various companies and individuals.

In addition, supply chain management typically spans many functional areas within a company and is affected by the way the various groups communicate and interact. Thus in this chapter we also will discuss topics that relate to company IT infrastructure, supply chain applications, and intercompany communications and collaboration.

For many firms, IT provides a competitive advantage. Athough this has been true for some time in service industries such as banks, it is also becoming more relevant for firms such as large retailers, airlines, and manufacturers. Prominent examples include Wal-Mart's satellite-connected information systems, American Airlines' innovative Sabre reservation system, Federal Express' superb tracking system, and Cisco's "virtual manufacturing environment."

Indeed, as we observed in Chapter 3, when applying supply chain strategies that reduce cost and lead times and increase service level, the timeliness and availability of relevant information are critical. In addition, an increasing number of companies are providing value-added IT-based services to their customers as a way of differentiating themselves in the marketplace and developing strong long-term relationships with their customers. Of course, once these kinds of services are offered by even one company within an industry, they can very quickly become a basic requirement for all others.

In many cases the IT that currently supports the components in the supply chain process is diverse and disconnected. It typically has evolved throughout the years based on various local and companywide requirements that were rarely integrated. This issue must be addressed if a company is to position itself to manage its supply chain effectively. We will see how companies use various strategies to overcome these problems and create systems that can use the multitude of data in the system effectively.

Information flow among suppliers, manufacturers, and customers is critical for effective supply chain management. This entails information flow between different companies [e.g., e-mail, electronic data interchange (EDI), and exchanges]. We also will discuss how developing standards for communications and user interfaces, particularly through the use of the Internet, are facilitating fairly inexpensive, simple-to-implement solutions to problems that previously would have required massive investments of time and money.

The implementation of advanced IT solutions typically requires changes in organizational structure, as well as in employee job descriptions and behavior. Although these issues are not the focus of this chapter, they need to be kept in mind.[1]

Specifically, in this chapter we will discuss the following questions:

- What are the goals of IT from the perspective of supply chain management?
- What IT components are needed to achieve the goals of supply chain management?
- What are the supply chain component systems, and how should they be approached?
- What are the trends in IT, and how do they affect supply chain management?
- What are the stages in the development of enterprise IT?

10.2   GOALS OF SUPPLY CHAIN IT

Consider some of the ultimate goals of IT as it relates to the supply chain. Some companies and industries are currently far from achieving these goals, whereas others are well on their way to accomplishing many of them. To use information, we need to collect it, access it, analyze it, and have the ability to share it for collaboration purposes. Supply chain management system goals in these areas are

- Collect information on each product from production to delivery or purchase point, and provide complete visibility for all parties involved.
- Access any data in the system from a *single point of contact.*
- Analyze, plan activities, and make tradeoffs based on information from the entire supply chain.
- Collaborate with supply chain partners. As we have seen in Chapters 1, 2, and 5, collaboration allows companies to manage uncertainty, e.g., through information sharing, and achieve global optimization.

The primary goal of IT in the supply chain is to link the point of production seamlessly with the point of delivery or purchase. The idea is to have an information trail that follows the product's physical trail. This allows planning, tracking, and estimating lead times based on real data. Any party that has an interest in the whereabouts of the product should be able to have access to this information. As we can see in Figure 10-1, products flow from the supplier to the manufacturer, internally through the manufacturer's distribution system, and then on to the retailers. Information flows in the opposite direction. Below we discuss each IT goal:

- *Collect information.* The retailer needs to know the status of its orders, and the suppliers need to be able to anticipate an incoming order from the manufacturer. This entails access to data that reside in other companies' information systems as well as across functions and geographic locations inside a company. Furthermore, the participants need to see data in their own terms; i.e., if suppliers of cotton are looking at the demand for Q-Tips, they need it translated into pounds of cotton consumed. Therefore, translation tables, such as bills of material, are required throughout the system.

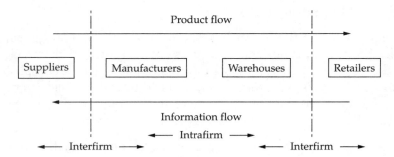

Figure 10-1   Flow of information and goods in the supply chain.

The availability of information regarding the status of products and material is the basis on which intelligent supply chain decisions can be made. Furthermore, it is not sufficient simply to track products across the supply chain; there is also a need to alert diverse systems to the implications of this movement. If there is a delay in a delivery that will affect production schedules, the appropriate systems need to be notified so that they can make the proper adjustments by either delaying the schedules or seeking alternative sources. This goal requires standardization of product identification (e.g., bar coding) across companies and industries. For example, Federal Express has implemented a tracking system that provides ongoing information on the whereabouts of any package handled by the company and makes this information available internally as well as to customers.

- *Access data.* The *single-point-of-contact concept* is critical for effective IT. The goal is that all the available information, either information provided to a customer or required internally, can be accessed in one stop and be the same regardless of the mode of inquiry used (e.g., phone, fax, Internet, or kiosk) or who is making the inquiry. This requirement is complicated by the fact that to satisfy a customer's query, information may be required that resides in various locations within one company and, in some cases, across several companies.

  In many companies, information systems tend to be islands, depending on their functions within the company. Customer service will work with one system and accounting with another, and the manufacturing and distribution systems are completely separate (Fig. 10-2). Occasionally, there may be a transfer of some crucial information that needs to be accessed across systems, but if the transfer is not done in real time, then the systems never have exactly the same data. The customer service representative receiving an order may not be able to provide shipping status information, and the plant may not be able to inquire about current outstanding orders.

Ideally, everyone who needs to use certain data should have access to the same real-time data through any interface device (Fig. 10-3). Banking applications are advanced in this respect: You can access the same account information the bank tellers use from almost anywhere over the telephone, computer, or automatic teller machine (ATM). Nevertheless, these systems

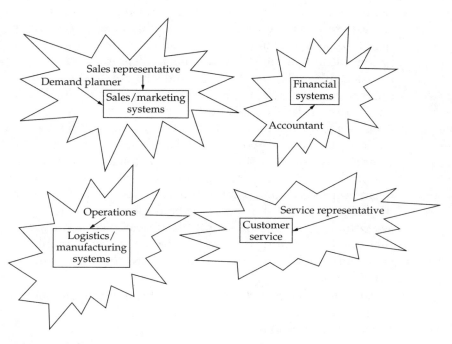

Figure 10-2 Current information systems.

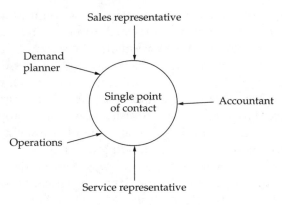

Figure 10-3 New generation of information systems.

may still be weak at linking all of a customer's accounts into a single point of inquiry—e.g., accessing mortgage information at the same time as a bank account.

- *Analyze based on supply chain data.* The third goal is related to analyzing the data, especially in a way that takes into account the global supply chain picture. In addition, the information system must be used to find the most efficient ways to produce, assemble, warehouse, and distribute products—in other words, the best way to operate the supply chain. This entails various levels of decision making: from operational decisions involving the way to fulfill a customer order, to tactical decisions related to which warehouse to stock with what product or what the production plan for the next 3 months should be, to strategic decisions about where to locate warehouses and what products to develop and produce. To facilitate this, systems need to be flexible enough to accommodate changes in supply chain strategies. To achieve this kind of flexibility, they need to be highly configurable, and require new standards. We will discuss these issues in detail below.

- *Collaborate with supply chain partners.* The ability to collaborate with supply chain partners is essential to a company's success. Indeed, as observed in Chapter 1, an important objective in supply chain management is replacing sequential processes with global optimization. This requires not only sophisticated alignment of IT systems but also the integration of business processes. Depending on its supply chain role, a company may be required to either integrate with a customer's procurement system or require its own suppliers to link into its own systems or collaborative platforms or both. The level and type of collaboration vary between industries. For instance, collaborative forecasting was initiated in the consumer packaged goods industry, whereas supplier integration is more common in the hi-tech industry, where outsourcing of critical components requires systems that support the product and logistics coordination.

In recent years, collaboration has become the focus of supply chain systems. The ability to link and work effectively with suppliers has produced new systems called *supplier relationship management* (SRM). In addition, the various exchanges that were developed during the Internet boom of the late 1990s are becoming collaboration platforms, whether private or public. On the other end of the supply chain, customer relationship management (CRM) systems are evolving to provide better contact and understanding of customer needs (see below).

As we will see, the four goals of supply chain management do not all have to be achieved at the same time and are not necessarily dependent on each other. They can be targeted in parallel, with the order of importance depending on the industry, company size, internal priorities, and return-on-investment (ROI) considerations. For instance, a bank could not survive without single-point-of-contact capability, a delivery company without a sophisticated tracking system, and a high-tech manufacturer without a production planning system.

To achieve these goals and to master the decisions and problems that arise when considering how to address them, it is helpful to understand many of the major issues in IT development, particularly as they relate to supply chain management. As we see in Figure 10-4, the following are the means toward achieving these goals.

- *Standardization.* IT standards are what allow systems to work together. They drive the cost and sometimes the feasibility of implementation.

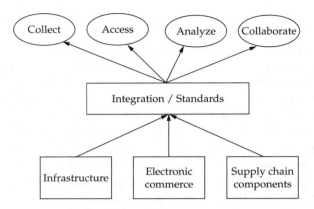

Figure 10-4 Goals and means of supply chain management.

- *IT infrastructure.* The IT infrastructure, whether internal or external to a company, is a basic component of system capabilities. Without this communications and database base, most of the goals outlined cannot be achieved.
- *Electronic commerce.* Electronic commerce has been the most important emerging IT field in the last few years. It has enabled not only internal efficiencies but also the ability to collaborate with partners in the supply chain.
- *Supply chain system components.* These components comprise the various systems that are involved directly in supply chain planning. These are typically systems that combine short- and long-term decision-support system and intelligence elements.
- *Integration-related issues.* How should priorities be set in order to achieve the goals just discussed? What kind of investments should be made in the short term and in the long term?

10.3 STANDARDIZATION

The push toward IT standards is a strong and growing trend. Although some issues are specific to logistics and supply chain management, most developments are occurring across industries and application areas. The IT field is evolving to a high level of standardization for the following reasons:

- *Market forces.* Corporate users need standards in order to reduce the cost of system development and maintenance.
- *Interconnectivity.* The need to connect different systems and work across networks has pushed the development of standards.
- *New software models.* The Internet has produced the need for network software that has new purchase, development, and deployment characteristics.
- *Economies of scale.* Standards reduce the price of system components, development, integration, and maintenance.

The standardization of IT has gone through four major phases:

- *Proprietary.* Computer development until the early 1980s involved proprietary systems, mostly mainframe computers that were accessed through key punches and later terminals with no processing capabilities (so-called dumb terminals). There was little communication between systems, and that was performed through private networks or physical media.
- *Stand alone.* The IBM personal computer (PC) software and hardware, introduced in the early 1980s, became the first standard platform called *Wintel,* the Microsoft Windows and Intel standard. This eventually created a large user base and a large market for applications. Communication standards also were developed mostly for local networks—Ethernet and IBM Token Ring were the leading contenders. For business networks, some standards were developed, but mostly private networks were used for file transfers.

  Electronic data interchange (EDI), a common transaction format, was introduced at this time. It allowed companies to electronically transmit data that used to be handled by paper and data entry. A further development, client-server technology, integrated PC capabilities and standards with business systems, applying the PC computing powers to create a more sophisticated client-controlled interface.
- *Communications.* The Internet provided the missing link in communications and display standards beyond the local network. Initially developed by the U.S. government and

used primarily in research institutes, the development of the
browser in the early 1990s created a standard and accessible
interface and caused the spread of use to individuals and later
companies. Another benefit was that the Internet enabled
forms of communication that heretofore existed internally in
many companies to work across companies and to become as
ubiquitous as phone calls. The most obvious example is
electronic mail (e-mail), but this is by no means the only
form. File and information transfer between individuals and
companies was greatly simplified by the Internet. The
Internet then spawned expanded electronic commerce from
shopping, bidding, and exchanges to shipment tracking and
collaboration between companies. In the meantime, due in
large part to year 2000 fears, many companies replaced their
legacy systems with client-server–based enterprise resource
planning (ERP) systems, which have become the standard
backbone of company IT. These systems typically covered
manufacturing, finance, and human resources applications
with some distribution functionality. Supply chain
management systems have been more varied and less
standard, although ERP vendors have added these capabilities
to their offerings.

- *Collaboration.* The next phase of standards, which is currently
largely under development, will address collaboration, a more
sophisticated form of communication between companies.
There are various efforts to address these issues—we will
describe some of the most prominent ones, although only
time will tell what will evolve to be the next standard. Indeed,
it is worth pointing out that in the previous phases, successful
developments came about quite unexpectedly, and hence it is
hard to predict which standard will succeed. The major issue
is specifying a common language format that will enable
diverse systems to understand each other. In addition,
software vendors are introducing technology that will
simplify integration and enable systems to access each other's
information and processes in a standard way.

The new phase of collaboration also has increased the importance of ERP systems as well as the need for a new generation of sys-

tems that support internal and external integration. The ability to expand processes and capabilities outside the company requires improved internal processes as well as new capabilities that the first generation of ERP systems do not have.

For this purpose, ERP systems are evolving into the so-called ERP II, a term introduced by the Gartner Group. ERP II is an application and deployment strategy that expands out from ERP functions in the following ways:

- *Role* has changed from enterprise optimization (in the first-generation ERP systems) to collaborative commerce and supply chain management (in ERP II).
- *Domain* has changed from a focus on manufacturing and distribution (in the first-generation ERP systems) to include supply chain, customer-facing, and supplier facing systems (in ERP II).
- *Function* has changed from internal processes such as finance, manufacturing, and distribution (in the first-generation ERP systems) to addressing cross-industry and specific industry concepts (in ERP II).
- *Process* has changed from internal and hidden (in the first-generation ERP systems) to externally connected (in ERP II).
- *Architecture* is evolving from closed and monolithic (in the first-generation ERP systems) to a Web-based, open, and component-based environment (in ERP II).
- *Data* have changed from internally generated and consumed (in the first-generation ERP systems) to internally and externally published and subscribed (in ERP II).

One of the cornerstones of all new IT standards development is the eXtensible Markup Language (XML), which is a language description format that is fast becoming the standard for Internet transactions. XML was developed by the Standard Generalized Markup Language (SGML) Editorial Board formed under the auspices of the World Wide Web Consortium (W3C) beginning in 1996. Since gaining W3C recommendation status in February 1998, its text-based structure has proved easy to understand and use. In many instances, businesses can exchange information without intermediate format conversions, provided they use the same XML document formats.

XML is a general standard that does not address the issue of terminology in a specific industry. This is being addressed in one case by a high-tech company industry consortium called RosettaNet (see *www.rosettanet.org*) that views itself as an e-business equivalent of the Rosetta stone, which carried the same message in three different languages, enabling translation from hieroglyphics. The RosettaNet-based initiative is aimed at producing a flexible standard governing online business collaboration between manufacturers and suppliers. RosettaNet defines dictionaries and partner interface processes that handle multiple data transactions among partners. It is being used by some high-tech vendors but has proven expensive to implement. This could change if the standard is adopted widely and vendors provide systems that support it.

Another important challenge in the development of standards is the issue of application-to-application interaction across companies, i.e., the ability to allow the integration of various applications between different companies. Web services, touted by major vendors such as IBM, Microsoft, and Sun, are an emerging set of protocols and standards that reside on the Internet and allow applications to describe their function to each other so that they can integrate with no or minimal programming effort.

The Web services architecture is based on standards such as XML, Universal Description, Discover, and Integration (UDDI), a directory service for applications, and communication protocols such as Simple Object Access Protocol (SOAP).[2] Web services initially will address mostly integration issues such as access to data in systems that are currently closed. Eventually, if security issues are addressed, Web services will provide self-defined stand-alone applications. In addition, the ramifications of Web services will be critical to the way software is developed, paid for, and deployed. Since Web services are offered as components, companies can purchase only the functionality they need, possibly in the form of services purchased over the Internet. Software updates will be automatic, and payment will be on a per-use basis. Web service applications will make collaboration easier by deploying a loose-coupling approach to integration because the integration methods are part of the service and do not need to be tailored for each of any two applications that are being integrated.

For all the obvious advantages of standardization, we should mention a few of its drawbacks and challenges:

- *Availability*. Problems surround the cost of creating a standard and the power of those who hold standards, especially if these standards are proprietary. Proprietary standards are problematic because they may not necessarily be the "best" standards, just those belonging to the most powerful company. This happened in the video battle of beta versus VHS and in the PC operating system battle of Apple versus Microsoft. Proprietary standards limit competition and therefore selection and advances in products beyond what the company owning the standard is willing to offer. Even open group standards, such as EDI, sometimes may limit growth because of (1) the difficulty of making changes acceptable to a committee and (2) producing timely improvements.
- *Security*. The easy access to the Internet exposes systems that are connected to attacks by hackers and conceivably industrial spies. In addition, there are inherent security issues that arise when everyone is running the same software: If someone finds a problem or takes advantage of a security flaw, he or she can access or bring down every system of the same type.
- *Scalability*. Standards that work in a certain context or size of problem may not be adequate for a different set of industries or for a large number of users. For example, RosettaNet, mentioned earlier, which is being developed by the high-tech industry, may not be appropriate for other types of industries because of its cost and complexity. This is an important challenge because of the enormous variety of supply chain applications that cut across industries, companies, and specialized supply chain functions.

10.4 INFORMATION TECHNOLOGY INFRASTRUCTURE

The information technology infrastructure is a critical factor in the success or failure of any system implementation. The infrastructure forms the base for data collection, transactions, system access, and communications. IT infrastructure typically consists of the following components:

- Interface/presentation devices
- Communications

- Databases
- System architecture

10.4.1 Interface Devices

PCs, voice mail, terminals, Internet devices, bar code scanners, and personal digital assistants (PDAs) are some of the interface devices most commonly used. A key trend in IT is toward uniform access capability anytime and anywhere, and interface devices clearly play a major role in this area. The Internet browser is fast becoming the interface of choice for information access, although it is still not as sophisticated as Windows in displaying forms and graphic data. In addition, other devices such as PDAs and phones are also competing as access devices to user systems. Supply chain management requires a standard way to track products in order to provide participants with the information they need to perform efficiently.

The Uniform Code Council created the bar code system, Universal Product Code (UPC), in 1973, and it has been used extensively for scanning and recording information about products. Automatic data capture interfaces, such as bar code readers and radiofrequency (RF) tags, are standardized and commonly used. RF tags on products or packaging are used to locate items, particularly in large warehouses. The same technology, together with wireless communication devices and Global Positioning System (GPS) capabilities, enables tracking of tagged cargo while in shipment.

A more recent development in this area is being introduced at the Auto-ID center (see *www.autoidcenter.org*), where many companies are collaborating with MIT researchers to develop Radio Frequency Identification (RFID) technology. This technology will embed intelligence into physical objects that will allow them to communicate with each other and with businesses and consumers. A 96-bit code of numbers called an *Electronic Product Code* (ePC) will be embedded in a memory chip (smart tag) on individual products. Each smart tag will be scanned by a wireless RF reader, which will transmit the product's embedded identity code to the Internet, where the detailed information on the product is kept. The necessary information about the product will then be communicated back to the user.

The system also includes a Product Markup Language (PML) and an Object Naming Service (ONS). PML is a new standard language for describing physical objects to the Internet in the same way that HyperText Markup Language (HTML) is the common language for describing Web site information. The ONS tells computer systems where to find information about any object that carries an ePC code, or smart tag. ONS is based in part on the Internet's existing Domain Name System (DNS), which routes information to appropriate Web sites. The ONS likely will be many times larger than the DNS, serving as a lightening-fast "post office" that locates data for every single one of trillions of objects carrying an ePC code.

When this new technology is operational, it will help businesses save billions of dollars in lost, stolen, or wasted products. Shoppers will be able to point their scanner-equipped cell phones at a product and learn about its features from the manufacturer's Web site while they are in the store. Items will be scanned and billed to the customer's personal account as he or she leaves the store. In addition, another related technology called *smart shelves* will notify manufacturers when it is time to restock items. Finally, tracking products for supply chain purposes will be simplified, providing real-time information about inventory status.

However, the impact of the RFID technology on supply chain performance cannot be overstated. It includes

- Improved service level by reducing store/shelf stockout rate through an accurate inventory database that triggers an order when the inventory level is low.
- Reduction of the stockout level, especially for promotional and advertised items, can have a major impact on sales.
- Better utilization of store and warehouse space.
- Significant increase in the ability to locate items at the store and in the backroom.

The initial implementations of RFID tags on the product level in early 2003 by companies such as Benetton and Gillette have been met with privacy advocate criticism. These relate to the ability to profile and track consumers without their consent and will eventually be resolved with better education of the public on how the technology works. Implementation of RFID on the pallet side is less problematic and in fact, Wal-Mart and the government's Defense Logistics Agency (DLA) have mandated for all their suppliers RFID tags on pallets, cases, and cartons by January 2005.

10.4.2 Communications

Interface devices are connected to either an internal system (e.g., local area network, mainframe, intranet) or an external network—either a private company network or the Internet. Sometimes direct links to another company's system are used for efficiency and security. There are two major trends in communications: The first is wireless communications, which is fast replacing the hard-wired computer and phone links most of us use today; and the second is the single point of contact for communications.

Advanced communications capabilities enable many applications, including

Electronic mail (e-mail) can be internal to a company or external. The Internet provides for simple cross-company interaction that was unavailable until recently because every company had its own internal system. e-Mail allows for communication across time zones and transfer of information and data.

Data exchange, the ability to electronically exchange transactions such as purchase orders and status between supplier and vendors, for many years has been supported by EDI. Recently, XML technology is enhancing and replacing EDI as well as supporting new Internet-based technology for information exchange.

Groupware enables group work by allowing shared access to information and specialized software so that knowledge can be shared throughout the company. There are also applications that allow sharing of electronic whiteboards and work on joint documents.

Transportation product tracking is the ability to locate a truck or cargo at any time during distribution. This technology requires a combination of GPS and wireless communications. As we have seen, the Auto-ID technology aims to address this area in a comprehensive way.

Supply chain event management (SCEM) systems track predefined performance measures for inventory, transportation, or other events and alert users to problems in the supply chain such as stockouts or delays. The alerts can reach the user in any form he or she specifies, such as phone, e-mail, or pager. In addition, these systems can provide performance measures.

Exchange platforms are used to share information, track products, and trade with supply chain partners. The exchanges can be private or public and provide a means of communication between companies. They are typically Web-based and provide a means to share information and processes that is important for the development of collaboration and visibility in the supply chain. We expanded on exchanges in Chapter 6.

10.4.3 Databases

Data need to be organized in some form of a database, including transaction information, status information, general information (prices and so on), forms, and group work. Organizing these data is an extremely challenging activity and may require specialized databases depending on the type of data. Some types of databases are described below:

Legacy databases. These systems are usually built around a hierarchical or network database. These databases can store large amounts of data, typically transaction data, and perform extensive processing. They typically have an online and batch component. Programs are written in COBOL (*c*ommon *b*usiness-*o*riented *l*anguage), and reporting tools are somewhat cumbersome to use.

Relational databases. These databases allow the storage of related data in such a way that standardized reporting and querying of related data are facilitated. For example, Structured Query Language (SQL) is designed only for relational databases. Relational databases may be centralized on a mainframe computer or server, or they may be distributed across a network of personal or minicomputers.

Object databases. These can hold not only numeric and character data but also more sophisticated objects such as pictures and graphic structures. Object databases are used to store different kinds of information in a way that relates them to database operations. These databases already exist for some applications but are not yet standard and are costly to maintain. Storing graphic and other nonstandard data requires considerably more storage space than text/numeric data and is more complicated to manipulate.

Data warehouses. These databases combine data from other
system databases to allow query by sophisticated analysis tools.
Data warehouses usually involve enterprise data and hold
extremely large amounts of data.

Datamarts. Datamarts are smaller versions of data warehouses
and usually store a smaller set of data and are more
departmental in scope.

Groupware databases. These are specialized databases designed to
accommodate group functions, such as keeping track of
updates, allowing multiple-user access, and so forth. Group
databases are also important in the age of telecommuting and
virtual companies, where keeping everyone up to date with
relevant data is impossible without a shared database.

10.4.4   System Architecture

System architecture encompasses the way the components—databases, interface devices, and communications—are configured. We
have added this topic to the section on IT infrastructure because the
design of the communications networks and choice of systems depend
on the implementation of these systems.

Legacy systems evolved as departmental solutions using mainframe
or minicomputers that were accessed through "dumb" terminals (Fig.
10-5). The PC was used initially apart from a company's main systems
for special applications such as word processing or spreadsheets. Eventually, the PCs in an office were connected by means of local area
networks (LANs) so that users could share files, e-mail, and other

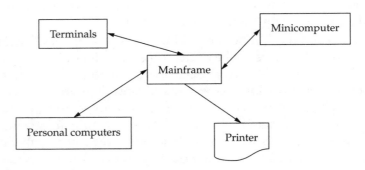

Figure 10-5   Legacy system architecture.

applications. These networks were then extended across companies with wide area networks (WANs) that connected the dispersed offices of a company. Finally, new systems were developed to take advantage of the PC's computing power and friendly graphic interface. In these systems, the PC is typically called the *client*, and the main processor is the *server*. *Client-server computing* is a form of distributed processing whereby some processes are performed centrally for many users, and others are performed locally on a user's PC.

Most current system design involves client-server structure (Fig. 10-6), although the sophistication and price of the client, the number and type of servers, and various other design parameters vary greatly from system to system. Examples of servers include database servers that allow Structured Query Language (SQL) requests from users, transaction-processing monitors, directory/security servers, and communications servers.[3]

The Internet is a form of client-server process where the local PC browser processes the HTML pages and Java applets (i.e., small applications) that are retrieved from servers—in this case from all over the world. The client-server model is now evolving toward a Web centric model where the client is a Web browser connected to a Web server.

The power of the client-server concept is in distributing functions among specialist servers that perform them efficiently; it is also easier to add new modules and functions. The disadvantage is the added complexity of navigating between servers and making sure that data are processed correctly and updated across the network. The implementation of client-server systems also has given impetus to the trend toward standardization because each server needs to be able to communicate tasks and processes

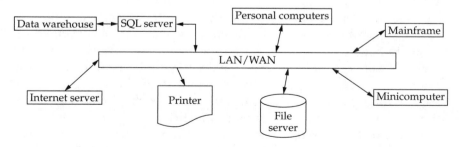

Figure 10-6   Client-server system architecture.

across the network. This feature is called *interoperability*, which means two systems are capable of interacting in a sophisticated way that is a built-in feature of their design. Many interfaces between systems are created through file transfers or other temporary schemes because the systems use different file formats and communications schemes. When standards for intrasystem operation become common, tools will be available to perform these interfaces and provide full data and process-sharing interface mechanisms.

The applications that reside between the server and the client collectively are called *middleware*, the hyphen in the term *client-server*. These are typically tools that facilitate communication between different system architectures, communication protocols, hardware architectures, and so forth. The parts of an application that reside on a server, client, or as middleware depend on specific implementations. This is the three-tiered architecture model now favored by many client-server designers.

Middleware can be important in the implementation of supply chain systems because in many cases the information for the planning tool exists in a number of locations and forms across the company. The appropriate middleware can be used to collect the data and format them in a way that can be used by various planning tools. This is how many supply chain applications are currently implemented. For instance, a telecommunications company may have billing information for the company's various services, such as long distance and wireless, stored on different systems. A customer service representative might have to search multiple locations for a customer's bills if the customer purchased more than one service. Middleware would perform the function of looking through the databases and combining the information. When these types of processes are applied between companies over the Internet, they are called *enterprise application integration* (EAI).

A more advanced generation of system infrastructure attempts to provide interconnectivity and collaboration platforms between companies. In Section 10.3 we reviewed the evolution from ERP to ERP II, which will provide extended support for these new infrastructure requirements. Earlier in this section we mentioned exchanges, Web-based trading platforms, that currently provide the technology used for collaboration across enterprises. Finally, we also described Web services, a technology that has the potential to provide flexible links between systems. This can improve the interoperability of diverse systems and allow processes to more easily communicate.

### 10.4.5	Electronic Commerce

Electronic commerce (e-commerce) refers to the replacement of physical processes with electronic ones and the creation of new models for collaboration with customers and suppliers.[4] e-Commerce can be used to facilitate the interaction between different companies as well as the interaction of individuals within companies. Examples include purchasing over the Internet, exchanges, order tracking, and e-mail.

e-Commerce has been in existence for many years, using private networks for corporations (e.g., WANs) and public ones at universities and government agencies. The acceptance of Internet standards has accelerated the adoption of e-commerce, especially between individual buyers and companies but also among companies. The initial use of the Internet, showcasing marketing materials, has expanded to allow user status and tracking inquiries as well as product purchases. Companies allow users to access their databases to troubleshoot product problems, thus saving the company money in support calls.

Companies use Internet standards internally—*intranets*—as well as externally—*extranets* and *exchanges.* The difference between the Internet, intranets, and extranets is explained mostly by who is allowed access to the system. Intranets allow companies to implement internal applications without having to develop custom interfaces and avoid incompatible types of hardware and special dial-in procedures. Internet applications typically allow unlimited access, but extranets allow limited access by restricting partners and customers from outside the company to certain applications and data. Internet standards have been used in recent years to create exchanges—private and public—that allow participants to trade or exchange information.

Another concept that has developed around internal company use of the Internet is the *portal*—a role-based entry into a company's systems. A portal aggregates all the applications and sources of information employees need in order to perform their job into a single desktop environment, typically through the Web browser. This capability not only empowers an employee to be productive individually but also makes it simpler for employees to interact with others, whether within the company or outside.

Portals require integration technology for structured and unstructured data sources, including databases, Java classes, Web services, and XML. As more organizations begin to deploy an enterprise portal framework, they are looking at ways to reduce the time and cost associated with building portals. The ability for end users to aggregate content and provide faster access to more information sources is critical to the success of building and maintaining portals.

10.4.6 Electronic Commerce Levels

There are various levels of e-commerce depending on the sophistication of the transaction and the level of data interchange. Table 10-1 illustrates the four levels of e-commerce based on the type of exchange and data and process sharing. Below we describe the various levels in more detail and provide additional information about each example.

EXAMPLE 10-1

At office furniture maker Herman Miller, Inc., approximately 300 employees who spend most of their days in contact with suppliers use a customizable portal that gives them fast access to news and information. This allows the employees to deal with business partners more effectively because they do not have to hunt for or combine various bits of data. The company was originally attracted to the technology from Top Tier Software (which was acquired by SAP in March 2001) because it provided a way for suppliers to interact with Herman Miller's enterprise resource planning system. Once the company saw how effective a portal interface could make employees, it began to roll it out for internal use as well. Today the company has several separate portals for various types of employees, but it is considering evolving its Web site into a sort of "superportal" that will then lead customers, suppliers, and employees to different subportals, depending on their needs. The benefits of collaboration are tremendous. For example, employees can decide what kinds of alerts they want to have fed to their screens ("Supplier X is 3 days late with a delivery") and then drill into data to identify the cause of the problem and the potential ramifications. The system has not been a panacea, however. While the technology is very good at sifting through structured data such as those contained in databases, it is far less effective in handling unstructured data, such as correspondence, computer-aided design (CAD) drawings, and the like. SAP recently combined its portals division with another business unit that dealt with online marketplaces, where unstructured data predominate, so, over time, all that functionality can be brought to bear in a single product.[5]

Table 10-1   Summary of Electronic Commerce Levels

Level Number	Description	Example
1	One-way communication	e-Mail, FTP, browsing
2	Database access	Inquiries, forms, purchases, tracking
3	Data exchange	EDI, clearinghouse
4	Sharing processes	CPFR, exchanges

Level 1: One-Way Communication This level has only one-way communication—the other party does not need to respond, as in the case of e-mail, file transfer, or Web browsing, or at least does not need to respond in real time. The browser or file data are usually for general use, through hypertext links, and cannot be accessed on the basis of any input data. This form of e-commerce has been around for more than 10 years, when Gopher and similar systems provided the browsing options before World Wide Web standards, developed at CERN, became widely used.

Level 2: Database Access At this level the user of e-commerce is accessing a database for personal or tailored information by entering data through data-entry forms. In addition, the user can make personalized requests and orders, such as status inquiries and purchases over the Internet. The database access level also includes searches in company knowledge bases for obscure error messages and problem reports, as well as use of vendor catalogs. Individual purchases can be made on the Internet using credit cards. This has raised some security issues, but it is no less safe than making a store purchase with a credit card. Business purchasing is typically more complex because there are restrictions concerning who can order and what configurations are acceptable. For this reason, Dell Computer created custom pages for businesses.

A more advanced application at this level is the creation of Internet sites that match buyers and sellers. These include electronic brokerages such as E*TRADE *(www.etrade.com)*, transportation exchanges such as the National Transportation Exchange *(www.nte.net)*, and auction and trading sites such as eBay *(www.ebay.com)* or ChemConnect *(www.chemconnect.com)*. These sites enable individuals and companies to either cut out the intermediary (in stock transactions), use available capacity more efficiently (as in the transportation exchange), or enlarge the market and force competition between suppliers (in public e-markets). See Chapter 7 for a detailed discussion.

Level 3: Data Exchange This level applies mainly to business-to-business (B2B) transactions and requires computers on both ends to exchange information typically using *electronic data interchange* (EDI) and more recently XML-based processes. Another form of data exchange is the automated clearinghouse, which enables an industry to consolidate data and allows inquiries by all parties. This approach is used in the banking industry, for instance, to process student loans and in health care to process claims.

The data exchange level of application will soon be applied more extensively to individual transactions, e.g., filing Internal Revenue Service (IRS) forms and receiving confirmation and corrections electronically. There are still many security issues, such as the use of digital signatures and authentication schemes, that need to be agreed on to make this effective. Another development that will allow individuals to participate at this level is the application of electronic cash. This will allow charging small amounts for various electronic transactions and will make it easier to use networks for low-cost transactions such as phone calls, reading an article, software use, and many others. Finally, because of the global reach of the Internet, issues such as taxes, tariffs, and exchange rates need to be resolved before the full global potential is unleashed.

Level 4: Sharing Processes The final level occurs when different entities share processes, not just data, electronically. For this to happen, standards need to be agreed on so that different applications can communicate with each other.

In recent years, companies have started to invest in systems that allow for collaboration with supply chain partners. Two types of systems have been developed—supplier relationship management (SRM) applications and customer relationship management (CRM) applications. These applications can span a variety of forms, including access, data transfer, trading exchange, and collaborative ventures such as product design and planning.

SRM drives the optimization of production goods and materials for manufacturers. These systems include the following capabilities:

- *Strategic supply management* ensures that a company has the right set of suppliers, that they are performing, and that the company is paying the best possible pricing across the board.
- *Supply chain collaboration* allows a company to share information with its suppliers in real time, cutting materials costs, minimizing inventory, and reducing shortages and expediting.
- *Direct materials procurement execution* uses the Internet to automate the process of dealing with suppliers. Benefits include cutting cycle times, increasing inventory turns, and allowing purchasing people to eliminate low-value activities and focus on important issues.

CRM systems aim to drive and optimize the interaction with clients. Typical applications include

- *Sales-force automation* provides the ability to track interactions with customers and have a single point of contact for all types of activities and customer access.
- *Sales-pitch customization* enables cross-selling opportunities using analytical CRM software. It provides the ability to understand what customers are buying and offer them complementary products.
- *Managing and using customer information* analyzes how customers interact with the company and the ability to centralize and take advantage of customer activities.

Another example for sharing processes is collaborative planning, forecasting, and replenishment (CPFR), a Web-based standard that enhances vendor-managed inventory and continuous replenishment by incorporating joint forecasting. With CPFR, parties exchange electronically a series of written comments and supporting data that include past sales trends, scheduled promotions, and forecasts. This allows the participants to coordinate joint forecasts by concentrating on differences in forecast numbers. The parties try to find the cause of the differences and come up with joint and improved figures. As we emphasized in Chapter 2, the results of multiple forecasts can be very expensive across the supply chain. Indeed, sharing forecasts with distributors and other parties can result in a significant decrease in inventory levels because it tends to reduce the bullwhip effect. To do this, systems need to be designed to allow data verification and to ensure standard practices of coordination.

CPFR was developed by the Voluntary Interindustry Commerce Standards Association (VICS) committee, made up of retailers, manufacturers, and solution providers. This group has developed a set of business processes that entities in a supply chain can use for collaborating along a number of buyer/seller functions toward improving supply chain performance. According to the committee, its mission is to create collaborative relationships between buyers and sellers through comanaged processes and shared information. By integrating demand- and supply-side processes, CPFR will improve efficiencies, increase sales, reduce fixed assets and working capital, and reduce inventory for the entire supply chain while satisfying consumer needs.

The VICS committee created the CPFR Voluntary Guidelines to explain the business processes, supporting technology, and change management issues associated with implementing CPFR. The committee published the CPFR Roadmap explaining how manufacturers and retailers can implement a CPFR partnership. This roadmap (see *www.cpfr.org*) includes the following nine steps:

1. Develop guidelines for the relationships.
2. Develop a joint business plan.
3. Create a sales forecast.
4. Identify exceptions for the sales forecast.
5. Collaborate on exception items.
6. Create an order forecast.
7. Identify exceptions for the order forecast.
8. Resolve/collaborate on exception items.
9. Generate orders.

EXAMPLE 10-2

Henkel is a large German company with over 57,000 employees worldwide and over 11 billion euros in sales. Henkel manufactures over 10,000 products, including detergents, cosmetics, adhesives, and many others. Eroski is the leading food retailer in Spain, with over 4 billion euros in sales each year. Eroski is one of Henkel's largest Spanish customers. In December 1998, the two companies decided to undertake collaborative planning and forecasting (CPFR) in order to address customer service and stockout issues relating to Henkel products in Eroski stores. The effort initially focused on detergents, with a goal of improving customer service, reducing lost sales, and increasing the turnover rate. Using commercially available software, the two companies collaborated on business and promotional plans and sales forecasts. The process was started in December 1999, and the companies have seen dramatic improvement in the quality of forecasts. Before the process started, half the sales forecasts had an average error of over 50 percent. Several months after the implementation, 75 percent of the forecasts showed an error of less than 20 percent. Similar improvements were seen in stockout levels. One of the challenges of implementing CPFR between these two firms was involving business organizations in the forecasting process that had not been involved in the past. For example, Henkel customer service personnel had to develop close working relationships with Eroski sales forecasters. Once initial reluctance was overcome, the benefits of this process were realized quickly. Forecasts could be developed that combined Eroski's knowledge of the dynamics of individual retail outlets and the impact of promotion at these outlets with Henkel's knowledge of the individual products and the impact of external factors on these product sales.[7]

10.5 SUPPLY CHAIN MANAGEMENT SYSTEM COMPONENTS

In the preceding section we covered developments in IT without focusing on supply chain management. The infrastructure issues, which ERP systems attempt to resolve, bring all business functions together and make an enterprise more efficient. They do not, however, help answer the fundamental questions of what should be made, where, when, and for whom. This is the role played by human planners with the aid of various analytical tools such as decision-support systems (DSSs). DSSs range from spreadsheets, in which users perform their own analysis, to expert systems, which attempt to incorporate the knowledge of experts in various fields and suggest possible alternatives. The appropriate DSS for a particular situation depends on the nature of the problem, the planning horizon, and the type of decisions that need to be made. In addition, there is frequently a tradeoff between generic tools that are not problem-specific and allow analysis of many different kinds of data and often more expensive systems that are tailored to a specific application. Within the various disciplines that make up supply chain management, DSSs are used to address various problems from strategic problems such as logistics network design, to tactical problems such as the assignment of products to warehouses and manufacturing facilities, all the way through to day-to-day operational problems such as production scheduling, delivery mode selection, and vehicle routing. The inherent size and complexity of many of these systems make DSSs essential for effective decision making.

As we saw in Section 10.2, where we analyzed the goals of IT, the first two goals, collecting and accessing data, require enterprise as well as interenterprise systems, which are not yet available in many industries. The third IT goal, data analysis, may be the most achievable and the one with the highest and most immediate *return on investment* (ROI). Such systems are much faster to implement and cause little disruption across the company because fewer people need to be trained to use a dedicated DSS.

The DSSs that various companies and industries employ depend, among other things, on manufacturing characteristics, demand fluctuation, transportation costs, and inventory costs. For instance, if a company's predominant cost is transportation, the first DSS implementation would be a fleet routing system or a network design project. On the other hand, if there is a high variability in demand and complex manufacturing processes requiring setups when switching between products, demand planning and production scheduling systems may be the most urgent.

These systems typically support the strategic, tactical, and operational levels. Some of the supply chain components predominantly support one level, while others may support more than one, depending on how they are defined and used.

In this section we describe the main IT capabilities required for supply chain excellence, as well as the relationships between the different capabilities. These capabilities are described in Figure 10-7. As you can see, IT capabilities are partitioned into four layers:

1. Strategic network design allows planners to pick the optimal number, location, and size of warehouses and/or plants; to determine optimal sourcing strategy, i.e., which plant/vendor should produce which product; and to determine the best

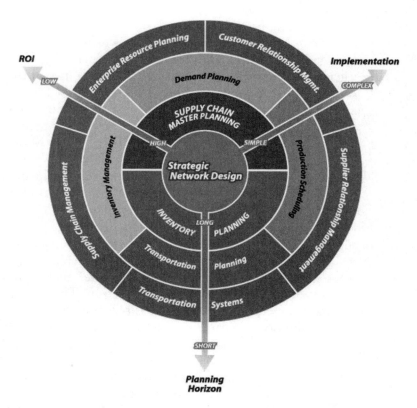

Figure 10-7   Capabilities required to achieve supply chain
excellence.

distribution channels, i.e., which warehouses should service
which customers. The objective is to minimize total costs,
including sourcing, production, transportation, warehousing,
and inventory, by identifying the optimal tradeoffs between
the number of facilities and service levels. The planning
horizon for these systems is typically a few months to a few
years using aggregated data and long-term forecasts. The
method most often used is optimization.

2. Tactical planning determines resource allocation over
   shorter planning periods such as weeks or months.

These systems include:

- *Supply chain master planning* coordinates production and distribution strategies and storage requirements by efficiently allocating supply chain resources to maximize profit or minimize systemwide cost. This allows companies to plan ahead for seasonality, promotions, and tight capacities. The planning horizon for these systems is typically weekly to monthly.
- *Inventory planning* determines the amount of safety stock and how to best position inventory in the supply chain. Network design and tactical planning combine into network planning described in Chapter 4.

3. Operational planning systems enable efficiencies in production, distribution, inventory, and transportation for short-term planning. The planning horizon is typically daily to weekly, and the focus is on one function; i.e., each system focuses on only one function, e.g., production. Therefore, these systems focus on generating feasible strategies, not optimized solutions, because of the lack of integration with other functions, the detailed level of the analysis, and the short horizon.

Operational planning systems include:

- *Demand planning* generates demand forecasts based on various historical and other pertinent information. It also allows users to analyze the impact of promotions, new product introduction, and other business plans. The method used is mostly statistical analysis.
- *Production scheduling* generates detailed production schedules based on the supply chain master plan or demand forecasts. The method used is constraint-based feasibility analysis that satisfies all production constraints.
- *Inventory management* generates inventory plans for the various facilities in the supply chain based on average demand, demand variability, and source material lead times. The methods used are statistical and computational.
- *Transportation planning* produces transportation routes and schedules based on availability of transportation on a lane, cost, and customer delivery schedules. There are a large

number of transportation planning options, so these systems can vary from fleet planning and transportation mode selection to routing and distribution planning. The methods used are mostly heuristic.

4. Operational execution systems provide the data, transaction processing, user access, and infrastructure for running a company. These systems tend to be real time in the sense that the data are current and are constantly being updated by users and events.

These systems include:

- *Enterprise resource planning* traditionally spans manufacturing, human resources, and financials but is now the backbone of most IT infrastructures. These systems are expanding to include new functionality covered by other components we discuss. They are also providing Web-based access and services and becoming more open to integration of other components.

- *Customer relationship management* involves systems that update and track interaction with customers. These systems connect to order tracking and other back-end systems to provide better information for customers and the service representatives who are trying to assist them.

- *Supplier relationship management* provides the interface to suppliers for transaction exchange as well as collaborative activities.

- *Supply chain management* systems provide tracking of distribution activities in plants and warehouses, as well as the event management that tracks exceptions based on performance measures. In addition, they provide lead-time quotations based on current supply chain status— called *available-to-promise* (ATP) or *capable-to-promise* (CTP).

- *Transportation systems* provide internal and external access and tracking of goods in transport. There may be some ability to route and plan at this level, but it would be on a smaller scale in terms of scope and horizon than the transportation planning systems.

Figure 10-7 illustrates the difference between the various layers of capabilities:

- *Planning horizon* for strategic network design is much longer than for an operational system. Indeed, companies typically make long-term investments in facilities over a few years. On the other hand, supply chain master planning develops a strategy for a few months to a year. Finally, operational systems have a very short horizon of days to weeks.
- *Return on investment* for strategic systems can be very high because the decisions impact large capital investments and major distribution decisions. Typically, companies report 5 to 15 percent cost reduction due to strategic network design implementation. Consider now operational planning and execution, which can have a significant cost impact as well. Unfortunately, they require a much larger investment for much smaller gain.
- *Implementation complexity* of a strategic network design is not high because the tools that are used and the processes employed do need to integrate with other systems or processes. Similarly, strategic network design does not require real-time updates, and few people in the company interact with it. Operational systems, on the other hand, are notoriously difficult to implement and integrate and require real-time data and extensive training.

10.6 DECISION-SUPPORT SYSTEMS

To use a DSS successfully, appropriate performance measures need to be selected. For example, reducing total cost may be a goal, but in some cases, improving customer service level may be more pertinent. DSS interfaces usually allow the user to select the relative importance of different objectives.

Once data have been collected, they must be analyzed and presented. Depending on the DSS and the particular decision being made, there are many different ways to analyze the data. It is important for the decision makers to *understand* how the DSS analyzes the data in order to assess the validity and accuracy of the DSS's recommendations. It is up to the decision maker to determine which analysis is most appropriate.

There are two main ways to analyze data. The first is using business analytic tools that are general-purpose methods on data that are extracted from ERP and other systems. These systems typically use the following techniques:

Queries. Often vast quantities of data make manual analysis difficult. Decisions are often facilitated simply by allowing decision makers to ask specific questions about the data, such as "How many clients do we service in California?" and "How many clients purchased over $3000 of a certain product by state?"

Statistical analysis. Sometimes asking questions is not enough. In this case, statistical techniques sometimes can be used to determine trends and patterns in the data. For example, statistical data such as the average inventory in a warehouse, the average number of stops and length of a route, and the variability of customer demand often can be useful to decision makers.

Data mining. Recently, as corporate databases have become larger and more all-encompassing, new tools have been developed to look for "hidden" patterns, trends, and relationships in the data. Data mining, for example, produced the marketing gem that men purchase beer and diapers on Friday afternoon, suggesting to retailers that these items should be displayed close to each other in the store.

Online analytical processing (OLAP) tools. Online analytical processing tools provide an intuitive way to view corporate data, typically stored in data warehouses. OLAP tools aggregate data along common business dimensions and let users navigate through the hierarchies and dimensions by drilling down, up, or across levels. OLAP tools also provide sophisticated statistical tools to analyze these data and tools to present them. Mostly they are generic tools—more sophisticated than spreadsheets and easier to use than database tools—for the analysis of large amounts of data.

The second method to analyze data involves DSSs that provide specialized interfaces that display and report based on the specific problem being solved. These DSSs employ analytic tools that have some specific embedded knowledge of the problem being solved. Since these problems are usually complex, the DSS employs its problem knowledge to find efficient solutions.

These systems typically use the following type of analytics:

Calculators. Simple decision-support tools can facilitate specialized calculations such as accounting costs. In many cases more than simple calculations may not be warranted, especially if the changes are predictable and easy to evaluate. This may be the case for forecasting or inventory management and for some product types, whereas others may need more sophisticated tools.

Simulation. All business processes have random components. Sales may take one value or another. A machine may or may not fail. Often these random, or stochastic, elements of a problem make analyzing it very difficult. In these cases, *simulation* is frequently an effective tool to help in decision making. In simulation, a model of the process is created on a computer. Each of the random elements of the model (e.g., sales, failures) is specified with a probability distribution. When the model is "run," the computer simulates carrying out the process. Each time a random event occurs, the computer uses the specified probability distribution to randomly "decide" what happens.

Consider, for example, a simulation model of a production line. As the computer runs the model, a series of decisions is made. How long does a job take on machine 1? On machine 2? Does machine 3 break while job 4 is being processed on it? As the model runs, statistical data (e.g., utilization rates, completion times) are collected and analyzed. Since this is a random model, each time the model is run, the results may be different. Statistical techniques are used to determine the model's average outcome and the variability of this outcome. Also, by varying input parameters, different models and decisions can be compared. For example, different distribution systems can be compared using the same simulated customer demand. Simulation is often a useful tool to understand very complex systems that are difficult to analyze analytically.

Artificial intelligence (AI). These are techniques that try to create systems that exhibit intelligence by incorporating some form of learning. For example, *intelligent agents* use AI to assist in decision making, especially in real-time decisions, such as determining how to supply a customer in the shortest possible time or to quote a delivery lead time as the customer waits on the phone. Following Fox, Chionglo, and Barbuceanu[8] we define an *agent* as a software process whose goal is to communicate and interact with other agents so that decisions affecting the entire supply chain can be made on a global level. For example, the intelligent agent that assists the customer service representative in determining the appropriate lead time could interact with the intelligent agent that schedules production to help ensure that the lead time is met.[9]

Expert systems also fall under the umbrella of artificial intelligence. These systems capture an expert's knowledge in a database and use it to solve problems. Expert systems rely on an extensive database of knowledge, usually expressed as a set of rules. Solving a problem involves applying the rules in the knowledge base and producing a conclusion that has the ability to explain how it was reached. Within the context of a DSS, this kind of expert system might suggest alternative solutions that the human decision maker has neither the time nor expertise to recognize.

Although not extensively used in logistics practice, these systems have an important role because of their capability to capture and explain expert reasoning. Indeed, a number of DSSs for supply chain management can be viewed as using intelligent agents to plan and execute different activities in the supply chain. These systems are characterized by the following interrelated issues:[8]

- The activities allocated to each intelligent agent (i.e., software processor)
- The level and nature of interactions between the different agents
- The level of knowledge embedded within each agent

For instance, a real-time supply chain planning tool involves the following components: intelligent agents that are located at each facility and collect information and enable planning and scheduling for the facility. In this case, facilities include manufacturing plants and distribution centers. Each agent interacts with other agents so that they can balance excess capacity at different plants, find missing parts, or coordinate production and distribution. A central planning agent communicates with agents that are located at each facility to collect status information and relate central planning decisions. The type and level of decisions made by the agents—as opposed to human operators—and the frequency and level of communications between agents depend on the specific implementation.

Mathematical models and algorithms. Mathematical tools, often from the discipline of operations research, can be used to determine potential solutions to problems. For example, these tools may generate the best set of locations for new warehouses, an efficient route for a truck to take, or an effective inventory policy for a retail store. These algorithms fall into two categories:

- *Exact algorithms.* Given a particular problem, these algorithms will find a solution that is mathematically the "best possible solution." In general, these kinds of algorithms may take a long time to run, especially if a problem is complex. In many cases it is impossible to find the optimal, or very best, solution. In other cases it may be possible but not worth the effort. This happens because the input data to these algorithms are often approximated or aggregated, so *exact solutions to approximate problems may be worth no more than approximate solutions to approximate problems.*

- *Heuristics.* These are algorithms that provide good but not necessarily optimal solutions to problems. Heuristics typically run much faster than exact algorithms. Most DSSs that use mathematical algorithms employ heuristics. A good heuristic will rapidly give a solution that is very close to the optimal solution. Heuristic design often involves a tradeoff between the quality of a solution and speed. It is often useful if in addition to the solution the heuristic provides an estimate of *how far the heuristic solution is from the optimal solution.*

The analytic tools used in practice are typically a hybrid of many of the tools just described. Almost all DSSs employ a combination of tools, and many will allow further analysis using generic tools such as spreadsheets. In addition, some of the tools just listed may be embedded in generic tools (e.g., spreadsheets).

There are many factors that dictate the appropriate analytic tools to use for a particular DSS. These include

- The type of problem being considered.
- The required accuracy of the solution—there may be no need to find the optimal solution.
- Problem complexity—some tools may not be appropriate for very complex problems, whereas others may be overkill for relatively simple problems.
- The number and type of quantifiable output measures.
- The required speed of the DSS—for operational systems such as lead-time quotation and vehicle routing, speed may be essential.
- The number of objectives or goals of the decision maker—for example, a DSS for truck routing may need to find a solution with the minimum number of vehicles and the least total distance traveled.

Table 10-2 shows a number of problems and the analytic tools that are appropriate for them.

Table 10-2   Applications and Analytical Tools

Problem	Tools Used
Marketing	Query, statistics, data mining
Routing	Heuristics, exact algorithms
Production scheduling	Simulation, heuristics, dispatch rules
Logistics network configuration	Simulation, heuristics, exact algorithms
Mode selection	Heuristics, exact algorithms

10.7   INTEGRATING SUPPLY CHAIN INFORMATION TECHNOLOGY

How do all the elements of information technology (IT) come together? Supply chain management is extremely complex, so there is no simple or cheap solution to the issues we have raised. Many companies do not think that it is cost-effective to introduce certain IT innovations because they are not sure there will be a significant return on investment. Trucking companies do not purchase sophisticated tracking systems because few clients would actually want to receive such detailed information. Warehouse managers do not invest in radio frequency (RF) technology because it is too expensive.

The key is to analyze what each component can contribute to the enterprise and then plan the investment according to the specific needs of the company and the demands of the industry. It should be noted, however, that the holistic solution is frequently greater than the arithmetic sum of the parts—i.e., installation of a warehouse control system and a transportation management system can do wonders for customer service performance.

Companies need to decide whether to automate their internal processes or agree to some industry conventions—which usually happens when investing in an ERP system from one of the major vendors (e.g., SAP, PeopleSoft, or Oracle). As more and more companies share information such as order entry, requisition, bills of material, and so forth and take part in joint planning, one can expect that standard approaches to sharing this information will lower everyone's cost of doing business. In supply chain management, no single standard has yet emerged because each ERP vendor continues to set its own de facto standards.

Due to the lack of standards, it is quite likely that in the near future middleware in the form of message brokers whose objective is to mediate between different systems and different standards will be developed. Eventually, supply chain standards will become part of the basic systems that constitute the infrastructure.

In the following subsections we will review some important aspects of supply chain system integration. First, we review SAP's "Stages of Excellence" model, a model designed for evaluating a company's stage of development in IT and its impact on supply chain management. As a major vendor of supply chain systems, SAP helps clients pinpoint their current state of development as well as points them toward goals for the future based on their industry and unique needs. In the next subsection we discuss implementation of ERP and DSSs. What are the priorities in implementation? What should a company invest in first? Finally, we will review the "best of breed" compared with the single-vendor package dilemma.

10.7.1   Stages of Development[3]

SAP, the leading ERP vendor, provides a supply chain management value calculator that can tell by a company's industry, stage of development, revenue, and profit margin how much it can save from an investment in various SCM systems. The Stages of Excellence, as the development stages are called, are divided into four levels (see *www.sap.com/scm/*). Note that at any point in time, different parts of a company's business may be in different stages of development. The model defines the IT capabilities of an organization in each stage. Thus the model is useful in evaluating current development and identifying where other companies are heading and where future competitive advantages lie.

Stage I: Disconnected Systems   Companies at this stage are characterized by the proliferation of many independent systems, manual and inefficient communications, and digitized internal data. Companies in stage I typically focus on automating existing functions and tasks. Companies are organized functionally, with a low degree of integration and nonleveraged Web capabilities. Organizations at this stage of excellence must focus on internal process standardization and address Internet readiness.

Characteristics of this stage include

- Functional (silo) strategies
- Lack of clear, consistent supply chain management processes
- Lack of qualified supply chain leadership
- Disconnected systems
- Measurements lacking or not aligned with company objectives

Stage II: Internal and External Interfaces   In this stage, companies are organized functionally, with a high degree of integration and nonleveraged Web capabilities. These companies operate with functionally focused e-business solutions, disparate information systems, functional "flow through" of data, and decentralized external links. Trading partners can exchange information and interact via the Internet. Organizations at this stage are transaction-focused on both buy-side and sell-side activities.

Characteristics of this stage include

- Integration of some functional information to decrease inventory and improve efficiency
- Documented processes that are followed
- Leaders who are supply chain professionals, and people providing data who are well directed
- Systems that are connected and generally provide accurate information about what is needed where
- Key measurements that are used departmentally

Stage III: Internal Integration and Limited External Integration Efficiency
In this stage, companies are cross-functionally organized. These companies operate with integrated systems within the enterprise and limited external value chain integration. One-to-one trading partner interactions have been established. Organizations at this stage have linked suppliers to their back-end systems and integrated with buyer front-end systems.

Characteristics of this stage include

- Visionary organization that integrates information from whole supply chain to plan product movement from supplier to customer
- Sophisticated processes that involve all affected organizations
- Visionary, professional leadership
- Highly capable systems that provide supply chain information to affected departments
- Sophisticated systems that provide real-time guidance

Stage IV: Multienterprise Integration Multienterprise systems/processes, common business objectives, seamless information sharing, knowledge organizations, and automated and interactive collaborations are included in this stage. In this stage, companies are cross-functionally organized. These companies operate with integrated systems within the enterprise and maximum external value chain integration. Total visibility into the value network is available as a result of end-to-end integration. Collaboration links trading partners and enables them to operate as one virtual corporation.

Characteristics of this stage include

- Collaboration across the supply chain
- Internal collaborative supply chain management's focus on key service and financial goals
- Executive leaders who foresee needs for functional and process skills that affect the supply chain and proactively drive skills development
- Systems that integrate appropriate information across the whole company
- Fully integrated performance management system that links supply chain results to company goals

Table 10-3 presents examples of different capabilities of supply chain management IT and how they evolve through the different stages of IT development. Of course, a company can be in a mix of

Table 10-3   SAP Stages of Excellence

Stage Capability	I: Disconnected	II: Interfaces	III: Integrated Internally	IV: Multienterprise Integrated
Internet	Visibility	Catalogs	Exchanges	Unattended trading
Integration	None	Batch	Interenterprise	Supply chain networks
Supply chain planning	None	Informal demand planning	Formal global demand planning	Integrated global planning
Production scheduling	None	Basic MRP	Constraint-based	Advanced planning systems (APS)
Integration with suppliers	FAX/phone	EDI/FAX/ phone	EDI with all large suppliers	VMI, online RFQ
Customer delivery	Research	Local inventory	Available to promise (ATP)	Capable to promise (CTP)

different stages based on its investment strategy and importance of a certain aspect to the business.

As we have mentioned before, the ultimate goal is to standardize processes across an industry so that companies can collaborate and cut costs. The ability to interact with as many business partners as possible in e-commerce projects makes this goal attractive. However, many companies report that the success of an application such as EDI requires that a large number of suppliers and customers use the system—a "critical mass"; otherwise, the expected cost savings cannot be achieved, and the system is not cost-effective.

10.7.2 Implementation of ERP and DSSs

Implementation of a system that supports supply chain integration involves infrastructure and decision-support systems. The ERP systems that are typically part of the infrastructure are different in many ways from the supply chain DSS. Table 10-4 compares enterprise resource planning (ERP) and DSSs based on various implementation issues.

What strategy should a company use in deciding what system to implement and when to implement it? IT goals suggest that a company first must install an ERP system so that the data will be accessible and complete. Only then can it start analysis of its entire supply chain processes using various DSS tools. This may be the ideal, but in reality, the data needed to achieve supply chain efficiencies already exist—maybe not in a single easy-to-access database, but it is worth the time it takes to assemble the database compared with the cost of waiting for installation of the ERP system.

These issues are illustrated in Table 10-4. An ERP implementation is typically much longer than a DSS implementation. The value of an ERP system to the enterprise involves the first two goals—visibility and single point of contact—and while these can imply improved operations, DSSs have an impact on the ability to perform strategic and tactical planning as well. This means that DSS projects have a much better ROI. Finally, DSS installations typically are cheaper and easier to implement, and they affect a smaller number of highly trained users compared with those of an ERP system, which has a large number of users who require less extensive training.

Indeed, companies do not necessarily wait for an ERP implementation to proceed with DSS projects. In many cases it makes sense to first implement DSS projects that provide a more immediate and

Table 10-4 ERP and DSS for Supply Chain Management

Implementation Issue	ERP	DSS
Length	18–48 months	6–12 months
Value	Operational	Strategic, tactical, operational
ROI	2–5-year payback	1-year payback
Users	All end users	Small group
Training	Simple	Complex

observable return. Of course, companies examine their financial and human resources before they decide on the order and number of projects they will tackle at a time.

The type of DSS implemented depends on the industry and the potential impact on the business. Table 10-5 includes some examples from various industries. In the soft drink industry, where distribution is a major cost factor, priorities are different from those of a computer manufacturer, which has a complex manufacturing process with many different products and whose distribution cost is only a fraction of product cost. Thus, in the latter case, the manufacturer can use expensive shipping solutions.

Table 10-5 Priorities When Implementing DSS

Industry	DSS
Soft drink distributor	Network and transportation
Computer manufacturer	Demand and manufacturing
Consumer products	Demand and distribution
Apparel	Demand, capacity, and distribution

10.7.3 "Best of Breed" versus Single-Vendor ERP Solutions

Supply chain IT solutions consist of many pieces that need to be assembled in order to achieve a competitive edge. They include infrastructure (ERP) and various systems to support decision making (DSSs). Two extreme approaches can be taken: The first is to purchase the ERP and supply chain DSS as a total solution from one vendor;

Table 10-6 "Best of Breed" versus Single
Vendor and Proprietary

Implementation Issue	Best of Breed	Single Vendor	Proprietary
Length	2–4 years	12–24 months	Not known
Cost	Higher	Lower	Depends on expertise
Flexibility	Higher	Lower	Highest
Complexity	Higher	Lower	Highest
Quality of solution	Higher	Lower	Not sure
Fit to enterprise	Higher	Lower	Highest
Staff training	Longer	Shorter	Shortest

the second is to build a "best of breed" solution, which purchases the best-fit solution in each category from a different vendor, thus producing a system that better fits each function in the company. While the best-of-breed solution is more complex and takes longer to implement, it may be an investment that provides greater long-term flexibility and better solutions to the company's problems. Of course, the long period of implementation also can cause the solution to be less useful at the end and cause difficulty maintaining IT staff and enthusiasm for the project. Many companies choose an interim approach that includes a dominant ERP provider; the functionality that cannot be provided by the vendor or does not suit the company is provided through best-of-breed or in-house systems. Finally, there are companies (e.g., Wal-Mart) that still prefer in-house, proprietary software development.[11] This probably makes sense for extremely large companies with expert IT departments and systems that already serve the company well. Table 10-6 summarizes the pros and cons of these approaches.

10.8 SUMMARY

We have identified four major goals for IT:

1. Information availability on each product from production to delivery point
2. Single point of contact

3. Decision making based on total supply chain information

4. Collaboration with supply chain partners

How are the four major goals achieved? More important, what is the impact on the logistics manager of achieving these goals?

First, standardization of processes, communications, data, and interfaces bring about cheaper and easier methods to implement the basic infrastructure. IT infrastructure will become more accessible for companies of any size and in the future will work across companies in an almost seamless way. This will allow access to IT and integration of the systems at every level of the supply chain—therefore, there will be more information and tracking of products at each level. New technologies such as RFID will allow products to be tagged and tracked through the supply chain and will be as easy to locate as a Federal Express package.

Second, data display and access in various forms are becoming more integrated in systems that do not require any specialized knowledge. This makes system interfaces more intuitive and relevant to the task at hand. The portal technology described in this chapter is one such example.

Third, various systems will interact in a way that will blur the current boundaries; Web service technologies, recently introduced by major vendors such as IBM, Microsoft, and Sun, are emerging technologies that allow different functions to integrate with no or minimal programming effort. As a result, systems purchased as "best of breed" by different people at various levels in the organization will become better integrated and use common interfaces. Similarly, there will be a proliferation of applications that can plug into a company's enterprise system to provide specialized functionality. The third goal will be achieved through development of DSSs and intelligent agents that are more sophisticated, rely on real-time data, and are interoperable.

Finally, electronic commerce is changing the way we work, interact, and do business. e-Commerce provides an interface to businesses and government that allows meaningful data comparison and transactions that follow through with error checking and correction capability. It enables access to data that exist in government, educational, and private databases and the ability to modify or correct these data. Private (and public) e-marketplaces now allow buyers to integrate their suppliers into their information systems. In the future, businesses will be able to expand their intercompany transactions into more sophisticated applications that can perform some basic processes and pass the information on to other applications. In a process as complicated as supply chain management, systems that not only perform their own function but also alert others in the system will be especially beneficial to fulfill the four goals we have outlined. We end with a quote from Lou Gerstner, former IBM CEO:[12]

> The payoff from information technology is going to be in making transactions and processes more effective and efficient, so it's not about creating a new economy, it's not about creating new models of behavior or new models of industry. It's about taking a tool, a powerful tool, and saying, "How can I make my supply chain more effective and efficient, how can I make my purchasing process more efficient, how can I make my internal employee communications more effective and efficient, how can I as a government deliver services to constituents more efficiently and more effectively?"

Notes

CHAPTER 1

1. Henkoff, R. "Delivering the Goods." *Fortune*, November 28, 1994, pp. 64–78.
2. *The Wall Street Journal*, October 23, 1997.
3. *U.S. Surgical Quarterly Report*, July 15, 1993.
4. *The Wall Street Journal*, October 7, 1994.
5. Anonymous. "Supply Disruptions May Linger as Quake Aftershock." http://www.eetimes.com, September 22, 1999.
6. Davis, D. "State of a New Art." *Manufacturing Systems* 13 (1995), pp. 2–10.
7. Delaney, R., and R. Wilson. "14th Annual State of Logistics Report," 2003.
8. *Journal of Business Strategy*, October–November 1997.
9. Keenan, F. "One Smart Cookie." *BusinessWeek E.Biz*, November 20, 2000.
10. Stein, T., and J. Sweat. "Killer Supply Chains." http://www.informationweek.com, November 9, 1988.
11. Kaufman, L. "Wal-Mart's Huge Slice of American Pie." *New York Times*, February 16, 2000.
12. Stalk, G., P. Evans, and L. E. Shulman. "Competing on Capabilities: The New Rule of Corporate Strategy." *Harvard Business Review*, March–April 1992, pp. 57–69.

13. Mottley, R. "Dead in Nine Months." *American Shipper,* December 1998, pp. 30–33.

CHAPTER 2

1. Lee, H., P. Padmanabhan, and S. Whang. "The Paralyzing Curse of the Bullwhip Effect in a Supply Chain." *Sloan Management Review,* Spring 1997, pp. 93–102.
2. Lee, H., P. Padmanabhan, and S. Whang. "Information Distortion in a Supply Chain: The Bullwhip Effect." *Management Science* 43 (1996), pp. 546–558.
3. Chen, F.Y., J.K. Ryan, and D. Simchi-Levi. "The Impact of Exponential Smoothing Forecasts on the Bullwhip Effect." *Naval Research Logistics* 47 (2000), pp. 269–286.
4. Chen, Y. F., Z. Drezner, J. K. Ryan, and D. Simchi-Levi. "Quantifying the Bullwhip Effect: The Impact of Forecasting, Leadtime and Information." *Management Science* 46 (2000), pp. 436–443.
5. Chen, F. Y., Z. Drezner, J. K. Ryan, and D. Simchi-Levi. "The Bullwhip Effect: Managerial Insights on the Impact of Forecasting and Information on Variability in the Supply Chain." In *Quantitative Models for Supply Chain Management,* ed. S. Tayur, R. Ganeshan, and M. Magazine. Norwell, MA: Kluwer Academic Publishing, 1998, chap. 14.
6. Nahmias, S. *Production and Operations Analysis.* 3d ed. Burr Ridge, IL: Irwin/McGraw-Hill, 1997.
7. Georgoff, D. M., and R. G. Murdick. "Managers' Guide to Forecasting." *Harvard Business Review* 64, no. 1 (1986), pp. 1–9.
8. Chambers, J. C., S. K. Mullick, and D. D. Smith. "How to Choose the Right Forecasting Technique." *Harvard Business Review* 49, no. 4 (1971), pp. 45–69.
9. Verity, J. "Clearing the Cobwebs from the Stockroom." *Business-Week,* October 21, 1996.
10. Hopp, W., and M. Spearman. *Factory Physics.* Burr Ridge, IL: Richard D. Irwin, 1996.
11. Lee, H. L., and C. Billington. "Managing Supply Chain Inventory: Pitfalls and Opportunities." *Sloan Management Review,* Spring 1992, pp. 65–73.

CHAPTER 3

1. Artman, L. B. "The Paradigm Shift from 'Push' to 'Pull' Logistics—What's the Impact on Manufacturing?" Northwestern University, Manufacturing Management Symposium, Evanston, IL, May 1995.
2. *The Wall Street Journal*, February 22, 2000.
3. Fisher, M. L., J. Hammond, W. Obermeyer, and A. Raman. "Making Supply Meet Demand in an Uncertain World." *Harvard Business Review*, May–June 1994, pp. 83–93.
4. Clark, T. "Campbell Soup Company: A Leader in Continuous Replenishment Innovations." Harvard Business School Case 9-195-124, 1994.
5. Hartman A. and J. Sifonis "Net ready," McGraw-Hill, 2000, pp. 259-263.
6. Stalk, G., P. Evans, and L. E. Shulman. "Competing on Capabilities: The New Rule of Corporate Strategy." *Harvard Business Review*, March–April 1992, pp. 57–69.

CHAPTER 4

1. Ballou, R. H. *Business Logistics Management.* 3d ed. Englewood Cliffs, NJ: Prentice Hall, 1992.
2. Johnson, J. C., and D. F. Wood. *Contemporary Physical Distribution and Logistics.* 3d ed. New York: Macmillan, 1986.
3. Robeson, J. F., and W. C. Copacino, eds. *The Logistics Handbook.* New York: Free Press, 1994.
4. House, R. G., and K. D. Jamie. "Measuring the Impact of Alternative Market Classification Systems in Distribution Planning." *Journal of Business Logistics* 2 (1981), pp. 1–31.
5. Patton, E. P. "Carrier Rates and Tariffs." In *The Distribution Management Handbook*, ed. J. A. Tompkins and D. Harmelink. New York: McGraw-Hill, 1994, chap. 12.
6. Hax, A. C., and D. Candea. *Production and Inventory Management.* Englewood Cliffs, NJ: Prentice Hall, 1984.
7. Blumenfeld, D. E., L. D. Burns, C. F. Daganzo, M. C. Frick, and R. W. Hall. "Reducing Logistics Costs at General Motors." *Interfaces* 17 (1987), pp. 26–47.
8. *The Wall Street Journal*, August 1993. *(Dell Computer ref.)

9. *The Wall Street Journal*, July 15, 1993. *(Liz Claiborne ref.)

10. *The Wall Street Journal*, October 7, 1994. *(IBM ThinkPad ref.)

11. Elecomp is a fictional company based on a 2002 LogicTools project. The name of the company and some of the data have been changed.

CHAPTER 5

1. Lewis, J. *Partnerships for Profit*. New York: Free Press, 1990.

2. Chesbrough, H., and D. Teece. "When Is Virtual Virtuous: Organizing for Innovation." *Harvard Business Review* 74, no. 1 (1996), pp. 65–74.

3. Delaney, R. and R. Wilson, "14th Annual State of Logistics Report," 2003.

4. Leahy, S., P. Murphy, and R. Poist. "Determinants of Successful Logistical Relationships: A Third Party Provider Perspective." *Transportation Journal* 35 (1995), pp. 5–13.

5. Bowman, R. "A HighWire Act." *Distribution* 94 (1995), pp. 36–39.

6. Davis, D. "Third Parties Deliver." *Manufacturing Systems* 13 (1995), pp. 66–68.

7. Andel, T. "There's Power in Numbers." *Transportation & Distribution* 36 (1995), pp. 67–72.

8. Harrington, L. "Logistics Assets: Should You Own or Manage?" *Transportation & Distribution* 37 (1996), pp. 51–54.

9. Troyer, C., and R. Cooper. "Smart Moves in Supply Chain Integration." *Transportation & Distribution* 36 (1995), pp. 55–62.

10. Anonymous. "Choosing Service Providers." *Transportation & Distribution* 36 (1995), pp. 74–76.

11. Maltz, A. "Why You Outsource Dictates How." *Transportation & Distribution* 36 (1995), pp. 73–80.

12. Anonymous. "Divorce: Third-Party Style." *Distribution* 94 (1995), pp. 46–51.

13. Schoneberger, R. J. "Strategic Collaboration: Breaching the Castle Walls." *Business Horizons* 39 (1996), p. 20.

14. Troyer, T., and D. Denny. "Quick Response Evolution." *Discount Merchandiser* 32 (1992), pp. 104–107.

15. Buzzell, R. D., and G. Ortmeyer. "Channel Partnerships Streamline Distribution." *Sloan Management Review* 36 (1995), p. 85

16. Davis, D. "State of a New Art." *Manufacturing Systems* 13 (1995), pp. 2–10.

17. Clemmet, A. "Demanding Supply." *Work Study* 44 (1995), pp. 23–24.

18. Andel, T. "Manage Inventory, Own Information." *Transportation & Distribution* 37 (1996), p. 54.

19. Andreoli, T. "VMI Confab Examines Value-Added Services." *Discount Store News* 34 (1995), pp. 4–61.

20. Pollack, E. "Partnership: Buzzword or Best Practice?" *Chain Store Age Executive* 71 (1995), pp. 11A–12A.

21. Huang, Y., A. Federgruen, O. Bakkalbasi, R. Desiraju, and R. Kranski. "Vendor-Managed Replenishment in an Agile Manufacturing Environment." Working paper, Philips Research.

22. Gamble, R. "Financially Efficient Partnerships." *Corporate Cashflow* 15 (1994), pp. 29–34.

23. Trunnick, P., H. Richardson, and L. Harrington. "CLM: Breakthroughs of Champions." *Transportation & Distribution* 35 (1994), pp. 41–50.

24. Robins, G. "Pushing the Limits of VMI." *Stores* 77 (1995), pp. 42–44.

25. Mathews, R. "Spartan Pulls the Plug on VMI." *Progressive Grocer* 74 (1995), pp. 64–65.

26. Narus, J., and J. Anderson. "Turn Your Industrial Distributors into Partners." *Harvard Business Review*, March–April 1986, pp. 66–71.

27. Fites, D. "Make Your Dealers Your Partners." *Harvard Business Review*, March–April 1996, pp. 84–95.

28. Narus, J. and J.C. Anderson. "Rethinking Distribution: Adaptive Channels." *Harvard Business Review*, July–August 1996, pp. 112–120.

CHAPTER 6

1. Schrader, C. "Speeding Build and Buy Processes across a Collaborative Manufacturing Network." *ASCET* 3 (2001), pp. 82–88.

2. Quinn, J. B., and F. Hilmer. "Strategic Outsourcing." *Sloan Management Review* 1994, pp. 9–21.

3. Lakenan, B., D. Boyd, and E. Frey. "Why Outsourcing and Its Perils?" *Strategy + Business*, no. 24 (2001).

4. Songini, M. L. "Nike Says Profit Woes IT-Based." *Computerworld*, March 5, 2001.

5. Chesbrough, H., and D. Teece. "When Is Virtual Virtuous: Organizing for Innovation." *Harvard Business Review* 74, no. 1 (1996), pp. 65–74.

6. Fine, C. H., and D. E. Whitney. "Is the Make-Buy Decision Process a Core Competence?" Working paper, Massachusetts Institute of Technology, 1996.

7. Ulrich, K. T. "The Role of Product Architecture in the Manufacturing Firm." *Research Policy* 24 (1995), pp. 419–440.

8. Swaminathan, J. M. "Enabling Customization Using Standardized Operations." *California Management Review* 43(3) (Spring 2001), pp. 125–135.

9. Fine, C. H. *Clock Speed: Winning Industry Control in the Age of Temporary Advantage*. Reading, MA: Pereus Books, 1998.

10. Singh, A. Private communication.

11. Kerrigan, R., E. V. Roegner, D. D. Swinford, and C. C. Zawada. "B2Basics." McKinsey and Company Report, 2001.

12. Copacino, W. C., and R. W. Dik. "Why B2B e-Markets Are Here to Stay. Part I: Public Independent Trading Exchanges." http://TechnologyEvaluation.Com, March 18, 2002.

13. Johnson, E. M. "Money for Nothing." *CIO Magazine*, September 15, 2000.

14. Hannon, D. "Online Buy Gains Speed." *Purchasing Magazine Online*, February 7, 2002.

15. Varon, E. "What You Need to Know about Public and Private Exchanges." *CIO Magazine*, September 1, 2001.

16. Temkin, B. "Preparing for the Coming Shake-Out in Online Markets." *ASCET* 3 (2001), pp. 102–107.

17. Anonymous. "Idapta: At the Core of E-Markets." *ASCET* 3 (2001), pp. 145–147.

18. Billington, C. "HP Cuts Risk with Portfolio Approach." *Purchasing Magazine Online*, February 21, 2002.

19. Martinez-de-Albeniz, V. and D. Simchi-Levi 2002. "A Portfolio Approach to Procurement Contracts." MIT, Working Paper, 2003.

20. Cachon, G. P. "Supply Coordination with Contracts." To appear in *Handbooks in Operations Research and Management Science*, ed. Steve Graves and Ton de Kok. Amsterdam: North-Holland, 2002.

21. Cachon, G. P., and M. A. Lariviere. "Supply Chain Coordination with Revenue Sharing Contracts: Strengths and Limitations." Working paper, the Wharton School, University of Pennsylvania, 2000.

CHAPTER 7

1. Lee, H. "Design for Supply Chain Management: Concepts and Examples." Working paper, Department of Industrial Engineering and Engineering Management, Stanford University, 1992.

2. Jones, H. "Ikea's Global Strategy Is a Winning Formula." *Marketing Week* 18, no. 50 (1996), p. 22.

3. "Management Brief: Furnishing the World." *The Economist*, November 19, 1994, pp. 79–80.

4. Pike, H. "IKEA Still Committed to U.S., Despite Uncertain Economy." *Discount Store News* 33, no. 8 (1994), pp. 17–19.

5. Nussbaum, B. "Designs for Living." *BusinessWeek*, June 2, 1997, p. 99.

6. Davis, D., and T. Foster. "Bulk Squeezes Shipping Costs." *Distribution Worldwide* 78, no. 8 (1979), pp. 25–30.

7. Schwind, G. "A Systems Approach to Docks and Cross-Docking." *Material Handling Engineering* 51, no. 2 (1996), pp. 59–62.

8. Swaminathan, J. M. "Enabling Customization Using Standardized Operations." *California Management Review* 43(3) (Spring 2001), pp. 125–135.

9. Signorelli, S., and J. Heskett. "Benetton (A)." Harvard University Business School Case (1984) Case No. 9-685-014.

10. Monczka, R., G. Ragatz, R. Handfield, R. Trent, and D. Frayer. "Executive Summary: Supplier Integration into New Product Development: A Strategy for Competitive Advantage." *The Global Procurement and Supply Chain Benchmarking Initiative*, Michigan State University, The Eli Broad Graduate School of Management, 1997.

11. Pine, J. B., II. *Mass Customization.* Harvard University Business School Press, 1993.

12. Pine, J. B., II, and A. Boynton. "Making Mass Customization Work." *Harvard Business Review* 71, no. 5 (1993), pp. 108–119.

13. Fisher, M. L. "National Bicycle Industrial Co.: A Case Study." The Wharton School, University of Pennsylvania, 1993.

14. McWilliams, G. "Whirlwind on the Web." *BusinessWeek*, April 7, 1997, pp. 132–136.

CHAPTER 8

1. Sliwa, C. "Beyond IT: Business Strategy Was a Problem, Too." *Computerworld*, January 25, 2002.

2. Fisher, M. L. "What Is the Right Supply Chain for Your Product?" *Harvard Business Review*, March–April 1997, pp. 105–117.

3. Crawford, F, and R. Mathews. *The Myth of Excellence.* New York: Crown Business, 2001.

4. Seybold, P. B. *The Customer Revolution.* New York: Crown Business, 2001.

5. Hof, R. "How Amazon Cleared That Hurdle." *BusinessWeek*, February 4, 2002, pp. 60–61.

6. Ries, A., and L. Ries. *The 22 Immutable Laws of Branding.* New York: HarperBusiness, 1998.

7. Brynjolfsson, E., and M. D. Smith. "Frictionless Commerce? A Comparison of Internet and Conventional Retailers." *Management Science* 46 (2000), pp. 563–585.

8. King, J. "The Service Advantage." *Computerworld*, October 28, 1998.

9. Pine, J. B., II, D. Peppers, and M. Rogers. "Do You Want to Keep Your Customers Forever?" *Harvard Business Review*, March–April 1995, pp. 103–115.

10. Peppers, D., and M. Rogers. *Enterprise One to One.* New York: Doubleday, 1997.

11. Pine, J. B., II, and J. Gilmore. "Welcome to the Experience Economy." *Harvard Business Review*, July–August 1998, pp. 97–108.

12. Leibs, S. "Deskbound for Glory." *CFO Magazine*, March 14, 2002.

13. Agrawal, V., and A. Kambil. "Dynamic Pricing Strategies in Electronic Commerce." Working paper, Stern Business School, New York University, 2000.

14. McWilliams, G. "Dell Fine-Tuned Its Pricing to Gain an Edge in Slow Market." *The Wall Street Journal*, June 8, 2001.

15. Kay, E. "Flexed Pricing." *Datamation* 44, no. 2 (1998), pp. 58–62.

16. Cook, T. "SABRE Soars." *ORMS Today*, June 1998, pp. 26–31.

17. Cook, T. "Creating Competitive Advantage in the Airline Industry." Seminar sponsored by the MIT Global Airline Industry Program and the MIT Operations Research Center, 2000.

18. Kimes, S. E. "A Tool for Capacity-Constrained Service Firms." *Journal of Operations Management* 8 (1989), pp. 348–363.

19. Duadel, S., and G. Vialle. *Yield Management: Applications to Transport and Other Service Industries.* Paris: ITA, 1994.

20. Federgruen, A., and A. Heching. "Combined Pricing and Inventory Control under Uncertainty." *Operations Research* 47 (1999), pp. 454–475.

21. Chan, L. M. A., D. Simchi-Levi, and J.Swann. "Effective Dynamic Pricing Strategies with Stochastic Demand." Working paper, Massachusetts Institute of Technology, 2001.

22. Yannis, B. J. "The Emerging Role of Electronic Marketplaces on the Internet." *Comm. ACM* 41, no. 9 (1998), pp. 35–42.

23. Baker, W., M. Marn, and C. Zawada. "Price Smarter on the Net." *Harvard Business Review* 79, no. 2 (2001), pp. 122–127.

24. Streitfeld, D. "Amazon Pays a Price for Marketing Test." *Washington Post*, October 2000.

25. Disabatino, J. "Priceline.com Reports $1.3 Million Q4 Loss." *Computerworld*, February 4, 2002.

26. Reichheld, F. F. "Learning from Customer Defections." *Harvard Business Review*, March–April 1996, pp. 57–69.

27. Supply Chain Council. "SCOR Introduction." Release 2.0, August 1, 1997.

28. Geary, S., and J. P. Zonnenberg. "What It Means to Be Best in Class." *Supply Chain Management Review*, July/August 2000, pp. 42–48.

29. Bovet, D., and Y. Sheffi. "The Brave New World of Supply Chain Management." *Supply Chain Management Review*, Spring 1998, pp. 14–22.

30. Narus, J. and J.C. Anderson. "Rethinking Distribution: Adaptive Channels." *Harvard Business Review*, July–August 1996, pp. 112–120.

31. Magretta, J. "The Power of Virtual Integration: An Interview with Dell Computer's Michael Dell." *Harvard Business Review*, March–April 1998, pp. 72–84.

CHAPTER 9

1. Dornier, P., R. Ernst, M. Fender, and P. Kouvelis. *Global Operations and Logistics: Text and Cases.* New York: John Wiley, 1998.

2. Levitt, T. "The Globalization of Markets." *Harvard Business Review* 61 (1983), pp. 92–102.

3. Ohmae, K. "Managing in a Borderless World." *Harvard Business Review* 67 (1989), pp. 152–161.

4. Kogut, B. "Designing Global Strategies: Profiting from Operational Flexibility." *Sloan Management Review* 27 (1985), pp. 27–38.

5. Lessard, D., and J. Lightstone. "Volatile Exchange Rates Put Operations at Risk." *Harvard Business Review* 64 (1986), pp. 107–114.

6. McGrath, M., and R. Hoole. "Manufacturing's New Economies of Scale." *Harvard Business Review* 70 (1992), pp. 94–102.

7. Markides, C., and N. Berg. "Manufacturing Offshore Is Bad Business." *Harvard Business Review* 66 (1988), pp. 113–120.

8. Wood, D., A. Barone, P. Murphy, and D. Wardlow. *International Logistics.* New York: Chapman & Hall, 1995.

9. Fernie, J. "International Comparisons of Supply Chain Management in Grocery Retailing." *Service Industries Journal* 15 (1995), pp. 134–147.

10. Byrne, P., and W. Markham. "Global Logistics: Only 10 Percent of Companies Satisfy Customers." *Transportation and Distribution* 34 (1993), pp. 41–45.

11. Mische, M. "EDI in the EC: Easier Said Than Done." *Journal of European Business* 4 (1992), pp. 19–22.

12. Handfield, R., and B.Withers. "A Comparison of Logistics Management in Hungary, China, Korea, and Japan." *Journal of Business Logistics* 14 (1993), pp. 81–109.

CHAPTER 10

1. Ross, D. F. *Competing through Supply Chain Management.* New York: Chapman & Hall, 1998.

2. Hagel, J., III, and J. S. Brown. "Your Next IT Strategy." *Harvard Business Review* 79, no. 10 (2001).

3. Guengerich, S., and V. G. Green. *Introduction to Client/Server Computing.* Dearborn, MI: SME Blue Book Series, 1996.

4. While there is a difference between the definition of *e-business* and *e-commerce* in general, in practice they are used interchangeably.

5. Leibs, S. "Deskbound for Glory." *CFO Magazine*, March 14, 2002.

6. CERN: Conseil Europeen pour la Recherche Nucleaire (the European Laboratory for Nuclear Research) in Geneva.

7. "Henkel-Eroski CPFR Pilot Case Study." Compiled by Thierry Jouenne, copyright 2000 by Jowen Editions, 2000, available at www.cpfr.org.

8. Fox, M. S., J. F. Chionglo, and M. Barbuceanu. "The Integrated Supply Chain Management System." Working paper, University of Toronto, 1993.

9. Zweben, M. "Delivering on Every Promise." APICS, March 1996, p. 50.

10. SAP and mySAP.com are trademarks of SAPAktiengescellschaft, Systems, Applications and Products in Data Processing, Neurottstrasse 16, 69190 Walldorf, Germany. The authors gratefully acknowledge SAP's kind permission to use its trademark in this publication.

11. Caldwell B. "Wal-Mart Ups the Pace." http://www. informationweek.com, December 9, 1996.

12. Lohr, S. "He Loves to Win. At I.B.M., He Did," *New York Times* March 10, 2002.

Index

About the Authors

David Simchi-Levi, Ph.D., is a professor of engineering systems at MIT, cofounder and chairman of Logic Tools, Inc., and the recipient of a number of awards for his work in supply, logistics, and transportation. Dr. Simchi-Levi is the coauthor of *The Logic of Logistics*, a book describing the theory behind logistics and supply chain management.

Philip Kaminsky, Ph.D., is an associate professor of industrial engineering at the University of California at Berkeley and a globally renowned consultant in supply chain and production management.

Edith Simchi-Levi is a co-founder and vice president of operations for Logic Tools, Inc. She has extensive experience in software development as well as logistics and supply chain management consulting.